ANALOGY AND ASSOCIATION

IN LINGUISTICS AND PSYCHOLOGY

ERWIN A. ESPER

ERWIN A. ESPER

ANALOGY AND ASSOCIATION

IN LINGUISTICS AND

PSYCHOLOGY

UNIVERSITY OF GEORGIA PRESS · ATHENS

Library of Congress Catalog Card Number: 72–86781
International Standard Book Number: 0–8203–0298–8

The University of Georgia Press, Athens 30602

Printed in the United States of America
by Heritage Printers, Inc.
Charlotte, N. C. 28202

ERWIN ALLEN ESPER

The author of this book died on 15 December 1972, while the book was in page proof.

Esper was born in Columbus, Ohio, on 14 August 1895, and received his early education in the public schools of that city. In 1913 he entered The Ohio State University, to receive the A.B. in 1917 (in Greek), the A.M. in 1920 (in Psychology), and the Ph.D. in 1923 (in Psychology). For the first year past the A.B. he was graduate assistant in Greek. In 1918 he married Ethel Marie Cooke, to whom he had been engaged since 1912 when both were students at Columbus's South High School.[1] For 1918–1919 he was graduate assistant in English. The following year he was an instructor in English, and thereafter through 1925 an instructor in psychology. At some point during the war years his academic career was interrupted for military duty, but only for eight months, during which he performed clerical tasks and rose to the rank of sergeant. For the summer of 1920 he was at Columbia University. In the spring of 1924 he was at the University of Vienna (attending the lectures of Paul Kretschmer, Wilhelm Schmidt, and Karl Bühler), and the summer of the same year was spent at the Phonetics Institute of G. Panconcelli-Calzia in Hamburg.

In 1925, Esper went to the University of Illinois in Urbana as Assistant Professor of Psychology. Two years later he moved on to the University of Washington in Seattle, in whose Department of Psychology

1. Ethel Marie was born in Manchester, England, and brought to Columbus by her parents at the age of five. At Ohio State she earned an A.B. and an A.M. in biology.

he spent the rest of his teaching career, as Associate Professor through 1934, thereafter as Professor. During the summer of 1930 he was on the staff of the (third annual) Linguistic Institute of the Linguistic Society of America, held that year in New York City under the joint sponsorship of the Society and of the City College of New York. In 1936 was born the Espers' only child, Hildegard.[2]

Statutory retirement came in 1960, whereupon Esper, with emeritus status but only a meager income, moved with his wife to Index, Washington, about fifty miles from the University. There, for a decade, he undertook the research and writing for which his teaching duties had not earlier allowed him adequate time. The fruits of that decade include a number of articles and reviews, and three books, of which that now in your hands is the third.

Ethel Marie died unexpectedly on 23 January 1971. A year later Esper remarried, but lost his new companion after a brief three months. What was left of him after this second cruel blow survived only for another eight months: his life was ended by a heart attack in Montreal shortly after he had arrived to spend the Christmas season with his daughter and her family. He was survived also by a younger brother, Harold C. Esper of Columbus.

Esper was a member of Phi Beta Kappa, of Sigma Xi, and of the Ohio Academy of Science, a fellow of the American Psychological Association and of the American Association for the Advancement of Science, and a foundation member of the Linguistic Society of America.

Esper's forebears came to Columbus from Germany in 1848, a ripple in the vast migratory wave that followed on the political unrest and bad economic conditions in Europe in the 1830s and 1840s:

By 1860, nearly a million Teutons had arrived in the United States. Among them were prominent "Forty-eighters" such as Carl Schurz and Franz Sigel. Most of the Germans settled in the newer parts of the country north of the Ohio or beyond the Mississippi. In some localities they held the balance of political power. Wherever they went they carried with them their zeal for education, their love of music, and the liberal social customs

2. Now Mrs. Mircea Enesco of Montreal, a Ph.D. in zoology and Associate Professor of Biology at Sir George Williams University.

of the Fatherland. In large degree, they planted the first seeds of aesthetic appreciation in the raw West.[3]

We need a reminder of this phase of our country's history, because the First World War—in which we participated on one side rather than on the other only by virtue of an initially almost imperceptible tipping of the scales—induced a nationwide amnesia from which we have still not recovered. During the second half of the nineteenth century and the first decade and a half of the twentieth, the learned culture of the Middle West, to some extent that of the whole nation, was overtly modeled on that of Central Europe. That was where scholars, scientists, and musicians went as a matter of course, if they could afford to, for their advanced training. American scholarship at its rare best still reflects this historic source.

If we do not talk much about this nowadays, neither did our predecessors seventy years ago—but for a very different reason: the Teutonic tie was taken for granted. Obviously that was especially so in the German enclaves, such as that of south Columbus where Esper spent his boyhood. German was the language of his parental home, probably the home language of many of his childhood companions, and the German community was so prominent and respected that, for the first three years of his education in the city's *public* schools, German was the language of instruction.

For the Ohio State years, we are fortunate in having a brief account in Esper's own words. The passage I am about to quote is from a letter written to me a few years ago when I was working on *A Leonard Bloomfield Anthology*.[4] I had asked him to recall what he could of Bloomfield and his colleagues in the early 1920s. Those mentioned in the passage, in addition to the linguist Bloomfield (1887–1949), include the Homeric scholar George Melville Bolling (1871–1963) and the psychologist Albert Paul Weiss (1871–1931). Bolling came to Ohio State in 1913 and remained until his retirement in 1940; his major life work was the philological demonstration of the multiple authorship of the Homeric poems

3. H. C. Hockett and A. M. Schlesinger, *Land of the Free: A Short History of the American People* (New York: Macmillan, 1944), p. 282.

4. Bloomington: Indiana University Press, 1970.

(those who held the opposite view were dubbed "Unitarians"). Weiss served at Ohio State from 1912 until his death; he had been a student of the behaviorist Max Meyer—the only one to earn a doctorate under Meyer's guidance. Bloomfield came to Ohio State in 1921 and stayed only until 1927, but those were crucial years: Bolling and Bloomfield were the prime movers in the founding of the Linguistic Society of America in 1925 (and Bolling became the first editor of its journal, *Language*); it was under Weiss's influence that Bloomfield abandoned his earlier adherence to the dualistic "psychology of language" of Wilhelm Wundt in favor of physicalism.

Here is Esper's account:

> ... I became Bolling's pupil in my sophomore year, 1914. There were not many true scholars at Ohio State at that time, and Bolling became my model, and I suspect still is. After we had got through the *Anabasis* and several of Plato's dialogues, the other members of the class disappeared, and for a number of years I was his only advanced pupil, sitting at his desk translating all of Homer, Euripides, etc. with no other interruption than Bolling's 'V-v-very good, go on.' After my graduation I became his assistant, and was allowed to teach the *Anabasis* and the *Apology*; my modeling had been so complete that in teaching I found it necessary to stutter. Bolling saw Thumb's article about association as related to *Annlogiebildung*, in the *Indogermanische Forschungen*, and suggested that I take a course in experimental psychology. Thus I came under the influence of Weiss. As I indicated in the Preface to my *A History of Psychology*,[5] both Bolling and Weiss were remarkable—especially in that environment —for their serious attitude toward scholarship, in the professional spirit of German scholarship. But both were also delightful persons. I wanted to continue in Greek, but Bolling was a one-man department, and thought I should go to Princeton for my doctorate. Dean West [of Princeton] came to the campus and Bolling arranged a meeting; West said he would adopt me as a son, etc. but when he found out that I had married, the bottom fell out; I was disqualified for West's graduate hall, for which, as at Oxford, celibacy was requisite. Bolling was becoming very despondent about the future of classical studies. . . . So on his advice I took my Ph.D. in psychology, although I spent my last year taking examinations in Greek. My first 'publication' was a column of numbers in an article by Bolling; I

5. See the bibliography, p. xix.

had counted the abstract nouns in . . . [a certain derivational ending] in the 'older strata' of the Iliad vs. the Odyssey and thus supplied ammunition for Bolling's war against the Unitarians. Then my master's thesis was a replication of Thumb and Marbe's *Experimentelle Untersuchungen über die psychologischen Grundlagen der sprachlichen Analogiebildung;* my thesis was published in the *Psychological Review* 1918, 468–487, after Miller had turned it down for the *American Journal of Psychology.* (I think that the hostility between Bolling and Miller was one of the reasons for the founding of *Language.*) My doctoral thesis followed a suggestion of Thumb's; Bolling, Bloomfield, and Weiss took an interest in this and helped me with suggestions.

All this was by way of a perhaps irrelevantly reminiscent explanation of how I came to see and hear a good deal of Bloomfield, although I was never his pupil. I might have become such if I had had more sense and had been less preoccupied with my work with Bolling and Weiss; Bloomfield invited me to his house and showed me his numerous files of Menominee material; the effect on me should have been like that of Prokosch on Bloomfield,[6] but Bloomfield was so modest and therefore tentative in his manner, and I was so overawed by this brilliant scholar that the occasion was rather aborted; when we had lunch together in his patio, his asking me my opinions on some linguistic matters . . . increased my shyness and awkwardness. I have always regretted that episode; I think that Bloomfield's aversion to imposing himself on others could make him seem formidable, because of the contrast between his modesty and his obvious stature as a scholar.

What a tangled trail, what a series of seemingly unrelated incidents and personalities, leads a scholar to his destiny! Esper might have followed in Bolling's footsteps to become undoubtedly one of the leading Hellenists of the mid twentieth century. Or he might have come into

6. Esper's allusion is to an episode recounted by Bloomfield in his obituary of the Germanicist Eduard Prokosch (1876–1938), in *Language* 14, 310–313 (1938): "In the summer of 1906 I came, fresh out of college, to Madison, to be looked over for an assistantship. Desiring to earn an academic living, I had developed no understanding or inclination for any branch of science. The kindly Professor Hohlfeld delegated Prokosch, one of his young instructors, to entertain me for the day. On a small table in Prokosch's dining room there stood a dozen technical books . . . and in the interval before lunch Prokosch explained to me their use and content. By the time we sat down to the meal, a matter perhaps of fifteen minutes, I had decided that I should always work in linguistics." —But let us note that in making the comparison Esper is unfair to himself. Bloomfield came to Prokosch with no commitment. Esper came to Bloomfield with a very firm one.

linguistics, strengthening Bloomfield's scientific integration and helping to pass it on (as it was, Bloomfield had no truly competent students until the mid 1930s). Or both. Although I realize that these remarks are a futile lament, I cannot help but feel that one more strong girder in the under-pinnings of American linguistics in the 1920s might have gone far towards forestalling the dreadful resurgence of mysticism in that field a few decades later.

Of course, Esper's move into psychology was not really a loss to the scientific study of language. It gave us a staunch ally in a sister discipline—all the more important after the untimely death of Weiss in 1931. And it was a gain for psychology, since by nature Esper could not be other than a profound and patient scholar, and a dedicated teacher, in any field into which he ventured.

I have no information on Esper's activities during the two years at the University of Illinois. As for his long career at the University of Washington, we are told[7] that he participated in few, if any, regional or national scientific conventions, and that his main concerns were the psychology of language ("associative interference, social transmission, and linguistic organization"), the history of psychology, and the investigation of the neural basis of behavior; in the last of these he developed a course and syllabus at the graduate level. A lesser man might have done such things with his left hand, meanwhile tossing off a half dozen ephemeral (if perhaps financially profitable) textbooks. Such was not Esper's style. A passage in his last letter to me, written 6 August 1972, primarily about his wife Ethel Marie and the emptiness of life without her, incidentally tells us all we really need to know about the University of Washington period:

> The fact is that after almost 60 years of marriage—counting six years of engagement beginning in 1912—I became a highly specialized human being, so that I just haven't known how—or why—to live alone. My wife was not only wholly devoted to me but she had the common sense and human touch which I lacked. (I had a good deal of the latter in the hun-

7. By his student, Professor Frank Wesley of Portland State University, in an obituary notice due for publication in *Journal of the History of the Behavioral Sciences.*

dreds of private sessions with students over the years, but not in other situations and not in practical affairs of private life.) So while I sometimes get letters from students of long ago, or meet them by chance, and they tell me how helpful my teaching or advice had been, or how I had even determined their careers, I gain some little feeling of worthwhileness. But against this, I know that hundreds of students found me boring or even hateful. My wife's despair was that I put in most of my time on my teaching, preparing mimeographed textbooks to be handed out gratis, etc. instead of writing for publication, and it was really her persuasion and pressure, conspiring with a publisher, that got me started finally on writing for publication after a lapse of many years, and her pleasure at handling my first book—my *History of Psychology*—was my chief reward.

We see why Esper's major writing was so long delayed, and also why it stopped when it did.

Esper's psychology, like that of his teacher Weiss and his teacher's teacher Meyer (and like that of the mature Bloomfield), was of the sort known in the teens and twenties as "behaviorism." Esper later came to prefer the term "objectivism," and Bloomfield "physicalism," but those shifts of label implied no basic change in orientation. Behaviorism was fashionable in the twenties, not only among professionals but also in "intellectual" parlor chatter and even in Sunday supplements. The popular brands derived largely from the writings of John B. Watson (1878–1958), whose scholarship cannot be impugned but whose facile pen titillated the senses and gave laymen an easier point of departure for distorting the doctrine in daring, though spurious, directions. Even the philosopher of education John Dewey (1859–1952) was classed as a behaviorist by some, though it is difficult to see why.

Shorn of irrelevancies, the debate between the behaviorists and their opponents boiled down to this. The tradition was dualistic—*psychology*, after all, is equivalent to German *Geisteswissenschaft* 'the science of mind', which contrasts clearly with *Naturwissenschaft* 'the science of nature'. Methods of investigation may be the same, or at least similar, but the findings will surely be different, since it is obvious (?) that the "laws of nature" and the "laws of mind" are different. The task of psychology is to investigate the "laws of mind," through observation of human conduct, through experimentation, and (perhaps) through introspection. The behaviorists said: introspection is personal and unreliable, and for our inferences about the "mind" of another we have absolutely no evidence except his overt behavior (including of course, his speech, and his special acts in experimental situations). Our real task, therefore, is to search for regularities in that overt behavior, and for correlations between the behavior of one person and that of another. In that enterprise we have no need for positing an unobservable and perhaps nonmaterial "mind," since we seem to be able to account for what we can observe entirely in terms of the "laws of nature." Thus psychology, despite the etymology of the word, turns out to be a branch of *Naturwissenschaft*. Accordingly, the behaviorists attempted to expunge from their vocabulary all terms with a "mentalistic" taint: *consciousness, awareness, idea, mind, soul.*

Unless conducted with great delicacy, this dispute can quickly incorporate spurious features—and it did, not only in parlor talk but also among the professionals. Some behaviorists and some of their opponents held that the behaviorist position denies the *existence* of a nonphysical mind or soul. In fact it does not. The rejection of nonphysical entities is an independent postulate. One who holds that postulate (as I do, and as many behaviorists in fact have) must be a behaviorist, but not vice versa. More confusing, really, was that the nonbehaviorists, noting the behaviorists' assiduous avoidance of certain common *words*, assumed that the behaviorists were leaving out *things*—that they were denying various realities of everyday life that are ordinarily talked about using those words. Weiss is particularly explicit on the point:

> When Watson maintains that he will not discuss consciousness, this is generally interpreted by psychologists to be an arbitrary elimination of the essential part of human behavior. To these it seems as if the behaviorists ignore consciousness because it is too difficult, or because it is a phase in the study of human behavior with which they do not wish to be bothered. Of course, no such inference is warranted. Behaviorism claims to render a *more* complete and a *more* scientific account of the totality of human achievement *without* the conception of consciousness, than tra-

ditional psychology is able to render *with* it. The factors which traditional psychology vaguely classifies as conscious or mental elements merely *vanish* without a remainder into the biological and social components of the behavioristic analysis.[8]

Weiss's words, of course, were programmatic rather than a report of actual achievement. The antibehaviorists were wrong in their specific accusations of inadequate coverage of observable facts (at least in intent) by the behaviorists, but it is true that the latter did leave some things out. Neither they nor their opponents can be faulted for neglecting matters on which we were still largely in ignorance: for example, genetics, then still in its infancy. I have been mystified by the extent to which the behaviorists were satisfied by merely replacing the term *mental* by *social*, as though the great empirical problems of social behavior and its transmission had been solved; but here, the investigation of the cultural mechanism of transmission and of its corollary, cultural relativism, had just barely been begun by anthropologists. Esper has commented[9] on the danger of the "empty organism" stance of most of the early behaviorists, who in their eagerness to discard "mind" also ignored the brain; yet what has been learned of the workings of the central nervous system in the last half century does not really seem to help much.

But on one score most of the behaviorists, along with all the nonbehaviorists, made a serious mistake: they did not make adequate provision for human *communicative* behavior—preeminently language, which is unique to our species.

It is just on this score that the collaboration of Weiss and Bloomfield was so vitally important; and Esper was there to observe and learn from it.

In the absence of transcripts of their consultations, we can nevertheless outline what must have happened. Weiss believed that human psy-

8. A. P. Weiss, *A Theoretical Basis of Human Behavior* (2nd ed., Columbus, Ohio: R. G. Adams, 1929), p. vii. Among linguists the accusations of the "mentalists" were even more absurd; some of them are quoted, together with appropriate rejoinder, by Bloomfield in "Secondary and Tertiary Responses to Language," *Language* 20, 45–55 (1944).

9. *Mentalism and Objectivism*, pp. 182ff.

chology can be accounted for only in terms of human language (Meyer had been insistent on this point, and all the early behaviorists at least gave lip service to the notion). Bloomfield had held the Wundtian view, then current among linguists: that human language can be accounted for only in terms of human psychology. If either of these proposals is partly true, then the other must be partly false. Weiss could not back up his thesis in detail because he lacked the technical tools of linguistic analysis, but Bloomfield supplied those in abundant measure. In turn, Weiss helped Bloomfield to realize that the traditional psychological "explanations" of this or that feature of language were nothing more than paraphrases, in mentalistic terms, of what could be (and often enough already had been) perfectly well described in purely linguistic terms.

The upshot was a special brand of behaviorism which can be summarized in three propositions:

(1) Human language behavior (indeed, human communicative behavior of all sorts) can be fully accounted for in terms of physics and biology (*Naturwissenschaft*), properly developed and extended, without positing any nonmaterial or "mental" entities.

(2) Such aspects of human conduct as belief systems, artistic endeavors, law, ethics, science, and mathematics, obvious realities and yet difficult to dissect and explain, can also be understood monistically—*provided we allow for the unique role of language.*

(3) Conversely, however: a linguistically naive monism or physicalism is as impotent as any dualism, for it cannot explain the differences between human behavior and that of other animals.

The wording here is mine, and more explicit than any formulation of the 1920s that has survived in print. But it was explicit enough then to enthrall a young scholar of Esper's stature. And it was sufficiently different from the program of any other version of behaviorism, or of any brand of nonbehavioristic psychology, to tell us why Esper could remain a steadfast behaviorist to the end, as divers of his colleagues and successors turned to other doctrines.

If Meyerian-Weissian-Bloomfieldian behaviorism, rather than Watsonian and the popular dilutions, had held the center of the stage fifty years ago, the subsequent history of psychology might have been different —and better.[10] Indeed, given a slightly incredible largesse of intellectual honesty, psychology as a separate discipline might have come to an honorable and unlamented end: once the *Geist* has been exorcised, *Geisteswissenschaft* has no subject matter. The scattered positive contributions that have been made by professional psychologists in the last half century would then have been made—doubtless with less fuss and bother—by professional something-elses.[11]

We know what actually happened. Meyerian-Weissian-Bloomfieldian behaviorism was forgotten by all but a very few. Its technical demands were too great; it violated our tribal beliefs too sharply; its special way of speaking ran too flagrantly counter to our inherited word magic. More dilute and palatable brands of quasibehaviorism had their flush of popularity in the 1920s, but then subsided to become just an inconspicuous few of the two and seventy jarring sects of psychology today. Psychology became all things to all men, and experienced a phenomenal expansion: in 1920 the American Psychological Association had 393 members, 0.00037 percent of the population of the country; in 1970, 30,839 members, 0.0149 percent of the population; the absolute growth in five decades was 78-fold, the percentagewise increase 40-fold. The intellectual history of our species records no more colossal failure.

Now we are in a better position to explain Esper's career.

He began it with superb training in an approach for which an increasing number of his professional colleagues had little sympathy and which few of them were even equipped to understand. He would have switched his theoretical stance had anyone ever given him adequate empirical reasons for doing so, but no one ever did, and a change merely for the sake of cheerful companionship was unthinkable in the German

10. I never checked this notion with Esper, but a year ago I mentioned it to my late colleague Prof. Robert MacLeod of Cornell's Department of Psychology, who was knowledgeable in such matttrs. His eyes lit up as he agreed.

11. Or, to be sure, the word *psychology* might have been retained with neglected etymology and a shifted meaning—which is what has happened to the perfectly respectable terms *atom, malaria,* and *warm-bloodedness.*

scholarly tradition to which he was heir. He became isolated because he was abandoned. The remoteness of Seattle may have contributed, but could not have been as important. It is fortunate that he had a remarkably warm family within which to find moral support, and not surprising that he sought it there. It is clear why he devoted the bulk of his attention to students, for whom there was some hope, rather than to his colleagues, for whom there was little or none.

The massive swing of psychology away from the objectivism of the 1920s must have dismayed him, but also puzzled him. Why should it happen? I suspect that this was what led him to his interest in the history of psychology. When he investigated, he discovered that the contemporary trend was nothing novel: as far back as the record carries us, we find the pendulum regularly moving between an emphasis on objective investigation and a reliance on philosophical dualism, sometimes with several swings in a single century. This is dealt with especially in *Mentalism and Objectivism*, but with occasional comment elsewhere (including his letters to me). As is so often the case, the enlargement of perspective merely replaced the original puzzle by a bigger one: what is there in human character that makes for the periodicity?

To that he never found the answer. But he did incline to become rather fatalistic about it, wondering whether any one scholar, no matter what his strategy, could ever influence the cyclicity in any major way. This growing conviction, though quite understandable, was Esper at his (remarkably good) worst. But it led to his valuable study of Max Meyer as a "scientific isolate," which in major outline, though obviously not in detail, is also autobiographical.

For his *History of Psychology* Esper made a bold decision: he chose to regard the periodic pendulum swings to the dualistic pole as interruptions, temporary setbacks in the development of psychology as an objective investigation. That would have been clear on the title page of the book had his publisher been willing to use Esper's intended full version; *The History of Psychology as a Biological Science*. When the publisher preferred a shorter form, Esper dropped the last four words, changed the initial definite article to the indefinite, and explained in the Preface. But the design and content of the book remained unaltered.

xvi

Before closing, I must explain why it fell to my lot to write the present account. As far as I am aware, Esper and I never met to face to face (I was raised on the Ohio State campus, but as students there he was nineteen years ahead of me). We began to correspond in 1967. He gave me help in an enterprise I had undertaken (p. vii); he then permitted me to help him get his second book into print. I found in him a close link with a period of scholarship for which I have deep respect but which I was too young to appreciate at the time; he found in me, I think, one of the relatively few people of a later generation who had not sold out to what he regarded as shallowness and deceit in pseudo-scholarship. We did not agree about everything (some of his criticisms of some of my proposals about language will be found in the present book), but our scientific predilections were the same. Also, we liked each other. We corresponded about many matters, at first only professional, later also personal. I tried hard to give him succor during his terribly difficult last two years. Perhaps I succeeded in some measure, since in his last letter to me he spoke, in terms that only he and I could fully understand, of my "sentimental rationality." He did not live to know the equally personal phrase I had chosen to describe him, but it appears in the Postface of a book I have just published and I shall repeat it here: "an uncompromising behaviorist with a beautiful soul."

Esper's teachings may not find many sympathetic listeners in the immediate future. But if his diagnosis of history was right (and if our species manages to survive), the pendulum will swing again. And then, just possibly, we will find that he has helped to transmit to us the essential clues for stilling the pendulum more permanently and for getting on more honestly with the real business of life, which is the business of trying to understand ourselves.

Charles F. Hockett

Ithaca, New York
8 May 1973

BIBLIOGRAPHY

The listing omits some reviews and brief notices that appeared in *Psychological Bulletin, Journal of Genetic Psychology, Journal of General Psychology,* and *Journal of English and Germanic Philology.*

1918. A contribution to the experimental study of analogy. *Psychological Review,* 25, 468–487.

1921. The psychology of language. *Psychological Bulletin,* 18, 490–496.

1925. *A technique for the experimental investigation of associative interference in artificial linguistic material.* Philadelphia: Linguistic Society of America, *Language Monographs,* no. 1.

1926. The bradyscope: An apparatus for the automatic presentation of visual stimuli at a constant slow rate. *Journal of Experimental Psychology,* 9, 56–59.

1930a. Review of G. de Laguna, *Speech: Its function and development. Psychological Bulletin,* 27, 65–70.

1930b. Review of G. de Laguna, *Speech: Its function and development. Journal of English and Germanic Philology,* 29, 140.

1933a. Polytactic manual movement apparatus. *Journal of Experimental Psychology,* 16, 161–174.

1933b. Studies in linguistic behavior organization. *Journal of General Psychology,* 8, 346–381.

1935. Language. In C. Murchison, ed., *A handbook of social psychology.* Worcester, Mass.: Clark University Press, 417–460.

1964. *A history of psychology.* Philadelphia: W. B. Saunders.

1966a. Max Meyer: The making of a scientific isolate. *Journal of the History of the Behavioral Sciences,* 2, 341–356.

1966b. Max Meyer and the psychology of music. *Journal of Music Theory,* 10, 182–199.

1966c. Social transmission of an artificial language. *Language,* 42, 575–580.

1967. Max Meyer in America. *Journal of the History of the Behavioral Sciences,* 3, 107–131.

1968. *Mentalism and objectivism in linguistics: The sources of Leonard Bloomfield's psychology of language.* New York: American Elsevier.

1971. Review of A. L. Blumenthal, *Language and psychology: Historical aspects of psycholinguistics. Language,* 47, 979–983.

1973. *Analogy and association in linguistics and psychology.* Athens: University of Georgia Press.

To my friend

CHARLES FRANCIS HOCKETT

Who has helped me over hurdles
both professional and personal

CONTENTS

PREFACE

When, in the early 1950s, the attempt was made to introduce psychologists and linguists to one another's terms, concepts, and techniques, both sciences had undergone great changes in these respects from the state of affairs which had prevailed during the period of their last previous lively interaction. In the period circa 1870–1910, psychology, particularly as applied to linguistics, had been for the most part mentalistic, and its method had been mostly that of introspection. Linguistics during that period was strongly historical and comparative. By 1950 psychology had become mostly objective and behavioristic. But presently, psychology, in its application to linguistics—as "psycholinguistics"—tended to revert to mentalism, particularly in America, under the influence largely of the logician Noam Chomsky, who sought to "revolutionize" both linguistics and psychology by returning these sciences to the state of affairs of an earlier period. Chomsky has called his doctrines "Cartesian" and declared that linguistic theory after Wilhelm von Humboldt was mostly wrong or inadequate. Unfortunately, it now appears that these allegations are a product of careless scholarship (see, e.g., Aarsleff, 1970); whether or how carefully he and his followers have read the works of the "neogrammarians," from Karl Brugmann to Leonard Bloomfield, seems questionable, in view of the contempt which they express for them. A. L. Blumenthal, a young psychologist convert to Chomskyanism, has sought to present Wilhelm Wundt as "the Master Psycholinguist"; although Wundt's "mentalism" was undoubtedly a form of psychophysical parallelism—if not of interactionism—Blumenthal and other Chomskyans deny that their "mentalism" is a dualism; e.g., J. J. Katz has asserted that the Chomskyan "mentalists" are referring to "brain mechanisms." But what linguists or "psycholinguists" have to do with the brain is far from clear; Blumenthal has denied that Chomsky and his coworkers have any pretensions to a knowledge of neurophysiology. Their vaguely spatial metaphors about "deep" or "underlying structures" are of course merely logical abstractions—which seem however to give many scholars a sense of a profound grasp of the nature of language. So too their talk about "competence" as being the main business of linguistics, and their disdain for actually spoken speech. Their contemptuous references to empiricism, positivism, and operationism seem to me ill-judged; I doubt whether at any time in the histories of psychology and linguistics we have been more in need of these controls on abstractions and metaphors. We have, of course, in psychology, been through all of this sort of thing before; C. L. Hull was assisted by some enthusiastic young men trained in the symbolism of formal logic and tried to present his theoretical views in such symbolism. This formidable presentation, though read by very few, impressed many as evidence of a growing sophistication in psychological theory, placing it abreast of the then triumphant mathematical physics—the demonstration working, I suppose, somewhat after the fashion of the legendary philosopher who in a disputation before a royal court wrote several mathematical equations and then wrote QED, thus defeating his opponent, who could not determine the relevance of the equations to the matter under discussion. Similarly, the relevance of Chomsky's formulae to the spoken language of the general population who are not linguists or logicians seems to me very dubious; in fact, the attempt to apply the Chomskyan technique to the description of a "native" language (Jamaican Creole) has been described as unfortunate (reference in Esper, 1968, p. 231). Had Chomsky presented his symbolic method, with the modesty appropriate in science, as a possibly convenient way of describing or comparing syntactic patterns, he would perhaps have made a useful contribution; but not content with that, he has delivered himself of a vast range of speculations and pronouncements, particularly about hereditary mechanisms and psychological theory—fields in which his professional competence is highly dubious. His review of B. F. Skinner's book *Verbal Behavior* has, as MacCorquodale (*Journal of the Experimental Analysis of Behavior*, 1969, 12, 831–841) has said, been "even more widely read [than Skinner's book] to judge by the subsequent uncritical acceptance of its misconceptions concerning *Verbal Behavior*'s content"; "his criticisms, although stylistically effective, were mostly irrelevant to *Verbal Behavior*." Skinner is of course a "peripheralist"; he followed his teachers in "resenting the nervous system"—at least, as it had appeared in the speculations of psychologists. I have discussed this matter elsewhere (Esper, 1964, 1968), pointing out that psychology must assume that behavior has a neural basis; this view has led J. R. Kantor (*Psychological Record*, 1970, pp. 275f.) to reproach me with "mentalism," a reproach which I can as little understand as I can Kantor's general principle that the nervous system is no more important in the behavior studied by psychology than are the muscles, viscera, etc. I have wondered where Kantor thinks all the knowledge, abilities, and prejudices are stored which have found expression in his books. But certainly, when we have said that the brain is the integrative and storage mechanism which makes more or less intelligent and coordinated behavior possible, we have said about as much as our present knowledge of neurophysiology—at least as applied to linguistics—justifies. K. S. Lashley did not, as E. G. Boring alleged, "discover the engram," nor did he, as the Chomskyans keep implying, discover the neurophysiological mechanisms governing syntactic sequences; he merely said that these were difficult and interesting problems which he had been unable to solve; he could not have solved them with the methods then at his disposal. *Nobody* has as yet discovered these things. Until neurophysiologists do arrive at discoveries which could have important applications in linguistics, linguists would do well to follow Bloomfield's suggestion that they express their findings in terms of their own data. In the meantime, both linguists and psychologists could benefit by a careful—though critical—reading of Skinner, while ignoring Chomsky's irrelevancies.

In linguistics, under the influence particularly of Ferdinand de Saussure, there had occurred a sharp separation of descriptive from historical interests, and in consequence the linguistics which psycholinguists learned in the 1950s was preoccupied with describing languages—or language "universals"—as static, rigid, rule-governed systems (cf. Hockett, 1968) in which variations were a form of "creativity" in accordance with rules developed on the basis of predispositions in the germ plasm of neonates. One result of these changes has been an absence of interest on the part of psycholinguists in the historical processes by which languages change, and in particular, in those processes which, under the name of *analogy*, had been considered to be the chief sources of order and organization in language. When, quite recently, psycholinguists have attempted to deal with such historical processes, they have been at pains to disavow the concept of analogy, and they have joined with colleagues in psychology in repudiating the related concept of association. Linguists, for their part, have mostly ignored the relevance of experimental studies by psychologists based on these concepts (but an exception is Stern, 1931). An unnecessary difficulty has been caused by the usual presentation of the process of analogy as a logical operation in the form of an equation, a presentation which exhibits the common tendency to "explain" linguistic phenomena in terms of supposed mental processes. Further difficulty has resulted from the attribution of analogical formations—particularly blends and contaminations—to the processes of word-association.

It is my hope—no doubt vain—that reviewers will read carefully at least my brief last chapter, and, if their time and prejudices permit, my longer second-last chapter. If, against all hope, they could be induced to read the last three chapters, momentarily suspending judgments based on preconceptions, they will understand why I define analogy as I do, why I regard word-association as resulting from the same tendency which also produces analogical formations, and why my definition of analogy excludes haplologies, metatheses, phonetic assimilations, etc. To have called these last phenomena *phonetic* was perhaps a mistake, since this term may suggest to linguists that I am confusing them with the operation of regular "sound-laws." A better term for me to have used would have been *articulatory* or *motor* phenomena. When someone says *evelate* for *elevate* or I *fool so feelish* he exemplifies an individual's momentary error of motor coordination, not an associative interference based on the similarity of meaning of two or more words. Such errors are commonly observed in the psychological laboratory in the form, e.g., of "anticipatory errors" in serial learning. I think that such momentary discoordinations should be distinguished from analogical tendencies which we might expect to be attested by the word-association responses of many individuals. Many "errors" of serial discoordination have of course become "naturalized" in languages; they can be distinguished from sound changes in that they do not exemplify the "exceptionless" property of phonetic "laws," and from analogy in that they are errors of motor discoordination within particular speech sequences rather than products of associative interference among words of similar meaning. Some linguists may also be disturbed by my exclusion of such changes as *mountain→mounting* (in my discussion, near the end of Chapter 7, of Thomason's classification) from the class of analogical changes. But I think that such changes had better be classed under borrowing, in which they are usually described as originating. They do not seem to me to be analogical; it seems very unlikely that there would be a semantic relation, e.g., between *mountain* and *going*—indeed, Thomason concedes that there is none. While in a word-association experiment one may occasionally elicit such associations as *noon→tune*, they are very infrequent in normal adults and are characteristic rather of very young children and of retardates (cf. Cramer, 1968). Since I wish to include semantic association among the criteria for analogical change, I must exclude changes of the kind here in question.

My purpose has been to arrive at a definition of analogy which would be in accord with and have heuristic value for psychological research. It has seemed to me that the term has been used much too loosely for it to serve this purpose; this is a matter, I think, in which linguists have paid too little attention to experimental psychology. It has been my hope that by reviewing the history, both in linguistics and in psychology, of the concepts of analogy and association, a sounder basis might be given for discussions of the processes whereby languages are learned and used, and whereby also they become organized into phonemically marked categories. I have been reinforced in this hope by my conviction that the literature which I have reviewed is unfamiliar to many of the younger practitioners both of linguistics and of psychology. It is unfamiliar also to several senior psychologists who have taken an interest in language but who, though they have lived through the great volume of theorizing and experimentation in association and learning, have been captivated by the Chomskyan doctrines; the atmosphere in which their conversion has taken place is very aptly conveyed by the description which I have quoted in Chapter 6 from J. J. Jenkins of a conference on verbal behavior. And so Deese (1970) has decided that "those who have tried to apply learning theory to the problem of how people use language do not really understand what language really is" (pp. 2f.). This implies that Deese now "really understands what language really is," an implication which I find difficult to accept. Some of the younger psychologists have been disturbed by my treatment of Wundt, although I gave rather extended treatment to his views about language in a previous book (1968). Blumenthal has presented Wundt as "the Master Psycholinguist," and J. C. Marshall (1970), having found it difficult to reconcile my estimate of Wundt's contribution to the psychology of language with his teachers' presentations of Wundt as "the founder of experimental psychology," has listed a great number of publications by Wundt and his pupils which he thinks that I have either missed or neglected to mention. So far as the present topic in the psychology of language is concerned, however, perhaps Marshall may be reminded that James McKeen Cattell took with him to Leipzig his problems in word-association, that he performed his association experiments at Leipzig in his own quarters so as not to be limited by Wundtian dogma, and that most of his experiments relevant to the psychology of language were performed after his return to America; further, that Wundt, with his customary arrogance, rejected the researches of Thumb and Marbe, for reasons which seemed rather frivolous (as described in my Chapter 4, where I also quote Thumb's reasons for rejecting the "Tiefsinn" of Karl Vossler, which are also the reasons for my distaste for Chomsky's "deep structures," and for all approaches, in natural science, by the "methods of formal logic" or by intuition, where a reference to a body of data—in the description of a living language, a "corpus" of recorded spoken language—is regarded as unnecessary; I have been astonished by the ready acceptance by many linguists of what is actually a form of "prescriptive grammar").

And now, as I lay down my pen and cover my typewriter for the last time, perhaps a few personal remarks may be pardoned. I regret the polemical tone of some of my recent writings; I regret the passing of the era of professional courtesy which Bloomfield thought he foresaw upon the founding of the Linguistic Society of America. And yet, perhaps Boring was right when he suggested that controversy supplies the motive power for science. Enthusiasms, and indeed fashions, come and go in both psychology and linguistics. In my first apprenticeship to scholarship, I enthusiastically counted the abstract nouns in the *Iliad* and *Odyssey* as a contribution to the war between the Separatists and the Unitarians, and I was proud to see my results printed in a column of figures in the *Classical Weekly* as evidence against the Unitarians. A little later I was inducted into the ranks of the behaviorists in their controversy with the— mostly Titchenerian—mentalists, in a university department that was divided into two ideologically hostile groups. Behaviorism, in its American form, had just been born, and though it claimed to be based on neurobiology, it was dogmatically peripheralistic; under the influence of Jacques Loeb, the central nervous system was thought to be no more than a system of "protoplasmic bridges" between sense organs and muscles. That was fifty or more years ago; it is since then that brain physiology has been developing techniques which may eventually tell us something of how the brain performs its functions in such an activity as speech. Until then, I think that linguists, psycholinguists, and most psychologists had better regard the brain as an area of intense technical activity surrounded by barriers labeled "Men Working" and refrain from uttering either peripheralistic dogmas or dogmas about deep structures or about what goes on inside a person's head when he speaks. I have, of course, during the past half-century, seen many other theories, fads, and fancies come and go, and while all the controversial literature which they produced may have supplied motive power, I am depressed by the thought of the enormous waste of energy, goodwill, and paper which they also produced, and I share Bloomfield's wistful vision of a more rational—and courteous—world of science in which workers could respect and mutually stimulate one another, and hostility would be expressed only for really careless and unscholarly publications and not for the work of those with whose point of view one happened to disagree.

It is a pleasure to express my gratitude to Professors Charles Hockett and David Olmsted and to Dr. Sarah Thomason for their reading of the manuscript of this book, and for their comments and suggestions; it would be unjust, however, to attribute to them approval of everything that I have said. I gratefully acknowledge a grant by the American Council of Learned Societies in aid of the expenses incidental to the writing of this book.

E. A. E.

Seattle, Washington
October 1971

Chapter 1
THE CONCEPT OF ANALOGY
IN ANCIENT GREECE AND ROME

Greek *analogía* (Latin *proportio* or *ratio* 'relation' or 'proportion') was used by Plato and Aristotle (e.g., *Poetics* 21) as a mathematical and logical term for "equality of ratios," as in $a : b = c : d$. Its application, in a transferred sense, to linguistic data is illustrated by Colson (1919, p. 25) with an example from Aristarchus:[1] "If the genitive plural of *thōs* was according to some *thóōn*, according to others *thōôn*, while the genitive of *thér* was undoubtedly *therôn*, it was reasonable to argue that *thōôn : therôn = thōs : thér.*" This example illustrates how the principle of analogy could be applied to the choice between rival forms, both in the emendation of texts and in the setting up of paradigms for prescriptive grammars. These were matters of concern to the grammarians of the several centuries before and after Christ when they were dealing editorially with the classics—especially Homer—of ages long past. In the writing of prescriptive grammars, based on the usage of "good" authors, the grammarians assembled noun and verb stems, classified them according to similarities, and sought to establish rules for their similarities and differences in inflection. When the term *analogy* was first applied to inflec-

---

1. Steinthal (1891, p. 103) says that Aristarchus used only simple comparison, i.e., two-member analogy, e.g., "*oiôn* like *aigôn.*" Varro (x.37) defines analogy in terms of a four-member proportion: "If there are two things of the same class which belong to some relation though in some respect unlike each other, and if alongside these two things two other things which have the same relation are placed, then because the two sets of words belong to the same *Lógos* each one is said separately to be an analogue and the comparison of the four constitutes an *Analogía.*" Lersch (1838, 1, 59f.) quotes Varro and others to the effect that Aristophanes of Byzantium (c. 260–180 B.C.), founder of the Alexandrian school of grammarians and teacher of Aristarchus, was the first to use the term *analogía* in the sense of "the complex of similar relationships in language."

tional paradigms, the regularities which they showed were perhaps interpreted as complexes of mathematical proportions between individual forms of individual words (Fehling, 1956). In the course of time, however, the term came to be used more generally for "inflectional regularity," or more specifically as a synonym for *declension* (Colson, 1919, p. 31n.).

There has been a tradition of a "controversy" of several centuries' duration between "analogists"—chiefly the Alexandrian grammarians, whose chief representative was Aristarchus (c. 220–145 B.C.), and who typically emphasized the regularities in the relations of forms to functional meanings—and "anomalists"—chiefly the so-called Stoics of Pergamum, of whom Crates of Mallos (fl. c. 160 B.C.) was a chief representative, and who typically emphasized the irregularities in the relations between forms and lexical meanings.[2] Lersch (1838) considered himself to be the first modern scholar to recognize the full historical importance of the supposed logomachy ("Strudel zweier gegeneinander ankämpfenden Bewegungen") which "for a thousand years was the preoccupation of the clearest heads in Greece and Rome"; other modern scholars had failed to notice the quarrel—except for Classen (1829), who had declared it to be *vix tanto hiatu digna*, "hardly worth a yawn." Fehling (1956, 1958) has made an exhaustive study of the evidence and has concluded that the "controversy" between two "schools" was an invention of the Roman polymath Marcus Terentius Varro (116–127 B.C.) and that none of the alleged adversaries were so stupid as to be unaware that there are systematic regularities in linguistic forms and that there are many exceptions to the regularities. Varro himself (IX.1) seems to make this statement with sufficient clarity. Perhaps Lersch qualifies more nearly as the inventor.

Steinthal (1891, pp. 124–126) makes statements which seem to place him on both sides of the question: "The controversy between

2. Compare the more general statement by Benfey (1869, p. 151): "The analogists . . . were intent on showing that language is ruled by a pervasive lawfulness, that conceptually similar categories are expressed by similar phonetic forms, and they succeeded thus in presenting language as in general a harmonious system . . . . The anomalists on the contrary . . . relied on the observation that in language analogy is often infringed and that the phonetic forms of categorically similar words differ in more or less essential degrees."

Aristarchus and Crates could not have had an empirical and practical but only a theoretical significance"; Aristarchus treated analogy as a general principle, but usually followed "usage"—either the best evidence of the texts or else his own "Sprachgefühl"; Crates and the Stoics considered usage to be the only general principle, although they were well aware of regularities ("Nicht darum sagt man *agathós, kakós, agathoû, kakoû,* weil dies die Analogie fordere, . . . sondern weil man tatsächlich so sagt, wie man denn auch hätte anders sagen können"). On the other hand, Steinthal and most later authors accepted the notion of a prolonged and vigorous controversy which furnished the motivation for the analysis and classification of linguistic forms into inflectional schemata and which ended in final mutual victory and defeat for the "antagonists": the "canons"[3] or rules which the analogists found necessary to account for apparent exceptions became so numerous that they demonstrated anomaly as much as analogy; the "fight" thus ended in a draw (Steinthal, 1891, pp. 153f., 160f.). Arens (1955, p. 18) remarks: "Bei so extremer Einstellung und verschiedenen Ausgangspunkten musste es notwendig ein Streit um des Kaisers Bart sein, und keine Partei konnte wahrhaft siegen."

The obvious difference between the Alexandrians and the Stoics was that the former were philologists interested in the editing of classical texts and in establishing prescriptive grammars of "correct" usage, whereas the latter were philosophers and logicians interested in the relations between speech, thought, and "reality." Steinthal (1891, p. 73) says that *analogy* and *anomaly* for the Stoics referred to the relation between logic and grammar, while for the grammarians they referred to the interrelations among linguistic elements. (Crates, however, was a grammarian, an editor of Homer, and was reputed to have introduced the study of grammar to Rome.) The Stoics had adopted the "naturalistic" position represented by Cratylus in Plato's dialogue: there is a natural affinity between word form and word meaning. They thus assumed a general principle of onomatopoeia or sound symbolism. But with this principle many phenomena, such as those of homonymy and polyonymy, were difficult to reconcile;

---

3. The term *kanónes* 'canons' was also used to refer to paradigms or inflectional schemata which conformed to given rules and which therefore were regular and in accordance with analogy.

the Stoics therefore declared that it was necessary to assume a condition of anomaly in language. This anomaly, however, could be attributed to processes of "corruption" of the original and "natural" form-meaning correlations, as "Socrates" suggested in the *Cratylus*. As a result of such processes, the relations of existing languages to thought—i.e., logic or dialectic—were imperfect. Thus the linguistic expressions for privation, negation, and opposition are not consistent: e.g., *blind* is a positive expression for a privation, while *immortal* is a negative expression of a positive attribute of the gods. The Stoic philosopher Chrysippus generalized the principle of anomaly by the statement "All words are by nature ambiguous"; the ambiguity was however said to be removed when words occur in syntactic contexts. Linguistic gender distinctions attracted especial attention; it was pointed out that they are often incongruent with "natural"—i.e., conceptual—classifications and may differ for the "same" word in different dialects. Thus Greek *to paidion* 'child' (like German *das Kind*) is neuter in form but common in meaning. Similar anomaly was found in expressions of grammatical number and in the temporal and other categorical forms of verbs. And finally, locutions are possible which are incongruent with reality: e.g., "I died yesterday."

According to Varro's account,[4] the "controversy" dealt chiefly with the declensions of nouns: "Analogie heisst das, was wir als 'regelmässige Flexion' bezeichnen würden" (Fehling, 1956, p. 237). The apparent "anomaly" of nouns of similar nominatives but dissimilar declensions was dealt with by the formulation of a set of rules: to have the same declensions, two or more such nouns had to be the same, not only in nominative and vocative, but also in gender, number, ending, number of syllables, accent, and in any other respects, ranging from cogent to absurd, which ingenuity could suggest in "explanation" for differences in inflection. The anomalists maintained—so said Varro—that a consistent and therefore valid principle of analogy would require, e.g., all nouns and adjectives to have forms for all genders, numbers, and cases—in short,

4. In his *De Lingua Latina*. Book VIII contains arguments for anomaly, Book IX, for analogy, while Book X is a sort of recapitulation and supplement favoring the analogist point of view. The text and translation of these books are contained in Roland G. Kent's *Varro on the Latin Language*, vol. 2, in the Loeb Classical Library; my quotations are from Kent's translation.

every word would have to have all the forms which other words of its category possessed. Varro pointed out that the degree of regularity in word-formations varied with cultural factors and usage; thus there was formerly only the feminine noun *columba* 'dove', but when doves had become domesticated, the masculine form *columbus* was analogically created; the gender distinction between *equus* 'horse' and *equa* 'mare' was not made for the less important *corvus* 'raven'. Unlike most other ancient grammarians, Varro distinguished between derivational and inflectional formations and showed that the latter tend to be more complete, analogically regular, and the same for all speakers, whereas the derivational formations are more irregular and variable.

The grammarians and rhetoricians applied the doctrine of analogy in a normative fashion, but they recognized limitations on regularity (i.e., analogy) imposed by usage. Thus in his Book IX, Varro says that "the people as a whole ought in all words to use regularity[5] . . . whereas the orator ought not to use regularity in all words, because he cannot do so without giving offense . . . . For the people has power over itself, but the individuals are in its power . . . I am not the master—so to speak—of the people's usage, but it is of mine" (IX.5, 6). Moreover, "regularity is sprung from a certain usage in speech, and from this usage likewise is sprung anomaly. Therefore, since usage consists of unlike and like words and their derivative forms, neither anomaly nor regularity is to be cast aside, unless man is not of soul because he is of body and of soul" (Varro, IX.3). Varro (IX.1) attributes this compromise view to Aristarchus (cf. Lersch, 1838, 1.65). In Book VIII.33 we find regularity described as dependent on usage: "But if we must follow regularity, either we must observe that regularity which is present in ordinary usage, or we must observe also that which is not found there. If we must follow that which is present, there is no need of rules, because when we follow usage, regularity attends us."

5. Kent's translation of *analogia* as 'regularity' was perhaps inspired by Benfey's (1869, pp. 154f.) suggestion that Herodian, the celebrated grammarian of the second century A.D., used the term *analogia* in the sense of *Gesetzlichkeit* 'lawfulness' and that modern linguistics owes a debt of gratitude to Herodian and the other analogists for "holding high the banner of analogy, which in those days represented the principle of *Gesetzlichkeit der Sprache*," the only sure principle of linguistics; we use the words *anomaly* or even *chance*, says Benfey, only as abbreviations meaning that the explanation of a given phenomenon is as yet unknown.

In such discussions by the Latin writers, analogy appears to have been re-garded as a deliberate, rational, or conscious process, whose force may be limited by usage, authority, etymology, and even by euphony or "suavity." Regular forms are in accordance with logical theory; irregular forms can only be justified as expedient concessions to usage (Varro, IX.8–20). But again, "the foundation of regularity (*analogía*) is nature and use taken in combination. That is singular which by nature denotes one thing, like *equus* 'horse', or which denotes things that by use are joined together in some way, like *bigae* 'two-horse team'. Therefore just as we say *una Musa* 'one muse', we say *unae bigae* 'one two-horse team' " (Varro, IX.63). "There is no regularity in those instances which lack a relationship in use or in nature" (Varro, IX.70). The Alexandrian Greeks listed analogy as one of the criteria for "correctness" ("Hellenism"); the other criteria were usage, age, authority, and relevant dialect (cf. Fehling, 1956, pp. 251–254). Quintilian recognized the philosophical validity of analogy, but for rhetoric recommended "the usage of the learned"—rather than that of the commonalty.[6]

Langendoen (1966) has cited passages in Varro which, by processes of "free association," might suggest that Varro was a forerunner of Hermann Paul, August Schleicher, and "the rationalist grammarians of the seventeenth and eighteenth centuries," and thus of Noam Chomsky. (Langendoen, however, actually suggests, not too seriously, only the last of these "anticipations.") Like Paul, Varro distinguished between the "voluntary derivation" of a lexical item "according to the whim of the innovator," and "natural derivations" which "are governed by statable

6. Concerning the later followers of Aristarchus, who were less inhibited by re-spect for textual authority and *Sprachgefühl*, Steinthal (1891, pp. 111f.) has a passage which may be of melancholy interest to us: "We know how easily pupils slip into the delusion that in the forms and manner of their master they possess the philosopher's stone. . . . The tendency toward transforming the world in accordance with universal laws was particularly strong in all fields, including the political, during the post-Alexandrian period. Subjectivity, in the ascendant, sought everywhere to revise objec-tive relations in accordance with a priori constructions. Thus the principle of analogy came to be regarded not merely as a means of explaining the facts but as a norm which was to govern the editing of texts." Moreover, in the application of the principle to the contemporary *Umgangssprache*, there was no clear recognition of the necessity of listen-ing to actual spontaneously creative speakers; "every deviation from literary language [well-formed sentences?] was regarded as a corruption" (Steinthal, p. 120).

6

rules of the language." "Therefore in the voluntary derivations there is inconsistency, and in the natural derivations there is consistency" (Varro, IX.35). Like Schleicher, Varro made use of a biological metaphor: "Naturally derived forms are produced by inflexible linguistic laws, just as the form of a plant is governed by the inflexible laws of its growth, according to kind." Like Humboldt and Chomsky, Varro declared that not only were there principles which governed particular languages but there were also universal principles which governed all languages: "syntactic derivation is an instance of a universal generative principle," and "given an expression denoting any underlying object or idea . . . it must be such that it can form the basis of further derivations." Thus, says Langendoen (whom I have just been quoting), the Stoic belief that only the level of *empeiría* 'practical knowledge' was attainable can be said to correspond to the empirical position concerning language. The Alexandrians thought that linguistics could be a *tékhnē* 'science'. Varro, says Langendoen, may be given credit for first raising questions about language at the level of *epistémē* 'understanding'. But Fehling (1956, p. 250) points out that in the Latin writers the definition of correct speech—"Latinity"—includes the word *observatio* 'observance', which is closely associated with *empeiría* as well as with *analogía*; he quotes Quintilian to the effect that analogy is not a law of language but an observance.

Steinthal (1891, p. 156) discusses Quintilian's view of analogy: "If analogy is only the product of usage, it can be based only on examples, not on logical consideration; hence it cannot serve as a law or means of emendation but only as an empirical fact. But in relinquishing logic and law and sinking to the level of mere observation, it lost its essential nature; it became indistinguishable from anomaly." Lersch (1838, pp. 77f.) had expressed the view that the analogy-anomaly controversy about the nature of language gradually became an argument about the nature of linguistics: whether the task of grammar was to organize everything rationally, under rules, or whether its task was to collect observations; thus arose "two new sects": the "technicists," who in the analogist tradition held grammar to be a science, and the "empiricists," who in the anomalist tradition held it to be an inventory of observed usage. (In medicine, a somewhat similar distinction was made between the "empirical" and the "dogmatic"

7

schools, although the former, in cases where "experience" failed, sought analogies in somehow similar cases.) In contemporary linguistics, the rationalistic "Cartesian" school has applied the term *taxonomic*—in a pejorative sense—to linguistic empiricism. Lersch (1838, pp. 176f.) quotes Klopstock: "The grammarian teaches the rules of language and notes the meanings of words. Because he must take the language as it is, and not as he thinks it ought to be, he must let usage alone be his guide with respect both to the rules and to his observations. . . . If he does not, he is a grammatical, even though sometimes a talented, prattler."

Our interest in all of the above arises of course from our desire to gain some notion of what the nineteenth-century linguists found in their conceptual toolbox when they began their efforts to create a scientific linguistics by tracing and attempting to account for linguistic change. We have seen that the ancient grammarians had introduced the proportional analogy pattern; that they assumed a basic orderliness in linguistic forms, to which they applied the term *analogy*;[7] that they sought to explain apparent irregularities by means of empirical or even ad hoc rules; that they regarded usage as both a limitation on and a source of regularity. Fehling (1956, p. 254) quotes a sentence from Sextus, attributed to a pupil of Aristarchus, which I translate as "Analogy arises from and in conformity with customary usage." From a Greek source, Fehling (p. 255) cites two different explanations for irregular forms: the first is that language was originally entirely irregular and only attained some regularity by the application to it of "science," whereby however many irregularities persisted; the second is that in language, as in all human affairs, there is continual change. Fehling considers these two explanations to be mutually contradictory, but they seem to be so only in that they are both offered as explanations of irregular forms. If continual change and the application of science were both considered to include the operation of analogic assimilation so as to produce regularities, the contradiction would disappear.

---

7. Thus in Charisius *analogia* = *regula sermonis*, and Quintilian (1,6,44) spoke of *regula sermonis* and (1,7,1) of *regula loquendi*. Curtius (1885) remarked that after *analogy* had come to mean "rule" it ceased to be used in this sense (e.g., in the famous grammars of Donatus [c. 350] and Zumpt [1818]), but that it began to be applied to deviations from a rule in the direction of a different formation; to such deviations the term *false analogy* was applied (Rogge, 1925, pp. 447f.).

We might then be tempted to attribute to the ancient grammarians the view that such continual change included a progressive increase in regularity and of form-meaning correlations by the operation of the associative processes which in the nineteenth century came to be regarded as the chief systematizing processes in linguistic history.[8] But it is doubtful whether we would be justified in attributing such an anticipation to the ancients; they noted the regularities and the irregularities and the fact of change, but they applied these observations chiefly to the emending of texts and to the prescription of rules of usage—of "correct" Greek or "correct" Latin—for the guidance of orators and authors; in both applications, the term *analogy* referred to acts of deliberate choice, of editors or of authors, or at most it referred to the observed paradigmatic regularities of language (although analogical regularity was said to be "natural" rather than "voluntary" [Varro, IX.33–35]). The concept of analogy as an associative systematizing process in linguistic history arose as a late by-product of the nineteenth-century need to explain, not regularities, but the apparent irregularities in the operation of phonetic "laws."

In view of the modern history of the concept of analogy, it is of interest to note the views of the ancients concerning its relation to meaning. The principle of analogy required that similar meanings be represented by similar forms. This raised the question—which has been bothersome ever since—of the definition and criteria of similarity or partial identity, of

8. We might so interpret Varro's statement (VIII.3), "Inflection has been introduced not only into Latin speech, but into the speech of all men, because it is useful and necessary; for if this system had not developed, we could not learn such a great number of words . . . ." The concept of synchronic analogical productivity is stated (VIII.6), "For the scheme by which you have learned to inflect in the instance of one noun, you can employ in a countless number of nouns; therefore when new nouns have been brought into common use, the whole people at once utters their declined forms without any hesitation." We could hardly expect an equally clear statement of analogy as a process of *historical* change. Robins (1967, p. 49) remarks that "one must regret Varro's failure to distinguish these two dimensions of linguistic study [historical etymology and the synchronic formation of derivations and inflections], because, as with other linguists in antiquity, his synchronic descriptive observations were much more informative and perceptive than his attempts at historical etymology." The latter could hardly succeed in the absence of an adequate technique of morphological analysis (cf. Benfey, 1868–1869, pp. 103, 149f.; Steinthal, 1891, p. 130n.), in particular, in the absence of a correct analytic notion of roots or stems. Historico-comparative grammar had to await the nineteenth century; until then, as Benfey says, historical etymology was "the derided Cinderella of the sciences."

"how the presence or absence of the likeness is wont to be recognized." This question was discussed by Varro (VIII.39ff.; x.3ff.). Sounds—of stem and inflectional forms—can be specified, as in the canons, but referential meanings are more troublesome; thus, "if that which is denoted by like words ought to be like, then *Dion* and *Theon*, which they [the analogists?] themselves say are almost identical, are found to be unlike if one is a boy and the other an old man." Varro defines similarity in terms of identical components; each named thing has a certain number of parts; several things may be said to be similar if more than half of their parts are identical. But there may be complete identity of form without any similarity of meaning: thus, *suis* 'thou sewest' and *suis* 'of a swine', the first being a member of a verb conjugation and the second a member of a noun declension, and the two differing completely in referential meaning. Words may show inflectional regularity (= analogy) even though their categorical meanings (gender, number, etc.) are quite arbitrary in relation to their referential meanings. "Therefore those which we use as masculines are not those which denote a male being, but those before which we employ [the pronominal adjectives] *hic* and *hi,* and those are feminines with reference to which we can say *haec* or *hae*" (Varro, IX.41). That is, the criteria of gender in such cases are grammatical rather than semantic.

Chapter 2

EARLY MODERN STATEMENTS
ABOUT ANALOGY

We may pick up the trail of the linguistic concept of analogy in what Robins (1967) has very aptly called "the eve of modern times," that is, in the eighteenth and early nineteenth centuries. Even before the strong impulse to historical and comparative linguistics given in 1786 by Sir William Jones's demonstration of the relationship of Sanskrit to European languages, and by the subsequent applications of Indian techniques of linguistic analysis in the work of Western linguists, the question of the origin and development of language had been the subject of lively discussion in which analogy was presented as an essential process. Thus Etienne Bonnot de Condillac (1715–1780), exponent of Lockian empiricism and antagonist of Cartesian "innate ideas," who in the second part of his *Essai sur l'origine des connaissances humaines* (1746) had presented a theory of the origin of articulate language—of morphology and syntax— from gestural communication, attributed, in the Preface to his *La langue des calculs* (1798, posthum.), to analogy the further development of language after "Nature"—that of human beings—had produced the first beginnings of articulate speech. Analogy, he said, is a relation of similarity. A thing can be expressed in many ways, since there is nothing which does not resemble many other things. But different expressions represent the same thing in different aspects, and our choice of expression depends upon our point of view. Because we are content with an approximate notion of what we want to say and are not greatly concerned to know what others are saying, natural languages exhibit a considerable arbitrariness, and their forms are determined by usage (which the grammarians formulate as laws). In contrast, algebra is a well-constructed language, the only one in which nothing is arbitrary and in which analogy determines the sequence of expressions; it is not a matter of speaking like other people but of speaking in accordance with analogy so as to attain the greatest possible accuracy. The whole art of thinking and speaking has its origin in analogy. The relation between analogy and usage which Condillac posits seems to be very like that which we found described by Varro and other ancient grammarians—analogy is the better way, but in communication among or with the commonalty, usage becomes a rival determinant. In view of the conceptual connection in nineteenth-century linguistics between analogy and association, it should be noted that Condillac, influenced by Locke, adopted as basic principles not only sensationism but also associationism: all experience arises from sensations and is organized by association; the arbitrary signs which constitute language facilitate the associative operations by which "understanding" develops. (Cf. Warren, 1921, pp. 182–186; Arens, 1955, pp. 88–93.)

Nicolas Beauzée (1717–1789), in his *Grammaire générale* (1767), made a logical analytic approach to language in the tradition of the Port Royal grammarians and thought thus to discover the "universal principles" corresponding to the nature of thought itself—the principles which underlie the superficial differences between languages. Among these universal principles were those governing syntactic relations such as the relation between accusative case and active verb, a relation which, he said, always implies a preposition: thus, "*Amo Deum* is *amo (ad* or *in) Deum* (I am in love with God)." This interpretation of the accusative is required by "the simplicity of the analogy which everywhere governs human language" (Arens, 1955, pp. 97–102).

"Poor Lord Monboddo," as Bertrand Russell called James Burnett (1714–1799) because of the ridicule excited by his premature Darwinism, presents an early example of the scholar who attempts to picture the origin of language in terms of spurious descriptions of the languages of "primitive" peoples or "barbarians." On the strength of such descriptions of several American Indian languages, Monboddo (1773) declared these languages to be wholly lacking in analogical systematization, lacking, that is, in phonetic marking of semantic similarities, in morphological and syntactic categories. Such languages, and hence the earliest forms of human language, were thus totally suppletive: e.g., in Huron there was no word for "bear," but different words for "little bear," "big bear," "strong bear," etc. For us, the significance of such absurd statements is, of course, the implication that, in contrast, the categorical organization of "developed" languages was considered to be attributable to or to exemplify analogy.

Theodor Benfey, in Part II of his history of linguistics, describes the developments from the beginning of the nineteenth century to his date of publication, 1869. He thus gives an account of the period during which the foundations of modern historical and comparative linguistics were being laid. His point of view, like that of many German *Gelehrte* of the time, is nationalistic; he celebrates the triumphs of German scholarship. Four great philosophers—Kant, Fichte, Schelling, and Hegel—had prepared the way for the worldview in which all human institutions arose and developed in accordance with laws founded on human nature. Unfortunately, the labors of this philosophical tetrad, and particularly those of Hegel, had resulted also in a separation of philosophical or theoretical from empirical or practical concerns: questions of causation and genesis were assigned to philosophy, whereas the other disciplines, including linguistics, were to base their teachings on traditional and arbitrary norms, for practical purposes. The philosophers, however, did not trouble themselves about actual facts, but "sucked their wisdom from their thumbs"; thus, not for the last time, the practitioners of the "rational" method declared their independence of empirical data. This situation gave way, during the first half of the nineteenth century, to the rise of the historical and scientific attitude and method. Psychology, to which philosophy still laid claim, was becoming a part of anthropology, and thus of zoology. Philosophy seemed fated to be left with speculative metaphysics, "the mythology of science" (Benfey, 1868–1869, pp. 320ff.). The powerful influence of natural science on linguistics was illustrated in the writings of August Schleicher (1821–1868), whose emphasis on objective observation was in strange contrast with his Hegelian beginnings.[9]

The most powerful stimulus within linguistics itself was the introduction into the Western world, in the last decades of the eighteenth century,

9. Cf. Esper, 1968, pp. 95–104.

of the knowledge of Sanskrit and the realization of its relation to the languages of Europe. During the first half of the nineteenth century, the principles by which true relationships among the Indo-European languages could be determined were in process of being established, and comparative grammar and the historical point of view thus came into being; before the criteria for similarity of forms and genetic relationships had been defined, it was possible for, e.g., Adelung in 1806 to find "similarities" between Sanskrit and Hebrew. Also being established was the fact that languages are in continual processes of change, and that the linguistic task is to note the history of these changes—rather than merely to set up a synchronic and static system of "correct" language. During the period 1833–1852, Franz Bopp (1791–1867) published his comparative grammar of the Indo-European languages and thereby established a claim to be called "the founder of comparative linguistics"; the inspiration which he gave to his contemporaries may be gathered from Benfey's (1868–1869) account: e.g., "And here in fact is one of his chief contributions: his researches and expositions showed incontrovertibly that these etymological questions, which had hitherto been considered to be objects only of lucky or unlucky divination, may, by means of an analysis—similar to that employed in the natural sciences—become objects of a methodical investigation, their explanations may become capable of rigorous proof, whose demonstration is essentially a purely mathematical one resting upon the equational form according to which if $A = B$ and $B = C$, then $C = A$" (p. 508).

During the early decades of the nineteenth century there were, on the one hand, the pioneer empirical studies by Rasmus Christian Rask, Jacob Grimm, and Bopp of the historical morphological relations of the Indo-European languages. Grimm said, in 1822, "I am hostile to general logical notions in grammar; they conduce apparently to strictness and solidity of definition, but hamper observation, which I take to be the soul of linguistic science." [10] On the other hand, there was the pioneer theoretical writing of Wilhelm von Humboldt (1767–1835), which may be regarded as the source of much of the subsequent application of "psychology," and hence of the principles of analogy and association, to linguistic explana-

10. Quoted from Jespersen, 1922, p. 42.

14

tions. Since Humboldt stood so near the threshold of these developments, his statements about analogy are of particular interest. The following is my translation of a relevant passage quoted by Arens (1955, pp. 151f.) from the *Gesammelte Schriften*, Bd. 3, pp. 295f.:

> We can assume, as a fundamental principle, that in any language everything is founded upon analogy, and that the structure of a language, even in its smallest details, is an organic one. Only where the linguistic development of a nation suffers disturbances, where a people borrows language elements from another language or is forced to make use of a foreign language in whole or in part, do exceptions to this principle occur. Such cases surely occur in all languages known to us—we are of course separated from the primitive languages and families by historical gaps—and even in the deepest forests of America there could hardly be found an example of a language which has remained throughout its history without admixture from any other language. But when a language adopts a foreign element or undergoes mixture with another language, there at once begins a process of assimilation and an effort gradually to transform the foreign material into the characteristic analogical formation, so that such mixtures result in shorter or longer analogical series rather than in an unorganized miscellany.
>
> But even the actually existing analogy cannot always be traced into its finest divisions. Its traces are obscured by the passage of time; intermediate members of series are lost, since linguistic elements are like living individuals in their rise and fall; indeed, the man himself who takes part in creating language is not always aware of the analogy which he instinctively follows, and the consciousness of a nation, divided among its individual members, cannot be brought into a single living focus.

Humboldt, said Benfey (1868–1869, pp. 520ff.), had one foot in the eighteenth and the other in the nineteenth century, so that the philosophical (Kantian), subjective, a priori tendency was often in conflict with the new historical and objective methodology, and this conflict was the source of many of his contradictions, obscurities, and erroneous assumptions; he worked "from above downward" and tended to pay too little attention to objective details. But he presented many insights which were valuable in the shaping of linguistic science in the first three decades of the nineteenth century: the importance for linguistics of the study of the languages of even the most "barbarous" peoples, the inadequacy of collecting peculiar fragments of grammar and word-lists, and the necessity of discovering the organic nature of a language. "The first rule is therefore to study every language in its inner organization, to follow and systematically arrange all of its discoverable analogies, and thus to arrive at a knowledge of its ideational connections, the range of the represented concepts, the nature of this representation and of its inherent more or less lively tendency toward extension and refinement" (Humboldt, quoted by Arens, 1955, p. 159).

Two Danish linguists, Holger Pedersen (1931, p. 294n.) and Otto Jespersen (1922, pp. 70f.), have called attention to a pamphlet published in 1821 by their countryman, Jakob Hornemann Bredsdorff (1790–1841). Of this little pamphlet, which went unnoticed, as did so many other publications in the Scandinavian languages, Pedersen says, "It could have had no influence even if it had been more easily accessible, for it deals with problems which at that time were not even raised elsewhere, or which at any rate no one understood how to bring into connection with the burning questions of the day." Jespersen says that "what constitutes the deep originality of his little book is the way in which linguistic changes are always regarded in terms of human activity, chiefly of a psychological character. Here he was head and shoulders above his contemporaries; in fact, most of Bredsdorff's ideas, such as the power of analogy, were the same that sixty years later had to fight so hard to be recognized by the leading linguists of that time." Wheeler (1887), in the chronologically arranged bibliography of his monograph on analogy, placed Bredsdorff's pamphlet first. The result of these citations has been, I suspect, a somewhat exaggerated notion among linguists—few of whom are likely to have looked up the original—of Bredsdorff's potential contribution. The single paragraph, of less than one page, which deals with analogy ("The Striving after Analogy") has been translated for me by my colleague, Professor Svere Arestad:

> We detect analogy daily in children's speech; they say, for example, *tiede* or *tee* instead of *tav*, *hvems* for *hvis*, *gaase* for *gaes*, etc., and it shows clearly its influence on every language where one does not retain the old form through written texts or other means. Thus it is that in our language

16

all genitives are formed in the same manner, and identically in the singular and the plural, while in the old language the singular was formed either in *s, r,* or in a vowel, and the plural differed from this. One also discovers that anomalously formed words are replaced by words that are formed in a regular manner (for example, *Sygdom* instead of *Sot,* both from *Syg*), or that a construction now follows analogy which previously was not followed (for example, in the Lord's Prayer we generally say V*or Fader* instead of *Fader Vor*). That, however, is not to say that languages are always improved or become more analogous; for, in part, the other causes of change quite often offset the force of analogy. We may also at times overlook real analogies, which previously were current in the language, and set apparent analogies in their stead. Thus one formerly said *Øien,* by analogy with *Øren* and *Ør̦en,* but later held that it should, like other plurals, end in *e,* and there thus resulted a form in *ne* which is without analogy.

Three linguists—Curtius, Whitney, and Scherer—definitively placed analogy alongside phonetic change as a fundamental linguistic process. Georg Curtius (1820–1885) represents the stage which linguistics had reached when the comparative and historical methods of Indo-European linguistics had been substantially achieved but had not yet been completely assimilated to the natural science model. Curtius, that is, spoke of laws of sound change which operated with "almost the necessity of natural forces" and declared that "only the lawful and intrinsically coherent can be studied by science," but he nevertheless recognized a class of "abnormal" or anomalous changes—of "exceptions to the sound-laws." Already in 1860 he had written what Wheeler (1887, p. 44) called "the earliest general statement of principle, so far as direct connection with the modern science of language is concerned." This was in an article in which he opposed the view that the rule, according to which the chief accent in Latin and in Greek never goes beyond the third syllable, had, in an earlier period of Latin, considerable exceptions. There was involved the question of the causal relation of accent to vowel weakening; Curtius argued that accent was indeed a factor in such linguistic change, but that there are other factors, above all analogy. "Language has a feeling for the association of related forms; each of these affects the others and there is an unmistakable tendency to make them similar, even identical, to level small differences. This tendency becomes even livelier in the course of linguistic history, with the result that anomalies progressively disappear, and in the course of time a continually increasing analogy prevails" (1860, p. 331). In 1870 Curtius made a statement which might seem to announce the program for linguistics in the last quarter of the century: "For linguistic research there are two fundamental notions which are of the highest importance: the notion of analogy and that of phonetic law. I do not think that I am mistaken in asserting that many of the differences of opinion on various questions depend upon the scope which is assigned to each of these notions in the life of language" (Curtius, 1870, p. 2). As Arens (1955, p. 247) says, this passage gives the impression that nothing separates Curtius from his juniors—the neogrammarians, including his pupil, Brugmann. "In reality, however, analogy plays practically no role in his [chief work, *Grundzüge der*] *Griechischen Etymologie.*" And of course he was bitterly separated from his juniors by his view of phonetic law. He was strong for lawfulness, but his juniors were stronger; he recognized the importance of analogy as a linguistic process, but his juniors applied it to the explanation of the "exceptions." In short, Curtius was one of those unhappy men who, after making great contributions, continue to live too long.

William Dwight Whitney (1827–1894) was in his youth "more than an amateur" in natural science (Seymour, 1894), having done important field work in botany, ornithology, and geography. But during the summer of 1849, when he was a member of the United States Survey of the Lake Superior region, he had Bopp's Sanskrit grammar with him. "Doubtless the accident of his finding various linguistic books [brought from Germany by his brother] ready to hand, at the time when his mental powers were most actively developing, had much to do with his turning in the direction of philology" (Seymour, 1894, p. 402). After less than a year of graduate study at Yale, Whitney went to Germany, where during the years 1850–1853 he studied with Weber, Bopp, Lepsius, and Roth; during this time he published, in collaboration with Roth, several textual Sanskrit studies. In 1854, at the age of twenty-seven, he became professor of Sanskrit at Yale. (He had "wasted" three postgraduate years as a teller in his father's bank, although his leisure time was devoted to the study of German and Swedish and to the practice of ornithology and botany.) In view of his early work in natural science, it is not difficult to understand why his work in linguistics could be described by the German adjectives which we frequently find applied to antimetaphysical scientists—*sauber* and *nüchtern,* 'clear' and 'sound'.

Misteli (1880), in the introduction to a 137-page critique of the neo-grammarians—and in particular, of their twin assumptions of exception-less sound-laws and of analogical formations as the necessary explanations of apparent exceptions—describes two men, Whitney and Scherer, as having been pioneers in these views. It is remarkable, however, says Misteli, how seldom Whitney is mentioned as a cofounder of the neo-grammarian movement; the credit rather is given to Scherer and August Leskien. And yet, observes Misteli, Whitney (1874), in his anti-Steinthal (and anti-Humboldt, antimetaphysical) paper, refers to "a whole school of linguistic students" who share his views, and moreover "he everywhere sets the power of analogy in the foreground." [11] And in 1901, Hanns Oertel, in illustrating his statement that "the development of linguistic studies at this very time [the 1860s] was forcing philologists to turn to-ward psychology. Two things especially have contributed to the produc-tion of this effect: first, the employment of analogy as a methodological principle, and second, the first beginnings of what we now term seman-tics" (1901a, pp. 68f.), calls attention to several passages in Whitney's (1867) *Language and the Study of Language.* Thus on page 27, Whitney speaks of children's analogical extension of English plural -*s* and past tense -*d*, and on pages 83ff. he speaks of the "extension of prevailing analogies beyond their historically correct limits," as illustrated by the spread of

11. Steinthal's reply (1874) was in the form of a "Socratic" dialogue and in a highly polemical spirit; in particular, he denounced, with the aid of a—fictitious?—interlocutor, Whitney's limitation of his critique to the section of Steinthal's (1871) Introduction on the origin of language. Whitney was repelled by Steinthal's rational-istic approach: "His point of view and method of treatment are distinctively and highly metaphysical . . . . He has been, in particular, the disciple, interpreter, and continuer of Wilhelm von Humboldt, a man whom it is nowadays the fashion to praise highly, without understanding or even reading him; Steinthal is *the* man in Germany, perhaps in the world, who penetrates the mysteries, unravels the inconsistencies, and expounds the dark sayings, of that ingenious and profound, but unclear and wholly unpractical thinker" (Whitney, 1874, p. 333). The quarrel was therefore similar to that between Bloomfieldians and Chomskyans in our own day; that is, between an inductive spirit and rationalism.

possessive -s. Any new word, such as *telegraph,* when introduced into English, is at once fitted with "a whole apparatus of English inflections," and alterations such as *spoke* and *broke,* for *spake* and *brake,* and even *I done* for *I did* "find support in one of the analogies of the language, which has doubtless done much to call them forth." Whitney is inclined to view most such changes as regrettable; they wipe out valuable distinctions; many of them are the result of ignorance and carelessness; they tend especially to be the work of the lower orders; he speaks of "corruption" and "linguistic degeneration." I suppose that he would not thus describe the addition of an -s or an -er to *telegraph,* but he does say that "historical congruency is the last thing we think of in all this." Thus analogy for Whitney, while recognized as a universal linguistic process, still carried somewhat the odor of error and ignorance. But in his article on philology in the *Encyclopaedia Britannica* he says, "Everything in language depends upon habit and analogy."

In his *The Life and Growth of Language* (1875), Whitney devotes the last page-and-a-half of his chapter on "Change in the Outer Form of Words" to "Change of form by extension of a prevailing analogy." Here he says,

> When phonetic corruption has disguised too much, or has swept away, the characteristics of a form, so that it becomes an exceptional or anomalous case, there is an inclination to remodel it on a prevailing norm. The greater mass of cases exerts an assimilative influence upon the smaller. Or we may say, it is a case of mental economy: an avoidance of the effort of memory involved in the remembering of exceptions and observing them accurately in practice. . . . But the tendency is ever at work, and on a small scale as well as a large; and, of course, especially among those whose acquisition of their language has not been made complete and accurate. Children, above all others, are all the time blundering in this direction— saying *gooder* and *badder, mans* and *foots, goed* and *comed,* even *brang* and *thunk*—and items of such products creep not seldom into cultivated speech. . . . The force of analogy is, in fact, one of the most potent in all language-history; as it makes whole classes of forms, so it has power to change their limits. (pp. 74f.)

Very interesting is Arens's estimate of Whitney's position in the history of linguistics: "His voice is that of common sense in linguistics, sound and unprejudiced (*nüchtern und unvoreingenommen*) with respect to any of the European directions of thought and methods of research, although well acquainted with them."

> And so: with a sound estimate of the possibilities of his science and with solid knowledge, and in everything undogmatic, the first representative of the new world entered the arena of the warring German defenders of principles, who tend to make a *Weltanschauung* of every opinion and an article of faith of every principle. It must also be said that, compared with the acute algebraic operations of Steinthal, the systematic aridity of Schleicher, and the labyrinthine exposition of Pott, Whitney's two books are distinguished by a mode of presentation which is pleasantly clear and smooth, but which is at the same time profound and captivating, a mode of writing, for books of this sort, which has been and still is rare in Germany. (Arens, 1955, pp. 260f.)

And finally, in the following is expressed Whitney's (1875, pp. 303f.) view of the relation of linguistics to psychology:

> The human capacity to which the production of language is most directly due is . . . the power of intelligently, and not by blind instinct alone, adapting means to ends. This is by no means a unitary capacity; on the contrary, it is a highly composite and intricate one. But it does not belong to the linguistic student to unravel and explain, any more than to the student of the history of civilization in its other departments; it falls, rather, to the student of the human mind and its powers, to the psychologist. . . . Out of this relation has grown the error of those who look upon linguistic science as a branch of psychology, would force it into a psychologic mould and conduct it by psychologic methods: an error which is so refuted by the whole view we have taken of language and its history, that we do not need to spend any more words upon it here.

In this passage, it was, I think, Steinthal whom Whitney had particularly in mind; in his paper "Steinthal and the Psychological Theory of Language," he says that, according to Steinthal, "the origin and history of language is a mere matter of states of the mind," and he continues,

> Neither here nor anywhere else in the chapter do we find acknowledgment of the truth that speech is made up of a vast number of items, each one of

which has its own time, occasion, and effect, nor anything to show that he does not regard it as an indivisible entity, produced or acquired once for all. . . . If such is to be the result of the full admission of psychology into linguistic investigation, then we can only say, may Heaven defend the science of language from psychology! and let us, too, aid the defense to the best of our ability. (Whitney, 1874, pp. 348f.)

For Whitney, linguistics is a historical and an inductive science, and he sounds like a premature behaviorist when he says,

Speech is a body of vocal signs, successions of vibrations produced in the atmosphere by the organs of utterance, and apprehended by the organs of hearing. Are the lungs, the larynx, the tongue, the palate, the teeth, the lips, even the air about us, parts of the mind? if so, what is the body? and what are its acts, as distinguished from those of the mind? So far as we can see, the word *jump* is just as much and just as little an act of the mind as jumping over a fence is; each is an act of the body, executed under direction of the mind indeed, but by bodily organs, namely the muscles. . . . An utterance is like nothing else in the world so much as a gesture or motion of the arms, hands, fingers. (Whitney, 1874, pp. 349f.)

We come now to the man who may be considered the last German link in the chain leading from Grimm to the neogrammarians: Wilhelm Scherer (1841–1886). A stumbling-block had been Schleicher's notion that linguistic change—"decay"—had been confined to the historical period. The admiration which Scherer's *Zur Geschichte der deutschen Sprache* (1868) [12] aroused, though hard to understand nowadays, "was fully justified by the intrepid energy with which Scherer liberated himself from the shackles of Schleicher's philosophy and appealed to the living source of experience" (Pedersen, 1931, p. 291). In particular, he explained many apparent anomalies in Indo-European forms in terms of analogy and applied this principle to the entire history and, contra Schleicher,

12. This was a young man's book—he was twenty-seven years old when he wrote it. J. Schmidt (1887, p. 484) says that "when he issued the second edition, ten years later, he was already so alienated from its contents that, in the Preface, he expressed regret at his inability to rewrite it in the manner required by the intervening advances." He had turned to the history of literature. All his work, says Schmidt, bore the stamp of subjectivity; he found careful detailed work somewhat depressing; he valued more highly work such as that of Grimm which suggests but does not exhaust possibilities.

prehistory of the Indo-European languages. His influence in Germany was in no small part due to the fact that he was author or coauthor of a number of works on German literature, and that he was an enthusiastic nationalist. In linguistics he was a positivist and an exponent of causal determinism.

> Among the phenomena which can be observed especially well in more recent epochs but which can be assumed also in prehistoric times, wherever they may offer explanation, form-transfer or "false analogy" is prominent.
>
> It would be very useful if someone were to treat this process in its general bearings, and especially were to try to establish the limits within which it must keep....
>
> It is the seldom used words and forms which are most readily influenced by false analogy. We can observe in ourselves how, in our native language, we sometimes hesitate and are doubtful and then must decide in accordance with an analogy which happens to present itself. But about things which occur daily there is no doubt; the most frequently used words resist the levelling influence the longest, and, as anomalies, lead an individualized but undisturbed existence.
>
> The following may be given as a preliminary rule which will be sufficient for many cases: When a form A defeats a form B and crowds it out, A and B must have one element x in common which distinguishes them from similar and related forms (thus, $A = x + \alpha$, $B = x + \beta$); but the supremacy of A and the displacement of β by α depend upon frequency of use. (Scherer, 1890, pp. 25f.) [13]

Scherer was a transitional figure in the history of linguistics. Just as Scherer's teacher, Rudolf von Raumer (1815–1876) prepared the way for the neogrammarians by insisting, contra Jacob Grimm, on the necessity of phonetic (physiological) knowledge as a basis for phonology, so Scherer introduced the "psychological" principle of analogy which was to play so large a part in subsequent linguistic history. How this contribution appeared to a linguist in 1901 may be seen in Oertel's statement (pp. 69f.) that "when, under the leadership of Leskien, the neogrammarians took the last, decisive step and forbade all and every exception to phonetic

13. P. 26 of the second edition of 1878. The two sentences of the last paragraph are in Oertel's (1901, p. 151) translation of the passage. With Scherer's "frequency" cf. Bloomfield's (1933, pp. 392ff.) "fluctuations in frequency."

law, the necessary corollary to the belief in 'mechanical sound laws' which operated without exceptions was the assumption of the *psychological* origin of many phonetic developments." The last paragraph of the above quotation from Scherer, says Oertel, is equivalent in modern terms to: Analogy presupposes association. This historical significance of Scherer's contribution will be missed by those who read, in Jespersen's (1922, p. 96) only reference to him, of his "wild fancies" about "Proto-Aryan." Johannes Schmidt, in his *Gedächtnisrede* (1887), spoke of the mixture of Austrian artistry and North German earnestness in Scherer, who, like Grimm, was strongly influenced by the Romanticist tradition in Germany; both men were strongly nationalistic, interested no less in the literary and ethnic than in the linguistic history of their fatherland. His goal, Scherer said in the Dedication of his *History of the German Language*, was "a system of national moral philosophy" in the sense of Buckle's *History of Civilization*. He was indeed, though a native Austrian, a Pan-Germanist, who "felt ashamed that our claims to notice among nations are based mostly on books" and who exulted at the Prussian victory in the war with France. It is perhaps not too much to say that for all German philologists, from Grimm to Brugmann, science was a religion, and that there was far less discontinuity in the historical development than has been supposed. Most German scholars shared the traditions of Romanticism—spontaneity, patriotism, freedom from necessity—and of science —universal order and determinism. But the ideal of order in linguistics became progressively predominant as the means of its establishment— phonetic laws and psychological processes—were progressively formulated. German scholars, before and afterward, were "men of principle." Those —e.g., Curtius—who polemized against the neogrammarians were merely a few steps back on the bipolar continuity along which the science of linguistics was moving.

Chapter 3
THE NEOGRAMMARIANS[14]

Linguists had in the course of the nineteenth century been becoming continually more rigorous in their methods; they had been learning to think of sounds and of articulations rather than of letters, and to apply the natural science principle of regularity in the sequences of phenomena to their data. Schleicher had made a false—though transiently not unuseful —start in this direction by his treatment of language as a "natural organism," but this was corrected by Whitney and Scherer, who emphasized the fact that languages were created and used by individual human beings in social interaction.

As Arens (1955, pp. 290ff.) has pointed out, the year 1876 is a landmark in the history of linguistics. Men born in the decade 1840–1850, who in 1876 were therefore quite young, initiated a movement which was to exert a dominant influence on the development of linguistics for at least the next seven decades. The main features of this movement were (*a*) the emphasis on speech-sounds and articulations as physical and physiological phenomena, occurring in the contexts of other such sounds and articulations; (*b*) the substitution of the natural science concept of "law" (Webster 2: "a statement of an order or relation of phenomena which, so far as known, is invariable under the given conditions") for the earlier notion of "tendency with exceptions"; (*c*) the view that apparent exceptions to phonetic laws must be explained by countervailing factors such as analogy and borrowing. Phonetic change was thought to be purely

14. For the first part of this chapter, I have found Wheeler's (1887, pp. 44ff.) bibliography most helpful. In the following, I shall occasionally quote his brief bibliographical notes.

physiological, a matter of "unconscious" changes in manners of articulation. Analogic change was viewed as a psychological process of word-association which was also for the most part "unconscious." Because these physiological and psychological processes were "unconscious," they could operate as natural science phenomena, and hence according to laws.

It was in 1876 that Eduard Sievers (1850–1932) published his *Grundzüge der Lautphysiologie*. In this work he presented the prescriptions for a scientific linguistics; in successive editions during several decades this work served, says Arens, as basis and standard for generations of linguists.[15]

> For the linguist, the physiology of sound is only an auxiliary science. He is concerned, not with the individual sound, but rather with the sound-system of the individual speech entities, their interrelationships and gradual shifts. In other words, it is the task of natural science, starting from the existing directly observed speech material, to discover and formulate the most general laws which constitute the essential basis for the further development of our science. With these basic discoveries the linguist must in the first place acquaint himself; on the basis which they furnish, his actual and higher task however is to trace the historical development of the present state of affairs from the earlier one. (Sievers, 1876, pp. 1f.)

The goal thus suggested "is at present still distant enough." The failure to progress results from inadequate interaction and failure of mutual understanding between natural science and linguistics. Scientific linguistics must be based on the direct study of spoken languages. The sound-system of a small illiterate closed community would offer a more reliable object of research than the written language of a large educated society, whose alleged unity is either a fiction or a product of the school-room. The linguist must have a thorough training of his organs of speech and of his auditory discrimination; only after such training, and reliability-testing with living languages and dialects, is he prepared to investigate the organization and gradual change of older sound-systems (Sievers, 1876, pp. 24ff.).

15. Sievers became a professor at the age of twenty-one and, after many other publications, produced his *Grundzüge* at the age of twenty-six.

All true sound-change depends on a gradually progressing and unconsciously consummated shift which affects either the whole or only particular parts of a sound-system, according as the underlying factors governing articulation determine a greater or lesser part of the system. Besides such more regular changes there of course occur, often enough, greater leaps . . . which cannot be subsumed under more general points of view. In such cases, sound-physiology can do little more than to seek the grounds which have conditioned, in the single case, the choice of the new sound or sound-sequence in place of the old; its truest field of activity is however the elucidation of the laws and principles which find expression in the regular and gradual sound-change which has just been described. (Sievers, 1876, pp. 126f.)

In 1876 was published August Leskien's (1840–1916) prize-winning essay in which he sought and failed to find satisfactory evidence for what had been assumed to be a close relationship between the declensions of the Balto-Slavic and the Germanic languages; this study was therefore an example of the application of detailed and rigorous research methods to the testing of loose or intuitive generalizations of such pioneers as Schleicher. In several places Leskien discussed the interrelationships of phonetic and analogic change:

In this research . . . I have started from the basic principle that the form of a case as transmitted to us is never the result of an exception to the elsewhere ruling sound-laws. To avoid misunderstanding, I will add: if by exceptions are understood cases in which the expected sound-change has failed to appear because of specific discoverable causes . . . where in some sense one rule collides with another, then naturally there can be no objection to the statement that sound-laws are not exceptionless. The law is not thereby abolished, but operates in the expected manner wherever these or other disturbances, the effects of other laws, are not present. But if we admit any arbitrary accidental deviations such as cannot be brought into any kind of relationship, we thereby basically declare that the object of research, language, is not accessible to scientific understanding. . . . (p. xxxiv)
The development of a specific inflectional paradigm, in this case a declension, is subject to the influence of two factors. Every language possesses at the time of its origin as a separate language a certain number of case-forms, inherited from the period of its coexistence with one or more

related languages. These forms, without exception, take on the configuration which the operation of the sound-laws—here in particular the laws pertaining to final sounds—must produce. So far, the development is simple and, we can say, regular. But actually, there occur formations, varying in number in different languages, whose form cannot and should not be explained by the working of the sound-laws; they are in origin foreign to the stem-class or the function to which usage seems to assign them; they have been borrowed from another stem-class or have had attached to them a wholly alien function—in a word, *analogical formations*. Both factors, sound-change in accordance with laws and analogy, explain the declensional configuration of a language in a given period as they do every kind of inflection, and only these two factors need to be considered. . . . (p. 2)

It is not unknown to me that such views still arouse strong opposition in comparative grammar; through the whole development of this discipline, it has become customary, in considering the individual forms of given languages, to think first of the *Ursprache* and to seek the channels which lead to it, neglecting the tendency toward form-building which is revealed in the individual languages by transferences and analogical formations. I regard it as essential, if we are to avoid false constructions, to begin always with the latter side, and only then to seek the primitive forms. If we had, what we unfortunately do not have, a history answering to the requirements of today's grammar, of those Indogermanic languages whose development we can follow for the longest time, . . . many a case of disbelief in analogy-formations would disappear. . . . (pp. 39f.)

In 1876, Reinhold Merzdorf, in discussing vowel-shortening before vowels in Ionic Greek, cited an apparent exception: the subjunctive forms *théōmen*, etc., which appear to be quantitative metatheses for Homeric *théomen*, etc.:

But only apparently; for they are nothing but analogical formations. More and more it is beginning to be recognized that analogy is a factor which is still far from being sufficiently appreciated; scholars have sought to derive and demonstrate organically, in terms of sound-laws, older language-stages, and primitive forms, a great deal which, examined closely, is found to have arisen by more or less mechanical, I might say stupid, form-transference whose various kinds, from the crudest to the most intellectual, we must properly separate. And just as this has long been regarded as an established fact in all more recent linguistic periods, so it is undoubtedly to be accepted for the older times, in which the language-process did not proceed differently from the way it does today.... Ancient Greek and Sanskrit, earnestly viewed from the standpoint of false analogy, will certainly yield many a wonderful result. And it is just in Greek verb-formation that the operation of analogy can be demonstrated in the highest degree, as Curtius, who is otherwise the most determined opponent of this explanatory principle, himself admits. (pp. 231f.)

To this reference to himself, Curtius appended an editorial footnote:

The author here exaggerates a little. Not only in the places mentioned but elsewhere ... I have recognized the explanatory principle of analogy, as I could hardly fail to do. My occasional warnings always concerned premature and unconsidered applications of this principle. Analogy always depends upon a force which one form or, as a rule, an entire group of forms exerts upon others. It is comparable to the disturbance of the course of a heavenly body by others crossing its path. To make such an effect credible, we must demonstrate the presence of such a force, whether it consists in a large number of forms attracting several isolated ones or in a much-used and therefore lively form causing the speaker to deviate from tradition. More fitting than an empty quarrel about yes or no would be research, supported by rich exemplification, into the very different phases and periods in which this linguistic phenomenon appears—an attractive task for such linguists as are of my opinion that synthesizing and methodological researches are an essential feature of our science. (Curtius, in Merzdorf, 1876, pp. 231f.)

Merzdorf, to his translation of an article by Ascoli on the origin of the Greek superlative suffix -tato-, prefaced the following note:

In this number of the *Studien* there has been discussion on several occasions of the principle of form-transference or analogy. When Prof. Curtius declares empty dispute about yes and no to be fruitless, and demands exact researches, everyone will agree, but especially those who are of my opinion that the configuration of every individual language is essentially conditioned by two factors: first, by the sound-laws which change the old traditional state of a language and, without altering it basically, bring it into a new form; and second, by the essentially new operation of analogy which creates formations quite special for the given language; as third factor we might no doubt add accent. It is with this in mind that I have translated the following article. . . . Of course, only a single important Greek form is here explained as an analogical formation; the chief signifi-cance of the article however . . . consists in the fact that such an authority as Ascoli has entered into the dispute, has opened a wide vista in the ana-logically ruled fields of the Indogermanic number and comparative system, and has thus provided a justification for the view that practically every linguistic new formation depends upon form-transference. (Merzdorf, in Ascoli, 1876, pp. 341f.)

And finally, in 1876 appeared a notable discussion of analogy by Karl Brugmann (1849–1919). This discussion was contained in a four-page footnote, which, in part, I translate as follows:

I find myself in agreement with Leskien [1876] on the question of "false analogy" . . . I venture the following additional remarks:

1. That many linguists still resist a more comprehensive application of this explanatory principle to the older languages, such as ancient Indic, Greek, etc., no doubt arises in large part from the tendency to regard "false analogy," that is, the transference of a language-form into a new track, as something pathological and degenerative in the development of a language. A little thought will show that this view is purely subjective and decidedly arbitrary. If we were to evaluate the forces which condition the develop-ment of languages in terms of their effects, . . . we could, with the same justification with which we have found the sound-shortening of English to give this language a great advantage over other, better preserved ones, describe the operation of false analogy as something highly advantageous for languages and declare that this force has, like "the victorious daughter of heaven who binds together things which are alike," brought about true harmony in linguistic structure.

2. As Merzdorf . . . has pointed out, many quite different things have been included under the term false analogy or form-transference. All these linguistic phenomena have three things in common:

a. They are never merely further developments, in accordance with phonetic laws, from older speech-forms.

b. They are always purely formal, not conceptual.

c. They owe their origin to the fact that the speaker, in the moment of his intention to speak, has in mind another form (association) from which the new formation results.

To use the term "false analogy" for all of these linguistic phenomena will simply not do. It fits only a part of them. Hence on this account alone the name is unsuitable. But still more for another reason: the name belongs to those unfortunate grammatical terms through which language is subjected to a quite subjective censorship and which sound as though the grammarian has the duty of prescribing in what ways language should change, whereas as a researcher he should surely take a purely passive attitude and simply accept the phenomena as they present themselves. It seems to me that now, while the term can still be eliminated, this should be done. Perhaps we might adopt the term "formal association" or "form-association." The classification of the phenomena is extremely difficult because they present the most varied principles of classification. [Here Brugmann suggests a number of classes, with examples, but concludes:] I carry this attempt no further because a comprehensive classification of the total material at present still eludes me. May others take up the task!

3. With regard to the effects of form-association, one language must not be treated in a manner essentially different from that applied to another. Above all we must free ourselves from the idea that form-associations can occur only in modern languages. . . . How can the age of a language be relevant here? Can it be supposed that the Indians of Vedic, or the Greeks of Homeric times still had an especially lively feeling for the antiquity and correctness of certain formations and therefore resisted the tendency for the involuntarily occurring form-associations to become habitual? Such a feeling for the actual nature and combination of language-formations was and is possessed only by analytic grammarians, not by the people who truly create languages. Our form-association is a purely psychological process which is as old as language itself. Most of the so-called primitive forms are perhaps already quite ordinary "false analogy-formations."

4. Anyone who, before thinking about the *Ursprache*, first examines the language-forms to see whether they may not be analogical new formations is far less likely to commit serious errors than is someone who always stumbles upon the thought of associative formation through immediate and obvious appearance, and who, if there is any imaginable primitive form from which the form in question can be derived through sound-laws, immediately so derives it. For whoever mistakenly sets up form-associations errs only in that he has not classified correctly an individual form, or a series of forms, but he who leaps at once from historical forms to an *Ursprache* and with the help of these forms infers primitive forms which never existed, errs not only in regard to those individual historical formations but also in regard to everything else that he is building on the inferred basic form.

5. It is of great importance to become clear about the relationship of form-association to what is called "phonetic law" or "phonetic tendency." A more detailed discussion of this point is not here possible. (Brugmann, 1876, pp. 317–320)

A "more detailed discussion" was prefaced by Brugmann to an article on Indo-Germanic nominal suffixes. Here he emphasized the necessity of greater agreement among linguists with respect to methodological principles. Every sound-tendency which appears in a language works blindly, i.e., without the conscious awareness of the speakers.

> We must expect that the entire linguistic material which the speakers of a language commit to their speech organs and which thus comes to expression becomes subject to this purely mechanical "sound-tendency." When for example a number of individuals at a particular point in time change a previously regular dental *r* into a guttural *r* . . .[16] this change does not begin in a few particular words and then spread to other words, but it begins in the speech organs themselves, and we must expect that *every* previously dental *r*, regardless of the word and word-category in which it occurs, undergoes the change. . . . An exception to the general rule may result from the operation of another speech-tendency. . . . But in that case we must not really speak of an exception . . . for the exception rather is evidence for a rule. (Brugmann, 1877, pp. 4f.)

Brugmann offered answers to the question: What is the reason that, beside the linguistic changes which can be described either as in accordance with a general phonetic law or as the lawful exceptions to the law, there are so many changes which seem to follow no law? Two kinds of process may be distinguished: dialect-mixture (which may occur even within the same language, since a given phonetic tendency need not appear in the same hour in all individuals, so that two different pronunciations—"mother" and "daughter" forms—of the same word may for a time co-exist, the older form persisting particularly in writing and in other conventional—e.g., ceremonial—uses).

> But in all other cases in which we find deviation from a general sound-law, we must look for an association. Most of the forms constituting the

16. The ellipses are mostly of examples from various Indo-European languages, especially from older historical periods of Greek, Sanskrit, Germanic, etc.

stock of forms of a dialect are felt by the language as members of a related form-complex or as related to other formations in some other way. Involuntarily and unconsciously one word leans on another, and thus, inasmuch as word-association, a psychical activity, transforms itself into physical activity, arise those speech-forms which we call analogical formations (or if they do not fit the grammarian's a priori schema, false analogical formations), and which, with reference to the philosophically usual term "association of ideas," I would prefer to call associative formations. Association is observable in language in a great variety of directions. It gives sometimes the appearance as if a sound-law which should have affected a form did not; sometimes it seems as if the language left a form no more intact than it did other forms of its class but gave its phonetic change a different direction . . . ; most often however it appears that there has been a complete derailment, so that every thought of a merely phonetic development is excluded. These last-mentioned formations are the ones usually called new formations or new creations. . . . All associative formations must actually be described as new words. . . .

The distinction between sound-law and sound-tendency is thus purely superficial. They are basically the same.

The basic methodological principle, however, which I wished especially to emphasize, is the following: *Excluding cases where doublets occur in the relationship of mother- and daughter-forms . . . or where dialect-mixture is demonstrable . . . or where it cannot be assumed that two forms, different from the beginning not only phonetically but also functionally came to coexist as doublets after a fading of the basic meaning of an element originally conditioning a difference of usage—except for such cases, one of the two forms must be regarded as an associative-formation. The operation of sound-laws in diverging directions in the same word of the same dialect, in other words, the purely phonetic origin of sister-forms from a mother-form in the same dialect, is never to be assumed.* (Brugmann, 1877, pp. 6–8)

Later in the article Brugmann declared that in his view it is a mistake to assume that one or a few forms cannot be the origin of numerous analogical forms. "For when [Latin] *auros raised its enticing cry, the seventy and more -as- neuters certainly did not come marching in a column in the same hour to don the new garb, but first one of them was newly clothed, the two words together served a third, the three together a fourth, etc." (Brugmann, 1877, pp. 5of.).

In 1877, Hermann Paul (1846–1921) prefaced (pp. 320–332) to a paper on the vowels of inflectional and derivational syllables of the oldest Germanic dialects a statement of his methodological principles. "Science is served only by necessary law, not by caprice." In the comparison of different linguistic stages or dialects, phonetically different forms did not offer much difficulty as long as the sound-laws were applied loosely. A stricter application however resulted in exceptions, of which some could be explained as the results of "false analogy," called "inorganic" formations by J. Grimm. But false analogy had been viewed with abhorrence in comparative grammar, to be resorted to only in dire need; this attitude was now giving way to the movement toward more consistent application of sound-laws. The original task of comparative grammar was to construct, from the oldest extant forms, the primitive forms and to analyze these into their morphological elements. But this approach, while a necessary beginning of linguistics, had become too dominant; the composition of roots, stems, suffixes, etc. had occurred in the Indo-European *Ursprache*; when the various members of this family began their separate histories, there were no longer roots, stems, and suffixes, but only words; the error of treating these analytic elements as real elements had prevented a correct understanding of analogy. An inflected language exists only in the minds of the individuals of a speech community, and its acquisition results from hearing how others use it. What is acquired is not morphological elements but words. The individual cannot hear and learn every possible form; he becomes capable of producing inflected and derivative forms after the model of other complete formations which he has acquired in intercourse with his fellows, and which have become organized in groups according to the laws of ideational association and in accordance with grammatical categories; these categories however never come into clear consciousness without assiduous thought or instruction. This grouping is an extraordinary aid to memory, and also makes possible new combinations; this is what we may call analogy-formations; thus everyone who speaks continuously creates analogy-formations. Failure to appreciate this fact has resulted from the tendency to regard a language, as it is summarized in grammar and dictionary—the totality of the possible words and forms, together with the concepts which may be connected with

34

them—as a complete actuality rather than as an abstraction without any reality; it has resulted, that is, from the failure to realize that the real language exists only in the individual. Thus, in order to understand the existence of every individual spoken form, we must ask, not "is it customary in the language?" or "is it in accordance with the laws abstracted by the grammarian?" but rather "did he who just now used it have it stored in his memory or did he himself create it, and if the latter, by what analogy?" The relative influence of the two factors, memory and analogy, may vary greatly; as memory increases and extends its scope, creative activity becomes superfluous; thus analogy-formation is extraordinarily active in the first years of childhood but becomes progressively inhibited with language-learning. Writing and grammatical consciousness also inhibit creative speech production.

But if the significance of analogy for the life of language is once understood, "false analogy" is seen to be no different from "correct analogy." If a speaker creates analogically a form which had previously been usual, or which is correct in terms of phonetic law, he thereby demonstrates no more consciousness of the laws of form-building than if he had produced a form incorrect in these respects. In the history of the Indo-European languages, phonetic changes produced extensive distortions of morphological harmony; analogical change is not only a necessary sequel to such distortions but also a reaction to them, whereby memory is freed from the threatened burden of a multitude of singularities.

Far more analogy-formations are produced than become current; as with phonetic changes, only those analogical formations become current which are psychologically so natural that they are independently created by many different individuals, are easily impressed in memory, and readily spread. They may begin as speech mistakes, which then compete for a time with the older forms; if they win out, the mistakes become the normal forms, regardless of the opposition of historical grammarians.

Thus it is today, and thus it has always been. When a comparativist attributes a higher value to a form which arose in a purely phonetic manner, he is making thereby a biased judgment in accordance with the usefulness for his special purpose of constructing the primitive form, and not in accordance with the usefulness for which grammatical forms chiefly exist, namely, as easy and convenient means of communication. But I think that the time is approaching when these false analogy-formations, these inorganic forms, will be regarded as objects equally worthy of consideration with the so-called organic ones. The conviction will grow that the former also constitute a large percentage of the total stock of forms even in ancient languages, and that perhaps in a strict sense actual organic forms are no longer to be found anywhere.

In consequence of the interaction between memory and analogy, those forms are least in danger of being displaced by new formations which are most strongly impressed in memory, whether through the ease of their association with other similar forms or through the frequency of their use. . . . Therefore the most common words best preserve their old inflections, even when in this they stand quite isolated. It may be observed in the most various languages that among the so-called anomalous forms uncommon words are only exceptionally found; it is rather the most necessary words of daily speech which are found there. And their anomaly consists in their having escaped the levelling tendency which otherwise rules the form-system of the language. (Paul, 1877, pp. 328f.)

Following the above passage, Paul proposes what Wheeler has called "the first mention of the classification which has since been so often employed; viz., as 'formalle' und 'stoffliche' Analogiebildungen." Paul says, "To me it seems that the most essential principle of classification is the determination of whether the model is furnished by the corresponding forms of other words (formal analogy) or by the other forms of the same word (material analogy)."

In his *Prinzipien der Sprachgeschichte*, Paul (1880) [17] presented, said Wheeler, "the profoundest and most thorough treatment of the subject [of analogy]." Here Paul presents language as a hierarchical system of associatively interrelated—overlapping and intersecting—groups of words, such as the members of grammatical categories, whose associative relations in the minds of individuals make possible continual creation, on models previously learned, of forms never previously heard or learned; syntactic collocations are similarly created on the basis of models. Such

17. I quote from the 5th ed., 1920, which was practically unaltered from the 4th, 1909. The passages to which I refer are also found in the 2nd ed., 1886 (except for the reference to Thumb and Marbe and the one to Herzog). The 1st ed., 1880, contains the essential arguments, but more briefly and differently organized.

creations may or may not be correct in terms of etymology or of prior usage; they become correct when many individuals coincide in the same tendency. In his Introduction, Paul strongly emphasizes the fact that language exists in the speech-activity of the interacting individuals—not in a "folk-soul"—of a community, and that linguistic explanations must be sought in the detailed psychological and historical study of such activity. In the Preface to his fourth edition, Paul says that one of the chief differences between himself and Wundt lay in the fact that "analogy, to which I, no doubt in agreement with all contemporary linguists, attribute so great a significance for speech-activity and speech-development, plays in Wundt's account [*Völkerpsychologie*, 1] practically no role at all."[18] Paul's *Prinzipien* differs also from the *Völkerpsychologie* of Lazarus and Steinthal in that the latter deals with only one of the ways in which the individual is influenced by and influences the community: the setting up of ideational complexes—the "psychological" way. But Paul includes in his science the physiological processes by which useful movements are learned and the physical processes whereby tools and other objects are made and transmitted and whereby individuals exert pressure on one another; thus, while Paul was hardly a proto-behaviorist, nevertheless he included behavior in his consideration, as well as the physical environment; "no culture rests upon a purely psychical foundation, and it is, to say the least, very inexact to describe the social sciences as *Geisteswissenschaften*."[19] "All intercourse between minds is only indirect, physically

18. In this connection, Paul expresses an opinion which seems to me to be applicable to a more recent "revolution": "In many reviews of Wundt's work, confidence is expressed that from it will arise a fundamental transformation of linguistics. I cannot share this expectation."

19. I have thought it worth while to call attention to these statements because Bloomfield (1933, pp. 16f.), it has seemed to me, was not quite just to Paul when he said that Paul's *Prinzipien* had two "great weaknesses" which "are significant of the limitations of nineteenth-century linguistics": (a) "neglect of descriptive language study. He admitted that descriptions of languages were necessary, but confined his actual discussion to matters of linguistic change"; and (b) "his insistence upon 'psychological' interpretation. He accompanies his statements about language with a paraphrase in terms of mental processes which the speakers are supposed to have undergone. The only evidence for these mental processes is the linguistic process; they add nothing to the discussion, but only obscure it." Moreover, "Paul and most of his contemporaries dealt only with Indo-European languages, and, what with their neglect of descriptive problems, refused to work with languages whose history was unknown."

mediated" (p. 12). Causal relations within an individual are wholly different from those in interactions between individuals; all psychology is individual psychology; to speak of "folk-psychology" (= our "social psychology") is to speak metaphorically. All linguistic creations are the work of individuals; a number of individuals may coincide in a creation, but the act of creation is still that of individuals.

In his first chapter (1920, pp. 23–36), entitled "Generalities Concerning the Nature of Language-Development," Paul presents a Herbartian picture of the mental organization of language. All expressions of linguistic activity flow from the dark recesses of the unconscious, in which lie all the linguistic resources available to the individual, the products of everything previously heard, spoken, or thought, the ideas which had entered consciousness. These ideas are organized in groups in the unconscious, in accordance with the manner in which they entered consciousness. Sounds, movements, and the word- and sentence-meanings which they symbolize become associatively interconnected. Thus arise the associatively organized groups of the cases of nouns, the moods, tenses, and persons of verbs, the different derivatives of the same stem, all words of the same functional class, etc., etc.; associations are also established between sentences of similar form or function. This associative organization is subject to continual change in each individual and it is different in different individuals, in accordance with variations in usage and experience; linguistic change is an inevitable result of such variability. The true cause of linguistic change is nothing other than ordinary speech-activity, in which the motivation is not to make changes in usage but only to communicate wishes and thoughts to others; in the development of speech-

---

Subsequent history has perhaps given a somewhat changed significance to these criticisms: Paul's writings on analogy were chiefly instrumental in the initiation of experimental work on linguistic change in psychological laboratories (beginning with Thumb and Marbe, 1901, and continuing to the present, as Ch. 4, 5, and 6 will show); his "paraphrases" may therefore be regarded, in effect, as hypotheses rather than mere circularities. As for neglect of description and overemphasis on history, we may set this "fault" over against the reverse state of affairs of the present time: elaborate and prescriptive—static and rationalistic—description of "competence" with a consequent neglect of the dynamic processes of variability and continuous change. Paul denies that there can be a science of language that is not historical, and in this I think he is right.

usage, the "fitness" of a usage is of the same sort as that which Darwin assigned to organic nature: greater or lesser adaptiveness.

In his chapter (1920, pp. 106–120) entitled "Analogy," Paul develops his notion of the associative organization of words in hierarchical groups. In "material" associations, the similarity in meaning is usually accompanied by a similarity in sound which usually represents an etymological relation, although material groups also occur which are based on meaning only: e.g., *ox—cow, man—wife, young—old, here—there, am—is—was,* etc. Formal groups include, e.g., the class of all action-nouns, all comparatives, all nominatives, all first persons of verbs, etc.; these are all classifiable into higher and lower classes; usually the smaller subgroups are marked by phonemic similarity. But associated groups may consist not only of individual words but also of analogous *proportions* between different words. The basis for a proportional equation is the correspondence in meaning both of the material element and of the formal element; there may be a phonemic similarity in both elements: thus German *Tag : Tages : Tage = Arm : Armes : Arme = Fisch : Fisches : Fische,* or, with the substitutions permissible in a proportion, *Tag : Arm : Fisch = Tages : Armes : Fisches,* or, with the phonemic similarity restricted to the material element, Latin *mensa : mensam : mensae = hortus : hortum : horti = nox : noctem : noctis,* etc. Of lesser significance are equations in which the phonemic correspondence is limited to the formal element, as *good : better = nice : nicer,* or in which there is no phonemic resemblance, as in *am : was = live : lived.* There are also proportional groupings of corresponding cases of singulars and plurals of nouns, of corresponding persons of the various tenses of verbs, and of the alternants in umlaut and ablaut. Syntactic collocations also become organized in analogical equations; thus Latin *pater : mortuus = filia : pulchra = caput : magnum;* from such groupings arise the functional word-classes. There is hardly a word in any language which is not a member of one or more associatively related groups; the ease of formation and the strength of the connections depend upon the degree to which the units have been impressed by virtue of the frequencies of occurrence of the individual words and the number of possible analogies. These proportional equations are not only operative in linguistic change; they serve also in the analogical creation of all those forms—words and syntactic collocations—which a speaker has never or seldom previously heard. Very few of the sentences which we speak have been learned by heart; most of them are composed at the moment of speaking. Rules are combined with examples in learning a foreign language, but in learning one's native language one is given only a number of models. Forms which are isolated or are members of small groups, unless they are of high frequency, tend to be assimilated to larger groups. Memory and heard usage progressively inhibit new formations in the course of language acquisition; hence new formations are most frequent in the speech of young children, but most of their deviations remain without effect in the development of a language. Analogical changes are not likely to be made "at one blow"; there is likely to be a period of competition between the new and the old form, during which some individuals continue to use the old form.

Since analogical creation is the solution of a proportional equation, there must be to begin with at least three members suitable for setting up such an equation; each member must be comparable with another—in the one case, there must be a material, in the other, a formal correspondence: thus in Latin, *animus* : *animi* = *senatus* : *x*, but not *animus* : *animi* = *mensa* : *x*. "The inflection of a word can, therefore, undergo the analogical influence of other words only if it corresponds in structure with them in one or more forms. There are indeed cases where such influence occurs in the absence of such correspondence, but such cases should not properly be called analogical formations" (Paul, 1920, p. 117).[20] Paul gives the example of the generalization of *-s* as a genitive suffix in English, Swedish, and Danish, "even in the plural." Beside the material-formal proportion-groups Paul distinguishes the "material-phonetic": e.g., the sandhi-alternants in French; he thinks that it is improbable that these have in their entirety been preserved in the memory of successive genera-

20. Cf. Bloomfield, 1933, p. 420: "For many new-formations we are not able to give a proportional model. We believe that this is not always due to our inability to find the model sets, and that there is really a type of linguistic change which resembles analogic change, but goes on without model sets. These *adaptive* new-formations resemble an old form with some change in the direction of semantically related forms." Bloomfield also applied the term *contamination* to such cases.

tions since the original sound-change, and that memory has been assisted by analogy.

In his chapter (1920, pp. 189–216) on "Isolation and Reaction Against It," Paul says,

> The symmetry of the form-system has in sound-change a ceaselessly working enemy and destroyer. One can hardly form any idea of the degree of the disconnectedness, disorder, and unintelligibility that would supervene if language had to endure all the devastations of sound-change, if no reaction against it were possible. A means of such reaction is however given in analogy. With its help language always works gradually back to better-adapted relationships, to a greater consistency and a more useful grouping in inflection and word-formation. Thus we see in linguistic history an eternal surging back and forth of two opposite currents. Every disorganization is followed by a reorganization. The stronger the attack on the groups, the more lively is the work of re-creation.

Paul (1920, pp. 160–173) has a chapter on "Contamination," which he defines as "the process whereby two synonymous or somehow related expressions both crowd into consciousness so that neither wholly prevails and a new form results in which elements of the one mix with elements of the other." Processes of this sort, like all deviations from previous usage, are initially momentary occurrences in individuals, and only those become established in usage which occur repeatedly in many individuals. Paul remarks that some writers, e.g., Thumb and Marbe (1901), had described contamination as not essentially different from analogy, but that he agrees with Herzog (1903), who wrote, "We shall define analogy-formation as the creation of a new form on the model of a definite proportion, whereby the original form is completely shut out of consciousness." "Contamination," said Herzog, "is the creation of a new form through the blending of parts of two forms which come simultaneously into consciousness." Paul adds that contamination occurs most readily between etymologically related synonyms and antonyms, especially those between which there already exists a phonemic similarity. A form may be contaminated by a formal group, or a group by another group, often with resulting pleonasms. Contaminations also occur at the syntactic level, as mixtures of constructions. Paul gives abundant illustrations of these processes from the histories of Indo-European languages.

In a paper of 1878, Hermann Osthoff (1847–1907) introduced the distinction between "physiological" (phonetic) and "psychological" (analogical) processes in linguistic change. He remarked that even those espousing a more rigorous methodology—e.g., Brugmann and Paul—spoke of forms' being "protected" from phonetic change by their associations with other forms. But Osthoff declared that form-associations work against the effects of phonetic laws, not against the laws themselves; thus analogical formations are always posterior and secondary; they are only apparently preserved older forms.

> Let us accept for the moment the crude but here most helpful notion that, on a certain day, 12 noon was the exact time at which in the prehistoric language of ancient Greece the loss of the intervocalic spirant *s* reached its final stage, and that immediately thereafter, perhaps at one second after 12, or even at the very moment at which sounded the last intervocalic *s*, someone pronounced the word *élūsa*, having in mind aorists like *éterpsa*: could one say that in this *élūsa* the *s* had survived the loss of the spirant, or isn't it rather, even after so slight an interval, a restored and necessarily new *s*? (Osthoff, 1878, p. 326)

In a monograph of 1879, Osthoff presented what Wheeler called "a semi-popular review of the relation between the psychological and physiological factors in language, illustrated by well-chosen examples."[21] He also discussed and illustrated the distinction which Paul had made between material and formal assimilation. His intention, he said, was "to arouse a general interest in two methodological principles of modern linguistics which have only in recent years begun to be accepted as the highest and most important guiding principles of research." These two principles he stated as follows:

> First: The historical sound-change of formal speech-material proceeds within given temporal and local limits in accordance with *laws which*

21. It should be remarked that the presentation was "semi-popular" only for the products of nineteenth-century German gymnasia and universities! The abundant illustrations were drawn from the histories of Greek, Latin, German, French, and Italian, and would require an educated reader's close attention.

operate without exceptions. This is the *physiological* side of linguistic form-building and form-reconstruction.

Second: All irregularities of phonetic development are such only in appearance. They result from the fact that the effects of the physiological laws undergo numerous interferences and suppressions by the *psychological* tendencies whose effect is to bring speech-forms into unconscious relations to other forms through ideational association, and thus to influence them formally and change them phonetically. (Osthoff, 1879, p. 3)

The term *false analogy*, Osthoff says, is objectionable because it implies an unjustifiable odium;[22] the unconscious and unreflective creative activity is not dependent upon a posteriori grammatical rules established by reflection.

Osthoff devotes the first nineteen pages of his monograph to discussion and exemplification of the exceptionless, mechanical, unconscious, and physiological nature of phonetic laws, for which he suggests changes in vocal organs related to changes of climate and culture as the most probable causes; he rejects the often-assumed factor of inertia or "laziness" as a general explanation. But he also speaks of practice in given speech-sounds as making pronounceable what had seemed unpronounceable, and of the great role of imitation whereby the members of a speech-community achieve, by progressive assimilation in childhood and by the influence and requirements of daily communication, a uniformity of speech only minimally subject to individual differences.

The last twenty-six pages Osthoff devotes to analogical change. Can the investigation of associative activity in speech be developed into a scientific method? The attempt had recently been made to discredit such studies by the phrase "the accidents of analogical formations." In so far as we can speak of "freedom of the will," there seems to be a variability of this sort; thus, in the history of German verb-ablaut, some singular forms were assimilated to plurals, some plurals to singulars; in numerous other cases, it seems as if any answer to the question, why must form A influence form B, rather than the other way round, must be at best a

22. "Sprach doch V. Henry in seinem Buch Étude sur l'Analogie 1883 von ihr als von einem chapitre intéressant de tératologie, was nichts Geringeres besagte, als dass es sich da handle um eine Lehre von den Missgeburten der Sprache" (Rogge, 1925, p. 451). In 1853 C. A. Lobeck had written a monograph on *De pathologia sermonis*.

lucky guess. To attain scientific validity for the principle of analogy, the attempt must be made to classify the heretofore most certainly established examples. The principle basis for classification must be sought in the prior associative relation between the forms in question. These relations may be classified into material and formal. In the material associations, a form which is much more frequently used will be more influential. In the formal associations, frequency—either the frequency of certain forms or the great number of similar forms—is also the most influential factor; the predominant systems and the most practiced forms have the advantage. "Many, or even most, of the forms which have become correct were originally nothing other than mistakes attributable to the levelling effect of psychological tendencies, until the tyrant usage raised them to a higher status."

In conclusion, Osthoff expresses the opinion that the distinction between the parts played by the physical and the mental organs in the development of speech-forms is essential to an answer to the question whether linguistics is a *Naturwissenschaft* or a *Geisteswissenschaft*; that it is both is becoming evident through the labors of those who have been dubbed the "young grammarians." But the concept of exceptionless sound-change brings it closest to natural science—closer in regard to the reliability of its results than all other historical sciences.

Brugmann, in the foreword to Osthoff and Brugmann (1878), gave what Wheeler called "a vigorous and clean-cut statement and defence of the general method employed by the Neogrammarians in linguistic investigation." He began with the statement that the older linguistics, of the period before Scherer's book had appeared, zealously investigated languages but gave far too little attention to the speakers. Only on the basis of a more exact knowledge of the psychophysical speech-mechanism— "not of the language on paper, for on paper almost anything is possible" —can the comparative linguist gain a correct notion of how linguistic innovations spread from individuals to a community, and, in general, of the methodological viewpoints which must guide him in all his historical researches; thus he will find a closer relationship with psychology helpful. Linguistics had been too preoccupied with setting up the forms of an Indo-European *Ursprache*—which are purely hypothetical—whose scientific probability depends upon whether they are based on correct assumptions about linguistic development. Since these linguists derived their notions of speech development from their own reconstructions, they moved in a circle. The principles of linguistics must be sought in living languages and in the natural unreflective speech of daily life. It was in this context that the author wrote the sentence which so enraged his opponents:

> Of comparative linguists, only he who once steps forth from the hypothesis-laden atmosphere of the shop in which the Indogermanic prototypes are forged into the clear air of the tangible reality of the present, there to learn what grey theory would never let him know, and only he who forever frees himself from that formerly wide-spread and still persisting method by which language is regarded only on paper, everything is resolved into terminology, formulae, and grammatical schematism, and the nature of phenomena is always thought to have been established when a name has been found for the thing:—only he can arrive at a correct notion of the mode of life and change of speech-forms, and achieve those methodological principles without which no believable results can be reached in historical linguistics and without which, in particular, an advance into the times before the historical records is like a voyage without a compass. (Osthoff and Brugmann, pp. ixf.) [23]

In their Preface, Osthoff and Brugmann refer to Leskien's lectures in Leipzig, in which he emphasized that language is not a thing existing outside of and above human beings; recognition of this fact had been hindered by the fact that linguists were accustomed to deal with language on paper and to speak of "the language" where they should have said "the speaking persons"; it is not the language which makes a linguistic change but those persons from whom the change spreads.

23. Pedersen (1931, pp. 292–294) has expressed the opinion that this "grandiose preface" was "extremely imprudent" in suggesting that Brugmann and his associates were "those alone amongst whom Scherer's words had fallen upon fruitful soil," and he points out that the principle of exceptionless sound-laws "had so long been developing that there was no holding it back in the seventies"; besides Scherer and Leskien he mentions Verner, who in 1872 wrote a letter in which he suggested reversing the proposition "No rule without exceptions" to "No exceptions without a rule"; "i.e. every exception to the rules prevailing in a language must have a cause." This last proposition of course gives the reason for the increasing interest in analogy. For the bitterness of the quarrel, e.g., with Brugmann's quondam coeditor, Curtius, see Pedersen, loc. cit.

Those who admit unmotivated or sporadic sound-changes, say our authors, become victims of subjectivism, and the constructions which they bring to market, however ingenious, cannot be found acceptable. Those who think that analogical formations only began to appear after the *Sprachgefühl* had become weak illustrate how metaphorical expressions can be substituted for reality, and merely grammatical notions can be imposed upon language itself. We can be as certain that our ancestors formed the ideational sequences of words and sentences under the influence of the association of ideas, just as we do, as we are that they used their speech-organs for the physical production of speech-sounds. The neogrammarians may reply to the charge that analogy-formations must be taken on faith by pointing out that recourse to a probable analogy is better than a stretching and bending of the phonetic laws. The serious application of the principle of analogy was of rather recent origin; with increasing study of modern languages, improved means will be found for judging the probability of the various kinds of associative connections.

In a section on form-associations between numerals (pp. 92–132 of Osthoff and Brugmann, 1878), Osthoff gives abundant illustrations of what Wheeler refers to as "the strong levelling tendency operating within compact series." Osthoff summarizes his survey as follows: there is a tendency for immediately neighboring numerals to influence one another; so, for example in the Indo-European languages, four and five, six and seven, seven and eight, nine and ten, eleven and twelve; so too the tens and hundreds, and the unit numbers and the corresponding tens or hundreds; also the cardinal and the ordinal numbers of the same value.

In 1880, Franz Misteli published, in two volumes of the *Zeitschrift für Völkerpsychologie und Sprachwissenschaft*, a 138-page critique of Osthoff and Brugmann's *Morphologische Untersuchungen*. This critique, written as he said at the request of one of the editors, was intended as the polemical reply of the Lazarus-Steinthal school, and thus of the Humboldt-Herbart tradition, to the statement of principles—particularly with respect to analogy—in the Osthoff-Brugmann foreword. The length of the paper is mostly attributable to the citation of an enormous number of illustrations from the histories of the Indo-European languages. The author seeks to show that the neogrammarians did not really make a revolution, that Curtius and Pott had made use of the principle of analogy, and that the growing evidence for the rigor of phonetic laws had made increasingly acceptable the analogy-explanation. "The new school did not raise a torch after a long darkness." "Thus phonetic laws and analogy are mutually supplementary; where the first ceases to work, the second takes over." A phonetic law is least likely to yield to analogy in the case of forms which are least related to others: e.g., particles, perhaps adverbs; but actually everything in language is interconnected. Misteli discusses at length the possible criteria for a phonetic law; the best, though subjective, one is that it should not require the assumption of too many or too complicated analogical processes, or such as are based on too few or seldom used words and forms. "When Brugmann says that two forms could create a third, three a fourth, and so on to a hundred or a thousand purely by analogy, that remains an empty although in the abstract a possibly acceptable statement, as long as the steps in individual cases cannot be demonstrated or at least made probable; for when has mere possibility ever sufficed as the foundation of a scientific proposition?" (p. 415). But in some of Osthoff's and Leskien's examples, the complication is so great as to give the impression of improbability.

Misteli states that analogy depends on sounds, meaning, and form, which are the causes of associative connections; of these, form is the most important, so that in linguistics *analogy* usually means, as Brugmann said, "form-association," whereas in psychology *association* usually designates the connections which result from temporal and spatial contiguity. The kinds of connections are described as sequences, intersections, and fusions; the most important, the form-associations, are expressions of intersections; that is, each word is by its form the intersection of numerous series, its form being determined by the joint influence of these, whose relative potency cannot be determined a priori. The analogical creations of children result from their simpler systems of intersection. Such influences are quite different from those experienced by pupils learning, e.g., *amo, amas, amat* in the schoolroom; this distinction, in the author's opinion, Paul overlooked.

The most important analogies are those whose grammatical unity, reflected by their phonetic unity, increases the system of existing functions or saves an old function by a new marker. In both cases there is evinced a creative vital force; for, in spite of all mechanism, free activity of the mind cannot be ruled out. Mechanism is only manner and form, not cause or essence of mental activity; the occasions and external incentives of these free creations must indeed be sought . . . but how little is thereby explained is seen at once when it is asked, why a given language exploits such an occasion while another language neglects or does not even recognize it. (pp. 464f.)

Misteli objects to Paul's notion of memory and creative fancy as the two factors in language, and his view that "the speech-forms gradually emerged from the isolation in which one after another they came to the speaker and became organized into groups according to the laws of ideational association; this process enormously aids memory and makes possible new combinations, and this is what we may call analogy-formation." This description, says Misteli, fits the learning of a foreign language by paradigms, but not the state of affairs in a native language. Paul's mistake was to confuse the association of speech-forms with ordinary association by contiguity; it is not the case that there exists to begin with a speech-material divided into groups, which analogy then seizes upon, but group- and analogy-formation are one and the same thing, which is a form of psychical activity. Or does anyone really think that the three persons of a plural verb become bound together after the fashion that smoke becomes associated with the idea of fire? This could only happen in foreign-language teaching. Misteli concludes with the assertion that it had best be left to psychologists to illuminate the findings of linguistics from the psychological point of view.

In 1885 appeared Brugmann's small book on "the present state of linguistics." This contained his inaugural lecture at Freiburg, in which he discussed the relations between linguistics and philology. Here he rejected as accidental and temporary the contrast whereby philology was said to deal with the "cultural side" of language (i.e., that of educated people as represented in literature), while linguistics dealt with the "natural side" (i.e., that of naive people as expressed in ordinary everyday speech). As Paul had said, every linguistic production is the work of an individual, and the speech of every individual is subject to the same physical and psychological principles and is equally an appropriate object of study. But it is natural for linguistics to start from the simpler conditions of everyday speech. Language exists nowhere but in individual human beings, in whom it exists as organizations of ideational groups; only in the psychical organization of human beings lie the conditions of historical development; what we are accustomed to call the forms and meanings of a language are empty abstractions.

The major part of Brugmann's (1885) book consists in his reply to Curtius' (1885) critique of the neogrammarian movement. Here Brugmann rejected the notion that tendencies to phonetic change could be inhibited in some word-forms by the factor of meaning; sound-changes proceed by minimal degrees, unnoticed by individuals, are dependent upon a general tendency in the members of a speech-community and are not subject to control by meaning. Apparent exceptions to sound-laws require explanation; the explanation in many cases may consist in showing the analogical influence of other forms which operated subsequent to the operation of the sound-change. Part II of this paper is devoted to the presentation of Brugmann's views on analogy. "The feeling for the etymological interconnection of words and for the rules of word-formation and inflection arises in individuals by the process of newly acquired speech-ideas being attracted by earlier acquired ones through partial identity of their elements" (p. 78). Brugmann follows Paul in the view that all the forms of a language become organized within individual speakers according to similarities of root, stem, derivation, and inflection. Not only in children but also in adults speech activity involves, besides memory, a large amount of creative production of forms according to the models and rules implicit in such organization. Particularly striking is the fact that individuals, although they have never heard or memorized most forms of the derivational and inflectional systems, nevertheless can produce them without consciousness of the analogical process which they imply. There tends to be a causal relation between analogical formations and phonetic change; the latter is, in the history of languages, continually destroying associated groups and creating useless differences between related forms; analogy is a means of reaction against such disturbances.

Every language is ceaselessly busy, by means of analogy, in eliminating useless differences and in securing similar phonetic expression for what is functionally similar.

> Thus analogy is today no longer the fatal drive which exists only to interrupt the straight course of phonetic development; rather, we know that it is, alongside the mechanical force of memory, a supremely important factor in the learning and practice of speech, in that it provides between earlier and later speech-activity an easier mediation than that which depends on the strength of memory, and that it moreover has the function of establishing, as against the form-splitting effects of phonetic change, a closer connection of what belongs together, and of countering the inexpedient loss of phonetic differences between functionally unrelated forms. (pp. 85f.)

Curtius had raised the question of the criteria for judging the probability of analogy-formations, in order to avoid subjective and arbitrary opinions. Brugmann points out that he had said in the Foreword to the *Morphologische Untersuchungen* (Osthoff and Brugmann, 1878) that the application of the principle of analogy had begun rather recently, that mistakes had undoubtedly been made, but that with the increasing study of analogy in modern languages more general viewpoints would be attained concerning the various directions of association, and measures of the probability of associations would be established; since then, Paul in his *Prinzipien* had done much in this direction.

In 1887 appeared Benjamin Ide Wheeler's *Analogy and the Scope of its Application in Language*. His purpose, he said, was "to attempt a coherent classification of the generally recognized products of the action of analogy in language." Previous classifications, such as that of Paul into material and formal, "describe only the results of the action of analogy, instead of referring back to the activities of the mind which produce the groupings, and, in accordance with the groupings, the forms. The classifications, in other words, have been grammatical rather than psychological" (p. 3). Wheeler adopts the distinction between physiological processes (sound-changes) and psychological processes (analogical changes) in language:

psychological laws ... are based upon the universal constituent principles of the human mind. The particular character of these laws is always determined by the relations existing in the storehouses of memory between the various word-pictures or the various thought- or sentence-pictures ... [but] the intervention of a *possible* analogy is never *necessary*. The Greek *oktṓ* ['eight'] was always exposed to the influence of its next neighbor *heptá* ['seven'] and *héks* ['six'] but accepted the [initial aspirate], as far as I know, only in the Heraklean dialect (*hoktṓ*), and the change of consonant only, if at all, in the Elean *optṓ*. ... In all linguistic investigation, the most rigid discrimination between the operation of the physiological factors and the psychological factors is indispensable. Under one of the two categories may be classed every case of change in language. In Latin *s* between vowels becomes *r*, and *arbŏrem* admits of a phonetic explanation; but *final s* does not become *r*, hence *arbŏr* beside *arbōs* must be referred to psychological action, namely, the association with the forms of the other cases. ... (p. 5)

The only satisfactory basis of classification will be that which arranges the resultant forms according to the psychological activities which produced them. These activities sum themselves up in the mind's effort to introduce into its material for expression a connected order, which shall reflect a corresponding order among the objects of thought to be expressed. Groups of forms shall correspond to groups of ideas; like modifications of form shall attend like modifications of idea. In opposition to this tendency stand the diversity and massiveness of the vocabulary, and the tendency to enrich it continually by borrowing and in other ways, and the destructive and confusing activity of the phonetic laws. (p. 7)

Wheeler's "Classification of the Phenomena of Analogy" is as follows:

I. *Likeness of signification and diversity of form.* "Two words entirely diverse in form, but which are capable of application to one and the same object or idea, may, through the influence of this limited likeness of signification, be confused into one word by the process known as 'contamination of form.'" "A Republican who is a Prohibitionist, or a Prohibitionist who is a Republican, might be designated either as *Republican* or as *Prohibitionist*; the mongrel *Prohiblican* was probably first suggested by somebody's 'slip of the tongue.'" "The two equally good expressions for the same thing spring into the mind simultaneously with the object of thought to be named, and in the hesitancy of choice each furnishes an

51

element to the name applied. It is to be noted that in this class of phenomena resemblance in *form* plays no part in suggesting the formation of the groups." "Syntactical phenomena of precisely analogous nature are common. Two equally good expressions for the same thought, but cast in entirely different form, occur simultaneously to the mind, and are merged in one. Cf. *I am friends with him* ... composed of *I am befriended with him,* or *I am on friendly terms with him,* and *we are friends.*"

II. *Affinity of signification and diversity of form.* "Words totally dissimilar in form, but expressing ideas of like category, are made to approximate slightly in form through the extended application of some sign of category, or through the extended use of some element or combination of elements of sound, which has come to be recognized as characteristic of the group." "This sort of grouping is especially traceable in changes of word gender. Thus Fr. *été,* m. (= Lat. *aestatem,* f.), follows the gender of the other names of seasons, as *hiver,* m., *printemps,* m." "An entirely analogous basis of grouping is found in the relation existing between certain word-groups or series, like the numerals. ... There, as in some other cases, it remains a question for the psychologist to determine how far the merely external relation of contiguity in use conditions the association of the members of the groups."

III. *Likeness of function and diversity of form.* "Words differing in *form* are reduced to groups upon the basis of likeness of function, i.e., of likeness of use in the economy of the sentence and for the expression of like modifications of thought."

A. *Like cases from different stems.* "The genitive ending -*s* in English, which is actually at home only in the *o*-stems, has by transfer come to be recognized as the almost universal sign of the genitive case; cf. *lady's maid, bride's cake.* ... " "Most of the cases of complete transfer must, furthermore, be classed under the head of that grouping by likeness of function which is mediated by a likeness of form in some part of the two systems involved; e.g., the adjective *Chinese* used substantively has the same form in singular and plural. ... As the form is, however, commonly used as plural, the analogy of *trees, seas, keys,* etc., led to associating the notion of plurality with the final sibilant, and caused the singular *Chinese* to be grouped with the singulars *tree, sea, key,* etc., with the result that the new form '*Chinee*' was developed."

B. *Like moods, like tenses, etc., of the verb from different stems.* "The same impulse which has led the child, by recognition of the preterite *-d,* as a convenient tense-sign, to say '*I see'd it,*' '*I know'd it*' has caused the 'weak' conjugation in all the Germanic languages to gradually encroach upon the old ablaut system inherited from the Indo-European mother-speech."

C. *Leveling in the formation of compounds.* "It is the tendency to establish a normalized method of connecting the constituent elements of a compound. The *s* in *daysman, birdsnest, Thursday,* etc., is old; not that in *doomsday,* O. E. *dômdaeg,* nor in *herdsman,* M.E. *herdeman.*"

D. *Origin and extension of suffixes.* "The Germanic suffix *-y* is in place in English *mighty,* but is analogically extended to Romance words, as in *noisy, easy.*"

IV. Contrast of signification and partial likeness of form. "Words of contrasted signification and of partly similar form are grouped in couplets, and a further approximation in the outward form is the result. A convenient illustration of this phenomenon is offered by the English *female* for *fēmĕl (= Fr. *femelle*), which has assumed the easy yoke of *male.*"

V. Likeness of signification and partial likeness of form. "Words whose stems have a like signification and are similar but not like in form are grouped together upon the basis both of meaning and form, and a levelling of the form of the stems is the result."

A. *Leveling between different cases of like stems.* "From peculiarities of accent or of other phonetic conditions, a diversity in the form of the stem grows up among the various case forms,—e.g., Greek *patḗr, patrós, patéra;* and it is in the direction of eliminating this useless diversity that the levelling activity operates. . . . The form most frequently recurring in use, as having the strongest hold upon the memory, is most liable to be the favored form in the process of levelling."

B. *Leveling between the different forms for person and number in the same tense of the verb.* "The common extension of the third singular -*s* has become an undeniable fact of the language in the phrase 'says I,' in which the -*s* is evidently felt to be the sign of the present tense, as -*d* of the pret. in *said,* and the proportion is completed: *said he : said I :: says he : says I.*"

C. *The leveling between the different parts (tenses, etc.) of the same verb* "is too common to require much illustration. Cf. *done* used as preterit; *took, drove* used as participles."

D. *Leveling between derivative and primitive.* "The primitive influences the derivative. Engl. *leafage* for *leavage shows the influence of *leaf.* The pronunciation of *nătional* as *nātional* is due to the analogy of *nātion.*"

VI. *Resemblance of form suggests a possible resemblance or likeness of signification* ["folk-etymologies"]. "Old English *brydguma* 'the bride's man, bridegroom' (cf. Goth. *guma* 'man' = Lat. *homo*) would regularly become Mod. Engl. *bridegoom; but the resemblance of the second component to *groom* suggests likeness of signification, and the form is changed to correspond."

VII. *Resemblance of form suggests a possible likeness of function.* "Elements of words like prefixes and suffixes are felt to have a definite use in the economy of expression, and parts of words which as unusual or as ordinarily conveying no definite idea in themselves cannot be classified and understood are often falsely identified by the mind with similar elements which are familiar and to which definite notions attach." Thus "French *plaisir* exchanges what would be in English an anomalous ending for the common ending of *measure, nature, picture,* and becomes *pleasure*"; and "In English the inherited prefix *en-* is often changed to *in-* through the influence of new-coming Latin words; as, *enquire* (M.E. *enqueren*) to *inquire, encline* (M.E. *enclinen*) to *incline.*"

VIII. *Likeness of form suggests a possible likeness of signification.* "This, the simplest, but yet the subtlest form of folk-etymology, involves, of course, no change of form, but only a shifting of the sense of signification, or the introduction of signification into elements to which heretofore no signification had been attached." "The German words *wahnsinn* and *wahnwitz*, 'madness' are compounded of the adjective *wan* 'empty' ... now out of use. The orthography shows that it has been replaced in the popular feeling by the substantive *wahn* 'delusion.' "

Near the end of his monograph, Wheeler gives sixteen "Principles," by way of summarizing his discussion. The key question concerning the process of analogical change is dealt with in the fifteenth principle: it is, "Why should the form A follow the influence of B rather than of C, or of C rather than of B?" "The explanation by analogy is never complete when the possibility of influence from a given source is indicated; it must also be shown how, out of many possible associations, the language was naturally impelled to choose the one in question; also why the retention of the old form was impracticable." "Reasons for choice of association may be: (*a*) Predominance in use; ... (*b*) Acquirement of an intelligible formation, so that, e.g., definite functions may be associated with definite elements of the form.... (*c*) Apparent acquirement of signification; our language had its choice between *an-ekename* (*eke*, 'additional') and *a-nekename*, and chose the latter because of *nick* = 'clip.' "

In 1892, Middleton published *An Essay on Analogy in Syntax*, "illustrated chiefly from the classical languages." He pointed out that while the principle of analogy had been applied freely, especially by the neogrammarians, in explanation of apparent deviations from phonetic— "physiological"—laws,

> The application of the principle to syntax, however, has been the theme of but few treatises; and this in spite of the fact that its operations are much more extended there than in morphology.... All syntactical change is psychological, and one of the chief agents of this change is analogy.... A sentence is the expression of thought, but an expression which proceeds not so much on the lines of logical rules as on the association of ideas.... Seeing that the association of ideas plays such an important part in the formation of sentences, it is not remarkable that the several members of a proposition should affect each other, or that syntactical forms, united in the mind by some internal connexion, should be found to exert a mutual influence. People are continually making analogical, and

55

therefore probably false enthymemes, and so in syntax the spoken language is continually making new formations on very slight points of similarity, and without a thought as to whether the new formations correspond with original forms. Thus analogy works, as far as formal grammar goes, illogically, until stereotyped forms arise, to depart from which would be mere pedantry. (Middleton, 1892, pp. 7f.)

Middleton distinguished three types of analogical assimilation in syntax. In *formal analogy*, "Two forms which have originally distinct functions are, through association of ideas caused by proximity or frequent union, assimilated to each other. The working of this influence is seen to be very widely spread, and comes up in tense, mood, voice, gender, number, and case. The assimilation may be either progressive or regressive, i.e., a form may be assimilated either to one which follows it or to one which precedes it." Agreement in gender between nouns and adjectives probably arose in this manner. Assimilation in number is illustrated by English *none of them were*, where the plural verb supplants the singular "on the analogy of *them*." As for tense, the more "primitive" parataxis often replaces hypotaxis in modern Greek and in English: thus *try to come* is supplanted by *try and come*. In mood, the assimilation of subjunctive to indicative is illustrated by *If this is so, all is lost*, where formerly the verb of the protasis would have been *be*. Double negatives, double comparatives, and other forms of repetition also are said to illustrate formal assimilation.

The second type of syntactic analogy or assimilation is *assimilation of meaning*, where "the psychological working of the inner meaning produces difference where likeness was to be expected. Thus a sentence like 'The populace were agitated' couples together a singular noun and a plural verb, the reason of the usage being that the noun is a collective one, and the speaker pays less attention to the fact of its being singular" (pp. 39f.).

The third type of syntactic analogy is *complex assimilation*, which "consists in the formation of a third syntactical form out of a mixture of other two. The two factors that go to make the new expression may be outwardly dissimilar, but are united by an inward bond of meaning, that is, by the psychological association subsisting between the two original

56

expressions." Such changes are classed as *contaminations*. Thus "the traditional grammatical gender of [Greek] nouns in *-os* is masculine, and of nouns in *-a (-ē)* feminine. It is probable that the exceptions to this rule are due to the working of syntactical contamination, i.e., a word in *-os* sometimes became feminine through psychological association due to similarity of meaning with a word in *-a*." Modern Greek *kalòn di' hēmâs* 'good for us' is "the result of phrases like *eprákhthē di' hēmâs* 'it was done on account of us.' Now, *eprákhthē hēmîn* can be used, and likewise *kalòn hēmîn*. Make a proportion, and we get the new form: *eprákhthē hēmîn : eprákhthē di' hēmâs :: kalòn hēmîn : kalòn di' hēmâs*." As Middleton says, this kind of assimilation "has a wider influence than either of the other two, and all languages are full of its results."

For experimental evidence of the tendencies underlying Middleton's first two classes of assimilation, we would probably find the sentence-completion method more appropriate than the word-association method. The latter method would however be expected to reveal some of the associations included in the third class, e.g., assimilations of gender endings. In Chapter 5 I shall have occasion to discuss Jenkins' distinction between "paradigmatic" and "syntactic" word-associations; by the latter Jenkins means to refer to word-associations resulting from frequent contiguity of words in sentences, as in *through thick and thin, here and there*, etc. Middleton's "syntactic analogies" are for the most part not expressions of word-associations but rather of the assimilative influence of word-patterns within sentences.

In 1895 Rudolf Meringer, a linguist, and Karl Mayer, a psychiatrist, published a study of *lapsus linguae*, "slips of the tongue." Meringer's purpose was to show that such slips could be ordered under rules and thus, by revealing the mechanism in which sounds and words are interrelated, could throw light on the historical development of language. Such mistakes, he thought, might be regarded as illustrating what can happen when the speech mechanism runs free, unsupervised by attention, so that "a glance at the wheels" becomes possible.[24]

24. As against the neogrammarians, Meringer took a gestaltish view of speech mechanisms. Paul had said that the "kinesthetic feeling is not formed separately for every individual word, but wherever in speech the same elements recur, their production

Most of the long lists of slips which Meringer and Mayer recorded exemplify metatheses, haplologies, assimilations, and dissimilations, and thus are not obviously relevant to analogy, since they are the effects of influence between the parts of a single word or of a momentary syntactic collocation rather than of the influence of one or more forms on other forms. Most relevant are the slips listed under "contaminations," in which elements of different words or constructions, similar in meaning or in form, are combined into a single word or construction; such combinations are particularly likely to occur when two different constructions intersect in a word or two different words intersect in a sound.[25] Particularly interesting are tendencies toward the elimination of ablaut and umlaut, and toward other levelings of irregularities. Thus Meringer and Mayer demonstrated that analogical tendencies are continually manifesting themselves in ordinary speech; the question of why certain of the resulting changes become habitual and general remains, of course, unanswered.

The work of Meringer and Mayer stimulated two American students —Bawden (1900) and Wells (1906)—to publish monographs on linguistic lapses; neither added significantly to the literature of linguistic analogy.

---

is ruled by the same kinesthetic feeling." Such a statement is based, of course, on the "ideomotor" notion that behind and causally related to overt articulatory processes are visual, auditory, and, particularly, kinesthetic "feelings" or images (*Bilder*) which, though "psychical," are nevertheless localized in the brain and constitute "inner speech." Paul's statement Meringer declares to be false; speech-sounds are not learned or used as separate entities but as unanalyzed parts of words; the internal images are not of phones but of words. Such a view would require quite a modification of the neogrammarian statement of exceptionless sound-change, since it questions the notion of "recurrent sames" of sound recurring under "the same phonetic conditions." Meringer suggests the analogy of writing; e.g., writing one's signature or familiar words occurs as a unitary act.

25. The numerous examples make upon me the same impression as do the ordinary informal conversations recorded by Dixon (1965); they suggest, that is, how far actual speech departs from the formal rules—e.g., of linguistic "competence"—which have been proposed by some grammarians. The uneasy foundation of formal and universal rules of language—e.g., phonetic laws—was emphasized by Oertel (1901a, pp. 258–273) and has been recently emphasized, as we shall see, by linguists reacting against formal syntactic rules. It should be noted that many of Meringer's examples were produced, not in careless speech in informal situations, but by scholars in formal lectures, often without being noticed or corrected by the speakers. Meringer remarks that slips of the tongue are analogous to absent-minded performances of other sorts; e.g., "One starts to put the penholder in the mouth and to write with the cigar."

Lapses for them were any sort of "error," mostly of assimilation, dissimilation, metathesis, etc. within words or phrases, whether these were spoken, heard, written, or seen. Bawden's monograph is interesting as exemplifying the "functional" movement in American psychology. "Every mental state is a complex of peripherally and centrally aroused ideas. . . . The question then becomes one in which psychology has to wait for physiology and neurology, rather than one which can be settled on the basis of mere introspection" (p. 17). "Just because ideomotor lapses [as distinguished from sensori-motor or 'imitation' errors] belong to the category of those mental processes which are centrally, rather than peripherally, initiated, they are the more baffling to investigation, because not admitting of experimental control" (p. 18). Lapses are products of associative processes, "best described by the term assimilation [defined as] that anoetic mental process in which presentations (or percepts) and images (or ideas) are fused, or coalesce." All ideas or objects have contexts in "marginal consciousness" which influence the "net result," as when a word previously called out determines the perception of another word (pp. 41ff.).

The studies by Laffal (1955) and Veness (1962) deal with the "faults" in word-association which, in the Jungian tradition, have been thought to be diagnostic of "emotional complexes," and are not relevant to our subject. In general, studies of slips of the tongue by psychologists and phoneticians[26] have treated them only as due to influences within words or phrases, and thus momentary and individual; analogical influences, such as might be predicted from high-frequency word-associations, have seldom been distinguished. Thus Goldstein (1968) lists the slip *too soon* where the speaker intended *too late,* and *eat* where he intended *drink,* but beside these he places such slips as *mawn lower* for intended *lawn mower.* Boomer and Laver (1968) define tongue-slips as "transient malfunctions of the sequencing system of the speech production process which obey stringent linguistic constraints." They illustrate their usage of the term "by reference to a characteristic example": "But these frunds . . . funds have been frozen." Boomer and Laver, however, follow Abercrombie (1965) in regarding conversation, which is "the overwhelming

26. Further references in Boomer and Laver, 1968.

bulk of man's daily use of spoken language," as the business of linguistics; they reject the limitation of linguistics to "spoken prose," the corpus of "well-formed" utterances; slips of the tongue are part of the daily spoken language, and they too conform to principles which can be discovered.

Linguists, of course, know the difference between momentary slips and analogical—historical—changes, but they do not all agree that the actual utterances of daily life should be included in the concerns of the linguist. One who does is Hockett (1967), who distinguishes between "speech marred by blunders and what I shall simply call 'smooth speech,'" and insists that the former requires study. But I am not sure that he makes a sufficient distinction between such a blend as *shell = shout + yell*, and such a one as *avord* or *affoid = avoid + afford*. In a word-association experiment, the associations *avoid⇌afford* would seem very unlikely, whereas the associations *shout⇌yell* might well occur. That is, the latter example is the sort which many people might share, both in word-association and in historical change, whereas the former was a momentary lapse of an individual on a certain special occasion.[27]

We are about to arrive at that landmark in the history of our subject which was the introduction, by Thumb and Marbe (1901), of the problem of linguistic analogy into the psychological laboratory. But before we enter upon this new chapter, it may be helpful to survey the scene as it appeared to a linguist, Hanns Oertel, in 1901 (Oertel, 1901a). Almost all of the linguists who have appeared thus far in our history were Indo-European scholars who were historically oriented; Oertel belonged to this tradition:[28] "The purpose of all scientific investigation is to understand its objects, *i.e.*, to learn how they came to be what they are" (p. 136). Oertel distinguished between "primary changes"—"those which originated in, and were created by, the individual," and "secondary changes" —"those which, having been originated elsewhere, are adopted by the individual" and are therefore "imitative" (Oertel had read Tarde, "who uses the word [imitation] without the usual implication of purpose or

---

27. Cf. the more generally probable *evoid = evade + avoid*, cited by Oertel (1901a, p. 167); phonetic similarity favors association, but only when there is also some semantic similarity.

28. But he was critical of the neogrammarians; see Oertel, 1901a, pp. 258ff.

intention"). The description of the primary changes also involves no implication of awareness or purpose. "The causes for a change can only be studied where the change is primary," whereas "in the case of secondary changes ... we must seek for reasons for their adoption" (p. 138). Oertel rejects Brugmann's dictum that "there must exist in a large number of individuals a tendency toward the alteration to insure its success"; for, says Oertel, "in many phonetic changes acceptance and rejection do not rest upon the character of the change itself at all, but upon external social considerations which have no inherent or necessary connection with the change. ... acceptance and rejection depend on causes which have nothing to do with the ease or difficulty or frequency of the sound. They are exactly parallel to the spread of fashions" (pp. 144f.).

As in "secondary" changes one individual imitates another, so in analogical changes "the same individual imitates himself."

> The basis of all analogy formation is association. Without previous association there can be no analogy formation, for we mean by this term the interference of one word or phrase with another word or phrase, and such interference is impossible without some sort of associative contact. But while every case of analogy formation presupposes an association, it is not conversely true that every association must result in an analogy formation. ... [Scherer had suggested frequency of use as a factor.] These questions, however, cannot be solved on the basis of analogy formations as they are recorded in language, but must be left to the psychological laboratory. (pp. 150f.)

In all cases of associative interference, says Oertel, there occurs a "shunting" or "derailment"—German *Entgleisung*—because the innervation of the muscles of articulation is switched from the track of the first word to that of the second. "Phonetic alterations which are the result of association by sense alone are comparatively small. ... But phonetic alterations will in most cases be found to involve a partial likeness of form as well as semantic similarity. The reason for this is that a sound or syllable which the two associated words have in common offers a point of contact, the switch, so to speak, by which the stronger innervation of the first word is transferred to the second, because in this particular sound or syllable the strong innervation of the first word reinforces that of the second" (pp. 166f.). This process is illustrated by the lapsus *evoid*, "immediately corrected to 'both avoid and evade,' " and diagrammed thus:[29]

$$\left\{ \begin{matrix} {\rightarrow} E {\rightarrow} \\ \alpha \end{matrix} V \begin{matrix} \alpha \\ {\rightarrow} OI {\rightarrow} \end{matrix} D {\rightarrow} E \right\}$$

"This is the reason why examples for Wheeler's fifth class (likeness of signification and partial likeness of form) are so plentiful and why analogy exercises so strong an influence over slightly different forms of the same stem in the inflectional system."

Where two words have all semantic elements in common, the associative tie between them must be proportionately stronger than that which binds together in a congeneric group terms which are semantically similar only. So that, even without any additional formal similarity, analogical interference might be expected. But here also analogical interference is usually connected with additional partial formal similarity . . . When the alteration produced by this association of homonyms is slight, and one of the two words retains by far the largest part of its original form . . . this process still goes by the name of analogy formation. When, however, the associative interference of the second word is stronger and both synonyms have about equal share in the creation of the new form, we are accustomed to speak of contamination [e.g., *whirlicane* from *whirlwind* and *hurricane*]. Yet the psychical process is the same in both cases. The difference lies merely in this fact, that in those cases which we call analogical changes there is a shunting back to the original word, or the shunting occurs at the very close of the word, so that the foreign element introduced is necessarily very small, while in contaminations the innervation of the speech-muscles once shifted from the original word to its associated synonym, continues to travel along the track of the latter, and as a consequence produces a more thorough change. (pp. 170f.)

Finally, I will mention that Pipping (1906) applied a suggestion of Jespersen, that analogical formations might be divided into two classes,

29. Oertel protects himself in a footnote against the charge of not knowing the difference between letters and sounds.

namely, the conservative (*erhaltende*) and the creative (*schaffende*), to a large amount of material of the North-Germanic languages, with the intention of showing that many problems are solved if it is assumed that conservative formations are produced more readily than are creative ones. He assumed that analogy could hinder—or, alternatively, subsequently reverse—the operation of a phonetic law. A sound-change such as umlauting would appear in the younger generation, while the older generation persisted in the old forms. But if one or more forms of an inflection were not subject to the law, association with these forms would produce analogical formations which would be reinforced by the practice of the older generation; creative analogies would not be thus reinforced.

Chapter 4

ANALOGY IN THE LABORATORY

Albert Thumb (1865–1915), who had been a pupil of Brugmann, was an assistant professor of comparative linguistics at Freiburg im Breisgau at the time of publication (1901) of the Thumb and Marbe monograph entitled *Experimental Researches on the Psychological Bases of Linguistic Analogy-Formation* (hereafter abbreviated T&M), but in that same year he moved to Marburg as *Ordinarius,* and in 1909 to Strassburg. Karl Marbe (1869–1953) was in 1901 a *Privatdocent der Philosophie* at Würzburg, where he later became a professor. In his autobiography (1936) he tells us that at the beginning of his student days at Freiburg he intended to study philology; he "was interested particularly in Old Norse, Middle High German, and Sanskrit"; his instructor in Germanistics was Hermann Paul. He then spent a semester at Bonn, where he continued his studies in philology, but also helped Götz Martius, who had been a pupil of Wundt, in "all sorts of reaction experiments." Next, Marbe spent a semester at Berlin, where, having decided on philosophy instead of philology as a career, he studied under the guidance of Hermann Ebbinghaus. He returned to Bonn for his doctor's degree; among his examiners was the classical philologist Bücheler. Next he went to Leipzig, where he worked in Wundt's Psychological Institute, in association with Wundt's first and second assistants, Oswald Külpe and Ernst Meumann. It was this association with Külpe that induced Marbe to join Külpe at Würzburg, where the latter had become a full professor. If we add to this history the fact that Marbe's friend Albert Thumb had interested him in the psychology of language, we may judge that he was well prepared to initiate psychological researches in that field. However, his contributions were almost wholly limited to the year 1901, in which were published the monograph with Thumb and the study of judgment which was one of the first of the studies of "imageless thought" for which Würzburg became famous. Thereafter Marbe turned to applied psychology—law, crime, industry, etc.—perhaps somewhat influenced by another friend of his Freiburg days, Hugo Münsterberg, for whom he had served as subject in association experiments. Marbe has said that he gave up research on the psychology of thought and judgment because he was disgruntled by Külpe's assigning subjects in this field to others and developing it in a manner of which Marbe disapproved; the result was a polemic which ended his association with Külpe. Another polemical article was directed against Wundt, with whose views he had become disenchanted.

The T&M monograph begins with an essay by Thumb on "Analogy-Formation in Language." He assumes that analogy—in Paul's sense—and contamination are products of the same psychological factors and may therefore both be subsumed under the term *analogy-formation*, defined (after Misteli) as "a kind of association of ideas (*Vorstellungen*) which gains phonic expression." He cites Curtius' statement, "Analogy-formation is in itself everywhere possible but nowhere necessary," and remarks on the danger of a vicious circle in which one postulates an association in order to "explain" a puzzle in linguistic history, e.g., an apparent exception to a phonetic law. "But even if the assumption of certain associations should appear, from a historical and psychological viewpoint, to be unobjectionable, we do not know why an analogical transformation took a particular direction. A form can be a member of various groups." Thus a verb-form can be associated with other forms of the same verb and with corresponding forms of other verbs. Paul had stated that the associations which would be effective would be those which were "strongest," but the relative strength of associations is a problem, not for linguistics but for psychology. But hitherto it had not occurred to anyone to investigate, by means of psychological experiments, the associations which are effective in language. Thumb mentions several experimental studies—by E. W. Scripture, M. Trautscholdt, and James McKeen Cattell—which suggested that such research might have linguistic significance.

The second section of the monograph, by Marbe, is entitled "A

Critique of the Doctrine of Association." Marbe cites a number of studies which had shown that associative reaction-time depends not only on the instigating idea but also on the constellation of consciousness before and during the associative process, a fact which Trautscholdt (1882), under the influence of Wundt's notion of "apperception," had failed to recognize. Marbe rejects Wundt's classification of associations; Wundt's "inner associations"—superordinates, subordinates, coordinates, and relations of causal and purposive dependence—constitute a classification, not of associations, but of semantic relationships between the associated words. This classification seems to assume that in the usual experiments with orally presented words the word heard by the subject releases in him a corresponding semantic idea which then arouses another idea which is then named by the subject. But this is not the usual course of events; in many cases the response is evoked directly by the stimulus-word, without intervening ideas belonging to the semantic sphere of the two words.

The third section of the monograph, also by Marbe, reports the association experiments performed by T&M. Previous studies by Kraepelin (1883), Münsterberg (1892), and Aschaffenburg (1895) had shown that the responses to stimulus-words of a given form-class tended to be words of the same class, but the classes used were limited to substantives, adjectives, and verb infinitives. T&M proposed to use a greater variety of classes: ten kinship names—*father*, *mother*, etc., ten adjectives, ten numerals from *one* to *ten*, ten pronouns, ten adverbs of place, ten adverbs of time. All sixty of these words were presented orally to each subject at one sitting. They were arranged in such an order that in no case would a word immediately follow another of the same category; miscellaneous words not belonging to the list selected for the experiment were frequently interposed. There were eight subjects, all students, teachers, or doctors of philosophy. In a later experiment eighty verb infinitives were presented to eight subjects. Still later finite verb-forms and participles were presented to several subjects; most of the responses were not verbal forms. Then the verb-forms were presented to three subjects with instruction to respond with another verb-form of the same or a different verb. A stopwatch was used to measure the reaction-time in the first experiment, and a Hipp chronoscope and voice-key in the later experiment.

66

Marbe summarizes the results of the experiments as follows: (*a*) The stimulus-words of each class elicited predominantly words of the same class, except that the infinitives elicited substantives about as often as verbs. (*b*) Except for the numerals, reciprocal associations occurred in all word-classes; that is, a word *a* which elicits word *b* as most frequent response is elicited by *b* when *b* occurs as stimulus. The numerals elicited predominantly the next higher numerals. (*c*) The more frequent a response—i.e., the greater the number of persons who gave the same response to a given stimulus-word—the shorter was its reaction-time. (In recent times this relationship has been referred to as "Marbe's Law.")

The remaining sections of the monograph were written by Thumb. Section IV is entitled "Linguistic Critique of the Experiments." Thumb distinguishes contaminations between synonyms, where two forms arise simultaneously and there results a mixture of the two, and contaminations between non-synonyms in which a word-idea (*Wortvorstellung*), which is in process of innervating the corresponding word, arouses another word-idea which then influences the articulation of the intended word. (Here is illustrated the awkwardness of mind-body dualism.) As Paul had stated, such a phonetic transformation of one word by another becomes customary (*usuell*) in a speech community when its individual members agree at least in their associations and in some degree in their tendencies toward slips of the tongue. Thumb states that the word-groups of the T&M experiments were selected because they had shown, in the history of the Indo-European languages, strong tendencies toward analogical changes. Thus, e.g., *father* and *mother*, *warm* and *cold*, etc., had undergone approximations to each other in various Indo-European languages. Thumb was of the opinion that the fact that most of the associations recorded in the T&M experiments were within the groups within which historical, and presumed prehistorical, analogical changes had occurred, confirmed the assumption of the role of word-associations; such experimental associations were not only most frequent but also of shorter reaction-time; moreover, linguists should be chary of postulating analogy-formations which are inconsistent with the most frequent associative responses. The reciprocal associations of adjectival opposites—e.g., old⇌young—have probably resulted in some degree from their use together in speech, but they have made the direction of analogical change less certain.[30] In the numerals one to ten, however, the order and hence the associations are unidirectional, and the analogical influences have been mostly from the next higher to the next lower number. So too with the series of months: *October* > *Octomber* in a number of Indo-European languages might be attributed simply to *November* (*December*) rather than to *September*, but there is another factor: these names of months are compounds of numbers and an element perceived as a meaningful suffix, and this suffix tends to be generalized to other months. Correspondences are found between the associative responses to adverbs and pronouns on the one hand and, on the other hand, the phonetic influences among these forms in the histories of Indo-European languages.

Section v concerns itself with "The Verbal System (Grammatical Analogy-Formations)." Some of the forms discussed in the preceding section, such as numerals and adverbs, in which conceptual or "material" —*stofflichen*—semantic relations were influential, were also found to develop, by means of similarity of endings, into grammatical—functional —categories. But the most elaborate functional systems are found in the verbs. Infinitives were selected as stimulus-words, says Thumb, "because the essential verb-meaning is best expressed by them." But the responses to them differed from those of the other word-classes in that they were not so predominantly words of the same class—i.e., verbs; almost 52 percent were substantives and only 42 percent were verbs. There were a few "most frequent" reciprocal associations: e.g., *nehmen*⇄*geben* ('to take', 'to give') which seems consistent with the history of Lat. *reddere*> *rendere* after *prendere*. The associations *gehen*→*laufen*→*springen* ('to walk, to run, to leap') are consistent with the semantic changes by which, in south Germany, the first was replaced by the second and the second by the third of these; these were however not analogical but semantic

---

30. Boer (1908) in a study of reciprocal associations found that "forward" associations—e.g., brother-sister, here-there—were more numerous than "backward" associations—e.g., sister-brother, etc., in the proportion of 1.5 to 1, and concluded that this could be attributed to "speech facility" (*Sprachgeläufigkeit*). Menzerath (1908b) found that 100 words from "facile combinations"—e.g., right-left, father-mother— elicited much greater commonality of responses and shorter reaction-time than did 100 words which were not members of such combinations.

changes, but it appears that for such changes also psychological studies are not without value. There was a tendency for strong verbs as stimuli to elicit strong verbs as responses, and for weak verbs to elicit weak verbs, but strong verbs showed a greater tendency than did weak verbs to elicit verbs of the other verb-class; these results were consistent both with the historical persistence of strong forms and with their slow yielding to the influence of weak forms.

Paul had assumed that in an inflectional system words were organized in a hierarchy of greater and lesser interacting groups which exist as effective forces in the unconscious.

> But if the reciprocal attraction and group organization of word-ideas are not to be merely an inexplicable psychophysical x or a mysterious physiological process in the neural paths, such concepts, from the standpoint of the phenomena of consciousness can only have the following meaning: a word-form is able to evoke another word-form, and the latter still another, etc., and these various associations can be arranged by us in series or groups which correspond to the nature of the psyche postulated by Paul. In every individual case only one association can actually enter into consciousness. Wundt speaks of the action of a "total force" (*Totalkraft*) of association and assumes that the associations of word-ideas or of their elements "are to be thought of only as dispositions of the mind which correspond to certain physical dispositions in the sensory centers, and which only then become possible psychic contents when they connect themselves to other elements"; that must mean, in terms of experimental psychology, that any word-idea, in consequence of such "dispositions," can evoke a particular association. Which association this is to be must be determined by observation or experiment, for only thus can such dispositions be revealed; the dispositions are psychophysical hypotheses intended to explain the occurrence of certain facile associations and their linguistic effects. (T&M, pp. 65ff.)

The experiments with verb-form responses to finite verb-forms were merely exploratory. "To Osthoff's dictum, 'in the declensional paradigm one case-form always influences the one next to it,' Misteli made the correct remark: 'This picture, taken from the printed grammatical paradigm, conceals an important and interesting question: what cases are chiefly interconnected by form-association?' " Paul's notion that, e.g., the forms of the present are more closely associated with one another than with those of the preterit, is merely a hypothesis abstracted from grammar, and needs to be tested by psychology.

The results of the experiments with finite verb forms were summarized by Thumb as follows:

A finite verb-form evokes
1. the same form of another verb ("outer grammatical assimilation")
2. another form of the same verb ("inner grammatical assimilation")
    a. the following person, less frequently another person
    b. the same form of another tense
    c. a form of the infinitive (participle or infinitive).

Here also the more preferred—in a group, *häufig* 'frequent'—associations are also, in the individuals who share them, more *geläufig* 'facile' as measured by reaction-time. Thus, while Paul's assumptions are in general supported, there are individual variations, and the associations are similar to those of the other word-classes in that a given form tends to evoke, in given individuals, a particular other form. Whether inflectional associations will result in analogical changes depends, as in the conceptual analogies (contaminations) previously considered, upon their frequency and facility in the community. But that verbs show inflectional changes in the different directions suggested by the above summary of association-types must be attributed, not to simultaneously operating associative processes in a given community at a given time, but to differences in the associations prevailing at different times or places; just as we say, "other times, other sound-laws," so we must say, "other times, other analogy-formations." Thumb supports this statement by references to the history of German verb-forms in the various dialects.

In a final section on "Association and Analogy," Thumb returns to the problem of the "vicious circle":

> For past speech-periods we have only the effects of associations; it is only through these effects that we infer the associative state of earlier generations. We do not thus arrive at an answer to the question, according to what law or under what conditions do certain analogy-formations come about. We lack the means to determine the associative state of earlier

speech-communities objectively and independently of the language. But if we were to assume that the question had been answered, what associations existed and why they were phonetically effective, we would still need, in order to establish the lawfulness of analogical innovations, to know in addition under what conditions particular word- or form-associations arise. These are questions, however, which linguistics by itself is even less able to solve—but psychology too has not got far in these matters.

Therefore we had better concern ourselves only with that aspect of the problem in which linguistics and psychology have most in common. From our standpoint, the question [in Delbrück's words], "why and under what circumstances such [analogical] changes occurred at a given time, and why in certain dialects but not in others," can only be formulated as, what characteristics must a word-association have in order for it to have a linguistic effect? (T&M, pp. 78f.)

From the T&M experiments Thumb draws the conclusion that analogy-formations result from associations which are preferred by and facile in the individuals of a group, and which are therefore, in association experiments, frequent and of short reaction-time. For these characteristics T&M have offered parallels in the histories of Indo-European languages. The psychological results however apply only to German, or strictly speaking, to the language of the T&M subjects. What associations may be universal, and which ones are dependent upon the peculiar phonetic, formal, or historical relations of a particular language or dialect, can only be determined by more extensive investigations. Thus the fact that the association *gravis*⇌*levis* resulted in *grevis* in Late Latin but the association *schwer*⇌*leicht* in German had no such effect might be explained by the initial phonetic resemblance in the former case, but the change *October* > *Octember* : *November* occurred in some Indo-European languages but not in others where the same phonetic and associative conditions existed. Moreover, even complete phonetic difference may not prevent assimilation; thus Greek *toûtos* > *etoûtos* : *ekeînos*. As Paul had declared, the occurrence of an analogical change depends upon the relative strengths of memory and association: "the least often used words are most, and the most frequently used words are least, subject to assimilation." Thus too the speech of children shows the strongest tendency toward analogical innovation.

The problems of association and analogy, says Thumb, should be studied in relation with linguistic studies of living languages and, particularly, dialects; this is where the relation between association and analogy can most directly be determined. Psychological research should be regarded as of equal importance for linguistics as the far more highly developed research in phonetics; as Misteli had said, nothing can be accomplished by "vague concepts" such as "psychical mechanism" and "association of ideas."

> The problem of the conditions under which facile associations can achieve linguistic effects—the question, that is, of the regularity [*Ausnahmslosigkeit*] of analogy-formation—can only then be successfully studied when a rich material of experiments in the psychology of language becomes available. For Wundt too knows no other answer to our question than that "in general a conceptual association always brings about an association of the phonetic elements"; thus the psychologist must for the present be as modest as the linguist. But this problem is also the last which still belongs in the realm of the principles of historical linguistics; in the question concerning the causes and conditions of associations, linguistics is involved only in so far as the linguistic—particularly the phonetic—form is influential in the occurrence of associations; this too is a task for united psychological and linguistic research. (T&M, p. 86)

The T&M monograph attracted a good deal of attention of both linguists and psychologists, to whose criticisms Thumb (1907a) replied. He noted that while psychologists refrained from passing judgments on linguistic matters, some linguists showed little hesitation in offering opinions about elementary facts, methods, and terminology of experimental psychology. Thus Oertel (1901b) was stimulated to report some association experiments which he had performed in 1899—presumably with the cooperation of E. W. Scripture, his colleague at Yale who was then director of the psychological laboratory.[31] Among the forty-seven words pre-

31. Oertel refers to Scripture's *Elements of Experimental Phonetics* which was then in press and which Oertel must have read in manuscript. Oertel had classified the associations which resulted in analogy-formations as (1) by sound, (2) by sense, and (3) by function. By the third of these he meant "the association of words which neither are related in meaning nor resemble each other in sound, but play the same or a similar part in the construction of a sentence"; these he calls "functional associations"

sented tachistoscopically to ten subjects were the numerals two, five, and seven. Each word was exposed for five seconds, and after an additional fifteen seconds the subjects were to report the chain of associations which they had formed during the total of twenty seconds. No reaction-times were taken. In only two cases was there an association with the immediately following numeral; most of the responses were not word-associations but phrases or sentences. "These figures," declared Oertel, "differ so materially from those obtained by Thumb and Marbe that a renewed examination of the associations with numerals seems advisable."

Marbe (1902) replied to Oertel, pointing out that "over and above his errors of procedure, [he] overlooks the fact that there is, a priori, not the least reason for expecting a coincidence of result in the two enquiries; they are concerned with totally different things. In the work of Thumb and Marbe, number words were pronounced to the observer, and he was required to answer by speaking aloud. Oertel, on the other hand, exposes printed number-words to his observers, and asks them to report upon the experiences which the words suggest." Thumb (1907a) in his comments on Oertel's study remarked that Oertel's visual presentation could not explain the divergence of his results, because Watt (1904) had shown that visual presentation gave the same results as the auditory presentation of T&M. Thumb quotes from a letter written to Oertel by Marbe:

> Whether a word evokes another word, and if so, what word, does not depend solely upon the word but also on the totality of conditions in consciousness, the so-called "constellation." A particular constellation was given our subjects by the instruction to respond to a given word with another word as quickly as possible. For anyone who wishes to study the influence of the facts of association on language must above all pay attention to associations in which one word evokes another without any sort of intervening members. This was the case for the constellation evoked by us.

Other linguists—Hugo Schuchardt, Karl Vossler, E. Herzog—had made criticisms which revealed their lack of acquaintance with psycho-

---

(Paul's "formal grouping" and Thumb and Marbe's "grammatische Analogiebildungen"). Oertel remarks in a footnote that Scripture in his *Elements* "denies the existence of 'functional associations'."

logical terms and methods. Vossler, who like Schuchardt was a leading "esthetic idealist" and thus a bitter enemy of the neogrammarians, attacked T&M for "a failure in logic," but Thumb said that he did not take this objurgation tragically, since the gulf between Thumb's notion of the task of science and the *Tiefsinn* of Vossler was so great as to make comment useless. The question of the generality of the T&M results was raised; thus Herzog (1903) pointed out that the T&M subjects were doctors and students—"Leute, die auf Schulbänken gesessen sind"—whereas linguistic change is attributable to the unschooled mass of a people. Thumb replied that the European masses are not unschooled and that moreover there is no reason to suppose that the basic psychological laws are not the same for the educated as for the uneducated; in fact, analogy-formations occur with less inhibition among the latter, and as for associations, Thumb had found by repeated experiments that there were no essential differences. Another linguist asked whether the T&M results were applicable to other languages; Thumb answered that it is reasonable to assume that the relations between association and analogy-formation found in one language have general validity; thus, the reciprocal relations of certain adjectives, such as *light* : *heavy*, Latin *levis* : *gravis* > *grevis* might well have general validity, although every language will also have its peculiar associations. These are matters which must be studied in the different languages, and particularly desirable would be the combination of association and linguistic studies in living dialects.

Wundt (1901) found little of value in the T&M studies; analogy-formations could throw light on association processes, but association experiments could not explain analogy-formations, because the conscious constellation in the T&M experiments was "as different as possible from that in analogy-formation." Thumb replied that analogy-formations may indeed throw light on the associative processes of bygone races of men, but that the question for which T&M sought an answer was that of the nature of analogy-formation and its relation to associational activity: what characteristics must an association have for it to have linguistic effects? The agreement between their results and the actual course of linguistic history—between the observed frequency-latency relations of associations and the relations which linguistic history suggests—allows us to assume

74

that the experiments and the processes in natural speech do not "occur under wholly different conditions"; the "conscious constellation" could hardly be "as different as possible" in the two situations. Wundt described the task of the T&M subjects as involving an effort of attention and a "volitional effort of memory," whereas these are not required in natural speech. Thumb replied that these operations are also not required in the T&M experiments; the subject gives his response "automatically" and thinks about it afterward; if he first thinks, this shows up in the reaction-time. Wundt's objection that the natural conscious constellation would be disturbed in the course of an experimental series by influences of previous members of the series is correct, but this objection can be raised concerning most researches in experimental psychology; T&M offset this effect by the intermixture of many non-experimental words; moreover, they found that subjects who gave the highly frequent responses, such as *father-mother, light-heavy,* did so in the very first words of the series, and experiments with many subjects subsequently convinced T&M that no special control of consciousness was necessary to elicit such responses from the very beginning of a series. Two other arguments advanced by Wundt may be noted: first, he rejected T&M's assumption that "in every individual case, only one association can actually enter into consciousness," in favor of his own notion of a *Totalkraft,* a joint influence of a group of associated forms; e.g., *gravis > grevis* was influenced not only by *levis* but also by *brevis;* so too with respect to a joint influence on a verb-form of a number of other verb-forms (Wundt however does not say how he knows this). Second, Thumb posits, on the ground of historical analogical changes, associations which were not revealed in his experiments. However, it seems that Thumb sufficiently emphasized the maxim, "other times, other analogical formations," and he would probably have accepted Wundt's "other times, other associations." That is, the occurrence or non-occurrence of a word-association at a given time does not by itself guarantee the occurrence or non-occurrence of an analogical change at any given other time; other factors are involved which may be revealed by further research (Thumb, 1911, p. 8). Thumb's goal was to discover under what conditions word-associations find expression in linguistic change.

Herzog (1903) too emphasized what he took to be the total difference between the conscious constellation in the T&M experiments and that in linguistic change; like Wundt, he erroneously assumed that the T&M instructions called for an interpolated thought-process. He objected also to T&M's adoption of Misteli's (1880) definition of analogy as including contamination. Herzog defined linguistic *analogy* as "the creation of a form on the model of a definite proportion, whereby the original form is completely eliminated from consciousness." Thus, $A_a : A_b = B_a : x$, where $x = B_b$ which replaces a prior B_c. *Contamination*, on the other hand, he defined as "the creation of a form through the fusion of parts of two forms which simultaneously enter consciousness." Thus, $A_{ab} + A_{bc} = A_{abc}$, or $A_{abc} + A_{dbe} = A_{abe}$. The T&M experiments, Herzog thought, could at most have significance for contaminations. Thumb could of course reply that associative processes underlie both sorts of change. Herzog and Schuchardt both asserted that such associations as *young-old* and *thick-thin* were the results, not of semantic relations but of syntactic contiguity—"through thick and thin," etc. But Thumb pointed out that finite verb-forms most frequently elicit other verb-forms, although they are usually syntactically contiguous with forms other than verbs.

The use of the fifth-second stopwatch had been criticized, but Thumb found that it gave the same relative results as the millisecond chronoscope with voice-keys. Thumb strongly recommended that the stopwatch be used for association studies of living dialects, so as to determine in what linguistic forms analogy is to be expected. While the existence of an association does not guarantee the occurrence of an analogical change, it would be an error in method to assume such a change if the required association is not found to exist.

In Part II of his 1907 paper, Thumb reported some further experiments which he performed in the Physiological Institute of Marburg with the cooperation of the psychologist Narziss Ach. In a study by two of Marbe's pupils, A. Mayer and J. Orth (1901), it had been found that associations could be classified into those with and those without intervening conscious processes—"mediated" and "spontaneous" associations, the latter having on the average shorter reaction-times. These results led Thumb to assume that associations in which there were, between stimulus and response, intervening sensory images or volitional or affective processes could not have linguistic effects, because their greater time requirement precluded an influence on the innervation and phonetic form of the words in question. Only the spontaneous associations need therefore be considered as being of influence in linguistic change.

In his new experiments, Thumb used 48 stimulus words, chosen from those of T&M, and divided them into three lists given on non-consecutive afternoons; non-experimental words were intercalated. Simultaneously with speaking each word he started a Hipp chronoscope by pressing a key; the subject stopped the chronoscope by speaking his response against a voice-key. The chronoscope was managed and read by Ach. There were seven adult subjects. In general, the results of T&M were confirmed. The most noteworthy new finding was that, in agreement with Mayer and Orth, the spontaneous associations had a shorter average reaction-time than did the mediated associations. Word-responses belonging to the same category as the stimulus-word showed a greater frequency of spontaneous associations than of mediated associations, in agreement with the fact that analogy-formations also most frequently involve words of the same category. Moreover, if among the same-category responses only the most frequent associates are considered, there is an even greater excess of spontaneous over mediated responses. Thumb therefore concludes that the liability of a word to analogical change is a function of three factors: namely, the frequency, latency ($=$ reaction-time), and type (spontaneous or mediated) of the associations which it induces. These relationships may be summarized in the formula $A_n = \dfrac{Ra}{H \cdot z}$, where $A_n =$ the liability to analogical change, $Ra =$ number of spontaneous (non-mediated) associations, $H =$ total number of associations, and $z =$ latency.[32] Similarity of sound and meaning and the number of influencing forms, says Thumb, are factors favorable to the establishment of associations, not to the occurrence of analogy-formations, as Herzog and others had claimed; these are matters for psychological research rather than for expressions of

32. In a later paper (1911), Thumb applied this formula to the associations *Vater→Mutter*, *Mutter→Vater*, and *Base→Vetter*, obtaining the values, respectively, of 0.69, 0.76, and 0.24; he concluded therefore that the probability of an analogical effect on *Vater* and *Mutter* was about three times as great as for *Base*.

opinion. Herzog and Schuchardt had emphasized syntactic collocations —e.g., *through thick and thin, light [as a] feather*—as sources of associations, since "words do not fly about free in the air" but occur only in speech which consists of sentences. All words may be combined in all sorts of collocations, but, says Thumb, such co-occurrence is not enough to guarantee facile associations. Most highly frequent associations are with words of the same category, not with words with which the stimulus-words have been syntactically linked.

In Part III of his paper, Thumb discusses the associations of children. Herzog had asserted that associations such as those between *I, you, he,* etc. would be characteristic of "people who had sat on school benches," and that the associations of children would be more interesting. Children's associations were studied by Friedrich Schmidt (1902), a pupil of Marbe; the subjects were eight ten-year-old boys who "had not yet been instructed in verb conjugation"; the stimulus-words were, like those previously used by Thumb, the indicative present and imperfect, the infinitive, and the past participle. The responses were chiefly (90 percent) verbal forms; this was interesting in that in syntactic collocations, which some linguists had declared to be the chief source of associations and analogy-formations, verbs are usually connected, not with other verb-forms, but with sub-stantives. Five subjects gave predominantly forms of the same verb as the stimulus-word, and three gave predominantly forms of other verbs. In responses which were forms of other verbs, both present and preterit stimulus-forms elicited predominantly the same form of the present. The responses which were forms of the same verb were more scattered, al-though the most frequent response to all forms of singular and plural present and preterit—except of course for the first person singular of the present itself—was the first person singular of the present. (In Thumb's study of adults, the associations had been most frequently with the next form of the paradigm; this was perhaps attributable to conjugation prac-tice in school; perhaps there is here a difference between child and adult.) The giving of the highly frequent (common) responses increases in fre-quency with increasing age of children (Saling, 1908 Reinhold, 1910); this seems to Thumb to argue against assigning a major role in analogical change—especially in contaminations—to the younger generation.

78

The general agreement between Schmidt's results and those of Thumb emboldened the latter to repeat his maxim: "other times, other analogies," which depends upon the rule, "other times, other associations," as Wundt had agreed. Various associations to a word may be present in an individual at a given time, but none becomes linguistically effective unless it becomes predominant at a given time and place. Thumb again raises the question whether linguistic change is to be attributed chiefly to the period of acquisition of language by children, as Schuchardt and Herzog had asserted; Thumb points out that children progressively give up their childish errors and that only such associative tendencies as are also present in adults can influence the speech of adults. The foregoing applies to formal associations within paradigmatic systems; in these, children's associations are similar to those of adults. But in material—*stoffliche*, i.e., semantic—associations and analogy-formations, Ziehen (1898, 1900) had found in boys 8-11 years of age few "pure" word-associations; most frequent were word-completions—e.g., post→card; the high-frequency associations of adults occurred much less often; therefore Thumb concluded that the conditions for analogy-formations are much less often fulfilled. Watt (1904), using Thumb's stimulus-words with five children and three adults, found that the adults gave the "most frequent" associations in 74 percent of their responses whereas the children did so in only 29 percent; the adults gave responses in the same grammatical category on 96 percent of the occasions whereas the children did so in only 39 percent. The children's reaction-times were much longer. Adult word-associations appeared to be gradually established during childhood.

Cattell and Bryant (1889) reported on the associations of the 363 girls of the third to sixth forms—average ages 12.7 to 17.8—of a London school; reaction-times decreased with growth and education, and the character of the responses seemed to be a function of age, education, and occupation. Of interest are the "Remarks on the Experiments" by six academic adults who had served as subjects; their retrospective statements indicate that their responses were mostly far from automatic; they reported a profusion of mediating processes, particularly visual imagery; G. F. Stout, deprecating the "psychological atomism of the English associationists" and "the limitation imposed on the subject of the experiments by the necessity of finding a verbal expression for his thought as soon as possible," declared that there was need of a method, imposing no time limit, of studying "the indistinct whole which mediates transitions between its component parts"; he obviously was following self-instructions for an experiment on thought-processes rather than on word-association.

Esper (1918) repeated the T&M experiment with English-speaking (American) subjects—100 educated adults, 11 children, and 15 uneducated adults. Of the 60 stimulus-words used, 50 were translations of the T&M words. The results confirmed those of T&M, thus tending to show that "the associations of English- and German-speaking communities correspond in the case of most words of familiar meaning and in universal use in both languages." The reaction-times of the children and of the uneducated adults were longer than those of the educated adults, but the favored associations were in most cases the same, and the essential character of the associations was similar; thus the results with children of Ziehen and Watt were not confirmed.

Cook, Mefferd, and Wieland (1965), in what no doubt was intended as a "historical introduction" to an article in which they demonstrated the unsurprising fact that an associative set can be established by previous stimulus-words in a list, state that both T&M and Esper "administered [the numerals] successively with no intervening non-numerals to break the resulting 'response set.' " This illustrates the vice of referring to publications which one has not read.

Thumb (1907a) concludes with some suggestions for future research. Is it perhaps possible to evoke analogy-formations artificially? Watt (1905) had reported that when the task was to respond to the name of a whole with the name of a part, associative interferences between two possible responses sometimes occurred; e.g., *Zimmer→Tusch = Stuhl + Tisch*. And so Thumb suggests:

> If it were possible to produce analogy-formations experimentally—of course in a linguistically neutral material, i.e., in artificial sound-formations—we should be able to study the operation of the hitherto recognized conditions of the process qualitatively and quantitatively and to discover additional factors in analogy-formation. Though many may regard this as *Zukunftsmusik* or shake their heads incredulously, I have the firm convic-

tion that further work in this direction will be not without profit. One must of course be a "positivist," i.e., strive for the scientific solution of the general problems of the mental sciences in the sense indicated by Wundt in his *Voelkerpsychologie* not only for psychology but also for linguistics, the history of art, and mythology. (Thumb, 1907b, p. 49)

In an appendix, Thumb refers to the association studies of Jung and Riklin (Jung, 1918), in which it was found that educated subjects gave more "pure" associations—i.e., high-frequency responses as in *young→ old*—than did uneducated subjects, although the uneducated seemed to exceed slightly in formal associations—same grammatical category, same ending, etc.—and in the latter respect to resemble children. When associations were given under conditions of distraction, the number of pure associations increased; Thumb suggests that attention is similarly distracted in speech because it is directed to the content of what is being said and so distracted from the actual words.

In two papers published in 1911, Thumb discussed the contributions which experimental psychology might make to linguistics. Many philologists, he says, erect a barrier between "mental" and "natural" sciences; they see the method of the former as that of intuitive valuation, while that of the latter is the establishment of causal laws. They are reluctant to avail themselves of the methods of statistics; they look upon measurement and counting with disdain and endeavor to make a joke of it; relying upon subjective judgments they make invalid statements in their grammatical works. "It is of course more pleasant to rise upon the wings of phantasy into the realm of hypotheses."

But natural science methods are not experimental unless they investigate specific problems by observations under known, purposefully varied, and measurable conditions. Thus phonetics, though it used physical and physiological methods, was not experimental, nor was zoology so long as it worked only with microscope, microtome, and stains. The nature of phonetic change can only be ascertained by direct observation and experiment performed on the living, speaking human being, for sound-laws and sound-changes are complex processes which can only thus be analyzed and described.

Psychology had been described by Paul as an essential aid to the understanding of linguistic history; the latter however could not perform a similar service for psychology. An opposite view had been expressed by Wundt: that psychology could benefit from the study of language, and that in fact the "higher mental processes," otherwise inaccessible to psychology, could only be approached by such study; Paul and Wundt were thus each disposed to yield priority to the other; the work of both, however, shows the close interaction of linguistics and psychology.

Thumb reviews his own studies of word-association. The only difference between momentary slips of the tongue and analogical—contaminative—changes is that the latter result from concurrences of tendencies in the members of a community. Contradicting Meringer, he states that the properties of an association which make it effective in analogy-formation can be better studied under conditions of experimental control than under the uncontrolled conditions of observation of daily life, as in the recording of slips of the tongue.[33] Thumb suggests that it would be useful to prepare "association dictionaries" for the various languages, in which the most frequent associate of each word would be listed.

Thumb found that while the majority of subjects gave the "most frequent" associative responses there were some who tended to give mediated, less usual, or idiosyncratic responses, with longer reaction-times. This observation might be thought to agree with my finding (Esper, 1933, 1966) of individual differences in the tendency toward analogical processes.

In the second part of his 1911 paper (Section III), Thumb again suggests the desirability of experiments with artificial material:

A research project which aims at the artificial production of contaminations would do well to operate with a linguistically wholly neutral material; that is, with meaningless sound-forms; for the word-forms of the mother-tongue are already determined in their associative relations with other

33. In another paper (1910), Thumb had replied to Meringer's assertion that observation of slips of the tongue would yield "more exact and better information" than would experiments. Thumb pointed out that "the observations of daily life" can suggest problems, but the testing of the conditions thus suggested can more economically be done by experiment.

word-forms—a circumstance which would make more difficult the quantitative and qualitative study of the artificially created linguistic disturbances. Concerning the possibility of such an experimental design there can be no doubt, now that P. Menzerath has already made pilot trials. Studies with nonsense syllables will make clear how sound-similarity of stimulus- and reaction-word has a favorable effect on the occurrence of a linguistic contamination. Pure sound-associations do not seem to play much of a part in the association process. It has been observed that the more familiar a word is, the less likely is it to elicit a sound-association, and that sound-associations occur more frequently in the normal individual only in a state of agitation (haste). (Thumb, 1911, p. 66)

Studies by Thumb and by Eberschweiler (1908) had shown that sound-similarity—of accented vowel or of initial consonant—had little or no effect on the selection of the response-word. Only in responses to foreign words, unfamiliar technical words, nonsense syllables (Peters, 1910), and in the responses of children (Stern and Stern, 1922, p. 138) does sound-association (e.g., folk etymology) play a greater role. But a strong influence on association is produced by the frequency of the response-words in the language, although such frequency does not seem to decrease reaction-time, and thus is not necessarily productive of linguistic change.

Thumb concludes rather dolefully, "My arguments have been intended to show, for a small area, that linguistics may not only stand in a platonic relation to modern psychology, but that it must enter, wherever possible, into an actual working partnership with psychology. Unfortunately however I stand alone in my psychological studies of analogy-formation; indeed, the interest in such matters is slight" (Thumb, 1911, p. 74).

Menzerath (1908a), who had been a pupil of Thumb, attempted an experimental test of Thumb's suggestion that linguistic contaminations might be studied in nonsense material. By the method of paired associates, he paired certain syllables alternately with either of two other syllables, and in consequence obtained a certain number of contaminations; e.g., *bäs*, having been paired with *zeg* and *gal*, elicited *zel*. Saling (1908) reported contamination-associations with ordinary meaningful words;

e.g., the response to *Mund* was *Mand* instead of *Hand,* and to *März* it was *Monart* instead of *Monat.*

The interest aroused by the work of Thumb and Marbe, together with that of Ebbinghaus, G. E. Müller, and others, was expressed by the study of Wilhelm Peters (1910), who was in 1909–1910 an assistant at the Frankfurt a.M. Academy for Social and Commercial Sciences during Marbe's tenure there. Peters attempted to demonstrate with nonsense-syllables that similarity is an effective principle of association. Similarity in the sense of partial identity had been illustrated by sound-associations, which were however of infrequent occurrence in experiments with meaningful words and normal subjects. In such experiments, the chief factors relating stimulus- to response-words were meaning and habitual syntactic contiguity. These factors would be eliminated and the factor of sound-similarity might thus be revealed as more potent if the stimuli were nonsense-syllables.[34] When subjects were instructed to answer such syllables with real words, sound-similarity was found to be the chief factor. Similarity in the sense of formal structural similarity—*Gestalt*—was thought to be demonstrated by the tendency to respond with words of the same number of syllables as were contained in the stimulus-words. In other experiments, Peters had subjects learn a series of visually presented nonsense-syllables and then respond to a series of syllables which had been altered from the learned syllables initially, medially, or finally, or—in other experiments—in one, two, or three phonemes; the responses were to be the corresponding syllables of the previously learned list. The results confirmed the principle of probability of association according to degree of similarity.

34. Eberschweiler (1908) had reported studies showing that the phonetic form (accented vowel, initial and final consonants) has little or no effect on the response-word unless there is distraction or evidence of an emotional "complex." There was however an influence with respect to number of syllables and grammatical form. The response-words were predominantly words of higher frequency in Kaeding's (1898) frequency tables, but the frequency values of neither stimulus- nor response-words had any marked influence on reaction-time.

Chapter 5

A HISTORY OF WORD-ASSOCIATION EXPERIMENTS

Word-association as a field of research is an offshoot of the theory of the association of ideas, which is the oldest theory of psychological organization in terms of learning. The history of the theory and of the experimental work on word-associations has been reviewed by Warren (1921), Robinson (1932), Fröbes (1923, pp. 518–614), Woodworth (1938, pp. 340–367), and Woodworth and Schlosberg (1954, pp. 43–71). Guthrie (1935, p. vii) remarked that "associative learning has been recognized in some form or other by every writer on psychology since Aristotle," and he made the Aristotelian principle of association by contiguity the basis of his influential doctrine of learning.

Early History

The concept of the association of ideas appears first in Plato, who exemplifies the principles of contiguity and similarity in a passage of the *Phaedo* (73–76): "So much is clear—that when we perceive something, either by the help of sight, or hearing, or some other sense, from that perception we are able to obtain a notion of some other thing like or unlike which is associated with it but has been forgotten." Aristotle emphasized the principles of contiguity and frequency, and he mentioned those of similarity and contrast. But he also mentioned properties of the individual— such states as we nowadays call set, emotion, attention, etc.—which reappeared more than two thousand years later among the "secondary laws" of association of Thomas Brown, and which are of course of prime importance in the word-association technique.

Beginning with Thomas Hobbes in the seventeenth century, a series of British philosophers adopted the concept of the association of ideas as a means of explaining the empirical origins of human knowledge—and of error, as well as of organization in general—in opposition to the doctrine, of which Descartes was usually taken to be the chief exponent, of innate ideas. "Associationism" thus came to be the name for a body of doctrine developed by the British empiricist philosophers of the seventeenth, eighteenth, and nineteenth centuries—Hobbes, John Locke, David Hume, David Hartley, Thomas Brown, James and John Stuart Mill, Alexander Bain. The doctrine varied with its various exponents, but might be summarized as follows. All mental life arises from sensations, the elementary experiences resulting from stimulation of the sense organs. Experiences similar to the sensations may subsequently occur in the absence of the corresponding sense organ stimulations; these derivative experiences are "ideas." Complex mental states or processes arise by the process of association. That is, a sensation or idea will arouse other ideas—simultaneously, as in perception, or successively, as in trains of thought—which had on previous occasions occurred in temporal contiguity with the instigating sensation or idea. Some writers made similarity, contrast, causality, etc. coordinate with contiguity; others reduced all of these to contiguity. It is obvious that the fundamentals of this scheme—the empiricism and the principle of associative connection—were anticipated by Aristotle. Hobbes recognized the difficulty which results from the fact that innumerable things occur in contiguity with innumerable other things: "But because in sense, to one and the same thing perceived sometimes one thing sometimes another succeedeth, it comes to pass in time that in the imagining of any thing there is no certainty what we shall imagine next; only this is certain: it shall be something that succeeded the same before at one time or another" (Hobbes, 1651, Ch. 3).

In the founding of experimental psychology, associationism was one of the great strands which united in the nineteenth century with Darwinism and with those other strands which could also be traced back to Aristotle: German functionalism and act psychology, from Leibnitz to Franz Brentano; and German biology, which appeared in a philosophical form in Rudolf Hermann Lotze and Friedrich Eduard Beneke, and became experimental with Johannes Müller, Carl Friedrich Wilhelm Ludwig, Hermann von Helmholtz, and Ludwig's Russian pupil, I. M. Sechenov.

The ideas of which Hobbes and Locke spoke were of course subjective phenomena, but David Hartley (1705–1757), who was a physician, extended the principle of association to include muscular movements and suggested a neurophysiological hypothesis to account for mnemic and associative processes. Thomas Brown (1778–1820) made an analysis of the variations in stimulating conditions and in the history and state of the individual which would influence the process of association. Alexander Bain (1818–1903), in his analysis of will, started from an assumed tendency of the organism to "spontaneous movements" and hypothesized that acts which bring pleasant results are retained while those which bring unpleasant results are eliminated. The introduction into the associationistic scheme of muscular movement by Hartley and of trial-and-error learning by Bain prepared the way for the experimental study of learning by Lloyd Morgan and E. L. Thorndike.

We now have before us the essentials of the philosophical background of the first *experimental* investigation of word-association, published in 1879 by Francis Galton. Little to our purpose would be added were we to search through the verbal aridities of the Mills, Bain, and Spencer.

Galton (1879) wrote 75 words (mostly nouns), each on a separate slip of paper. Having placed these slips under a book, he uncovered one at a time. He started a stopwatch when he perceived a word and stopped it when two different associations had occurred. The associations might take the form of words or of mental pictures; the latter were recorded in verbal form. He went through his stimulus list four times at intervals of about a month. His results may be summarized as follows:

1. The average reaction-time per association was 1.3 seconds.

2. There was a tendency to repeat the same association on the different occasions. Those which occurred more than once dated mostly from his earlier years.

3. The significance of early life was suggested by the fact that 39 percent of the associations could be traced to boyhood and youth, 46 percent to the period of manhood, and only 15 percent to recent events.

4. The associations could be classified into three kinds: (a) Visual and other images of past scenes or events (32.5 percent). (b) "Histrionic representations," acting out an event or attitude (22.5 percent). (c) Purely verbal: names, phrases, quotations (45 percent).

Concerning the significance of such data, Galton observed: "They lay bare the foundations of a man's thoughts with a curious distinctness, and exhibit his mental anatomy with more vividness and truth than he would probably care to publish to the world."

The research field thus opened up by Galton was immediately entered upon by Wundt and his students in the newly founded laboratory at Leipzig. Trautscholdt (1882), in research done in 1880, introduced the method of having an experimenter pronounce the stimulus-word and record the time; his main purpose, he said, was to measure association-time, "the time required for the reproduction of a memory-image by means of a given apperceived presentation." The task of the subject was described thus: the stimulus-word having aroused an idea, the subject was to associate with this idea another idea, and as soon as this other idea was apperceived he was to note and report it. The language of this description —which is not unlike that of our contemporary mentalists, some of whom are also Wundtians—is in part derived from the philosophical history which we have recounted and in part it is Wundtian. According to the philosophical tradition represented, e.g., by Hartley, a stimulus-word would arouse a brain process with which would be correlated a mental process or idea, and this brain process and idea would arouse an associated process and idea, which associated idea the subject would then report verbally. In the language of Wundt, the subject would report the associated idea as soon as he had "apperceived" it, that is to say, when, by active attention, he became clearly aware of it. This language has become unfamiliar to us; under the influence of behaviorism and of the literature of neural physiology and conditioning, associationism has developed into a group of stimulus-response theories according to which the items supposed to become associated are stimuli and responses rather than sensations and ideas. This change in language was a manifestation of psychology's struggle to free itself from its metaphysical and mentalistic heritage, and the principle that stimuli issue in motor responses became a canon of scientific virtue. But since among contemporary psychologists—except for the neomentalists—the need for defense against dualism is no longer urgent, and since we have gained a more sophisticated view of the nervous system, it is possible for us to re-examine the question of what happens in a subject when he hears a stimulus-word in an association experiment. We shall see that this depends on the word, on the instructions, and on the education, intelligence, present state, and prior experience of the subject. But in the present connection we may note that while it is possible in many cases for the stimulus-word to elicit an immediate, automatic word-response, it may instead arouse a "mental picture," a reproduction of a prior sensory experience; if the subject has been instructed to respond verbally, he must then either retrospectively describe this experience or find a single word which will represent it. Thus I doubt whether we must continue to regard as scientifically disreputable the assumption that the main physiological effect of a stimulus may often be a pattern of activity in the brain, and that motor effects may in such cases be relatively non-specific or inconsequential—e.g., postural changes—or may occur after a delay as a verbal report. (It has become fashionable recently to speak of "mediating processes" intercalated between external stimulus and overt response.) It is perhaps no longer necessary to seek the specificity of a perception or a memory image in a pattern of muscular contractions; the brain, though hitherto less accessible, is no less biological and objective than the muscles. We have seen that more than half of Galton's associations were "visual images" or "histrionic representations." This large percentage was, however, undoubtedly a function of his self-instruction and method. With subjects of adequate intelligence and education, with adequate instruction, rapport, and forepractice, and with familiar stimulus-words, it is usually possible to obtain mostly prompt one-word responses whose short latency attest to their verbal habit nature; such associations are of particular interest when we wish to study the interconnections of the symbolic behavior system which are shared by the members of a speech community; to call such associations "superficial," as some do, suggests a questionable valuative attitude. Of course, the exceptions to facile verbal responses—the individualistic responses and those of long latency—are of great interest in the study of individual differences, especially in clinical situations. Responses of high and low commonality may suggest connections of the symbolic organization to socially shared and to individualistic components, respectively, of manual, visceral, emotional, or attitudinal behavior.

Returning to Trautscholdt's study, we note that, characteristically for those pioneer days in the psychological laboratory, the data of only three subjects were utilized. The apparatus consisted of a Hipp chronoscope and two telegraph keys. Upon the ready signal of the starting of the clockwork, the subject closed his key; after an irregular interval the experimenter closed his key, thereby starting the clock hands, simultaneously with his pronunciation of the stimulus-word. The subject opened his key, thereby stopping the hands, at the instant when an idea was associatively aroused and apperceived; this idea was then orally reported, not necessarily by a single word.

Upon examining the longest reaction-times, Trautscholdt found three kinds of stimulus-words: (1) words of high frequency and familiarity which arouse so many different ideas that conflict results; (2) ambiguous words; (3) seldom used and relatively isolated words. Almost all of the associative responses of this latter group are of purely individual nature, not likely to be given by other subjects. Upon examining the shortest reaction-times, he again found three classes of stimulus-words: (1) words of frequent usage and rather general meaning which mostly occur in combination with particular other words, especially in the relation of opposites: e.g., *light→dark, war→peace*; (2) words which occur infrequently but which are unambiguous and have only one possible association for most persons: e.g., *Cologne→cathedral, arrow→bow*; (3) words which give rise to individual associations whose short reaction-time is attributable to the dominant interests of the individual: e.g., *time→ chronoscope*. Two factors determining the frequency and latency of associative responses which emerge from Trautscholdt's study and have been abundantly confirmed in subsequent work are the frequency of usage of the stimulus-word and the frequency and exclusiveness with which it has preceded a particular other word in speech. Examples of high-frequency, low-latency associations are *March→April, two→three, lightning→thunder*. Many associations are more facile in one direction than in the other: e.g., part→whole and subordinate→supraordinate associations tend to have shorter latencies than those in the opposite directions; this difference in facility is attributable to the two factors mentioned above; Trautscholdt notes that, e.g., in the whole→part direction there are more alternative and hence rival associations than in the reverse direction.

Trautscholdt found, in agreement with Galton, a preponderance of associations established in childhood and youth. This finding, he thought, confirmed the view that the stock of commonly available ideas is relatively limited, and that a large proportion of the most frequently occurring ideas and associations of ideas are established early in life.

Trautscholdt's remarks on the statistical handling of his reaction-time data might well have been attended to by subsequent researchers. He states that he did not employ "the method of least squares" for reasons given by Friedrich (1883). Friedrich had stated that this method gives false results if two assumptions are not justified: that the probability of large deviations is very small, and that positive and negative deviations are of equal probability. In psychophysiological processes, he said, these assumptions are open to question because of the operation of such factors as adaptation within an observation series, practice effects, fatigue, and variations in attention and set; he might also have mentioned the small number of highly selected but individually peculiar subjects used in those days (for which we have substituted "volunteer" college freshmen or sophomores). Wechsler (1935) published studies of distributions of human traits, including reaction-times, and reported that practically none of these conformed to the Gaussian normal curve; it is questionable, he says, whether "the assumptions required by the theory of probability . . . namely the independence of the individual factors and the absence of any inordinately preponderant ones" are justified for most kinds of trait measurements. "Weighting" and "transforming" scores may of course result in Gaussian distributions, but these are statistical artifacts (unless, as Chapanis [1953] remarks, there is a special—perhaps one might say, an extrastatistical—justification for transformation, as in the use of logarithmic transforms of visual stimulus intensities in many visual problems). We shall discuss this problem, so egregiously neglected in much of the word-association literature, under the heading of associative reaction-times.

Following the main part of his study on "free" association, Traut-scholdt (1882) had done a pilot study of "controlled" association (in which the subject is instructed to respond with a word bearing a specified relation to the stimulus-word, so that the responses are restricted by a specified set, as contrasted with "free" association, in which the instruction is simply to respond with the very first word, whatever it may be, suggested by the stimulus word). Cattell (1887) recorded the controlled associations of two subjects; the required relations between stimulus-word and response were, e.g., *city→country, month→season, author→language,* or the reverse of each of these. He remarks, "The mental processes considered above are by no means invented for the sake of experiment, but are such as make up a considerable part of life. We see that it took the subjects 2/5 to 4/5 sec. to call to mind facts with which they were familiar." (Cattell subtracted from his association-times "the time it takes the subjects to see and name words," in conformity with Wundt's technique of "mental chronometry"—which Cattell helped to invalidate.) Cattell then points out that the differences in time between the two subjects "are explained by the character and pursuits of the subjects, and in turn throw light back upon these. For example, B is a teacher of mathematics, C has busied himself more with literature; C knows quite as well as B that $5 + 7 = 12$, yet he needs 1/10 second longer to call it to mind; B knows quite as well as C that Dante was a poet, but he needs 1/10 second longer to think of it." The results showed also that the reaction-times tended to be shorter when the instructions were more restrictive; e.g., *month→season* and *author→language* gave shorter times than did *season→month* and *language→author*; the wider the choice of permitted responses, the longer was the reaction-time.

Like Galton, Cattell was impressed by the diagnostic potentialities of the word-association method; he wrote that associative reactions "lay bare the mental life in a way that is startling and not always gratifying."

Cattell (1886) introduced the automatic starting and stopping of the chronoscope, by means of a contact on the exposure apparatus for visual stimuli and by means of lip- or voice-keys for oral stimuli and responses. Cattell and Bryant (1889) carried out an extensive investigation of free association; they were the first to demonstrate that any familiar stimulus-word evokes the same response from many subjects, and they were the first to construct a frequency table, which gave the responses, occurring ten or more times, of 465 subjects to ten concrete and ten abstract nouns.

Hermann Ebbinghaus (1885) pioneered a quite different method of investigating verbal associations. This consisted in learning by heart series of nonsense syllables (or other material) and determining the relations between "strength of association" (as measured by number of repetitions required for subsequent relearning) and number of repetitions given in the original learning, length of time between original learning and relearning, etc. These were therefore experiments on serial verbal learning and retention; they involved the experimental establishment of serial verbal associations. They were an attempt "to penetrate into the inner mechanism" of association, of those processes which are described—so superficially that "every new presentation starts out with a reinterpretation of the contents of a few lines from Aristotle"—by the so-called laws of association, of which "there is one which has never been disputed or doubted. It has usually been formulated as follows: Ideas which have been developed simultaneously or in immediate succession in the same mind mutually reproduce each other, and do this with greater ease in the direction of the original succession and with a certainty proportional to the frequency with which they were together" (pp. 90f.). Historically, these experiments of Ebbinghaus stand at the beginning of a vast and ever-widening —if not deepening—stream of research which is nowadays called the psychology of learning, although, to be sure, "association" has become "conditioning" and "sensations" and "ideas" have become "stimuli" and "responses"—supplemented in recent times by "mediating processes."

It is obvious that such terms as *association* and *association experiment* are ambiguous—as we shall soon find if we look up references cited in bibliographical indexes. On the one hand, there is the use of the term *association* in the broad tradition of Aristotle and Ebbinghaus as the name of a general principle of mental organization and of techniques for the experimental study of learning and retention. On the other hand, there is the special field of research with which we shall be concerned, that of word-association, in the tradition of Galton, Trautscholdt, and Cattell. In this latter field we usually assume that the interconnections—"associations"—between various units of an individual's linguistic repertoire have been previously established in the course of his ordinary "non-experimental" life history, and our aim is to discover what the interconnections are. However, a combination of the two experimental techniques has been devised in which an artificial "language" is learned and the associations between its "words" are then tested (Esper, 1933); it thus becomes possible to study the conditions which favor the establishment of the verbal interconnections which appear in word-association experiments.

The paper by Mayer and Orth (1901), says Boring (1950, p. 402), "technically began" the Würzburg school. Their experiments—with four subjects!—were done at the suggestion of Marbe. Their method was oral stimulus and response, with introspective reports after each response. They found that in some third of the stimulus-response events there were no intervening conscious processes; in the roughly two-thirds with such processes the reaction-time was longer, especially when volitional or affective processes were involved. In some cases the subjects could not report any ideational or volitional content but only a "conscious attitude" (*Bewusstseinslage*). Their results were of course a function of the instruction to give introspections.

Arthur Wreschner (1907–1909) performed a much-quoted series of association experiments during the years 1900–1903. He used a Hipp chronoscope, a finger-key for the experimenter, and a voice-key for the subject. His subjects were 15 "educated adults," 5 "uneducated adults," and 2 children—the latter being boys aged 3¾ and 5¾; the various subjects served in varying numbers of experiments. The stimulus-words were adjectives, concrete nouns, abstract nouns, and, for some subjects, verbs. With this array of instruments, persons, and materials, he engaged in such detailed fractionation that he was left, in some of his cells, with, e.g., one child or one woman.[35] Moreover, the subjects were required to give reports of their "mental processes" after each response, so that the "set" and context for the successive responses must have been influenced in special and individualistic ways. However, we may recall that "Marbe's Law" was based on results from eight subjects, and the famous "forgetting curve" of Ebbinghaus on the performance of *one* subject. And so, in the six hundred pages which Wreschner required to present and discuss his dubiously based results, we may perhaps find some relationships which have, in some measure, stood the test of time. Of his numerous conclusions, the following are of especial interest:

1. The perception and interpretation of the stimulus-word, the set or expectancy governing this perception and the response to it, and the level of attention are variable both in different subjects and on different occasions for the same subject; moreover, many words are ambiguous.

2. "Centrally aroused"—i.e., mnemic or emotional—processes may determine individualistic responses.

3. The response may occur either automatically, without mediating processes, and with short reaction-time, or only after a blank period or after an active search for an appropriate response; it may be common to many subjects or individualistic; if the latter, its reaction-time will usually be lengthened. Mediating processes include visualizations and search in accordance with self-imposed tasks, as when the subject asks himself, "What is an example of . . . ?" Subjectively unsatisfactory responses may be rejected before becoming overt.

4. Recent events outside the laboratory, or preceding stimuli or responses in the experiment, may determine the responses; these factors may result in frequent repetition of the same response.

5. Responses are most frequently "symmetrical"—i.e., of the same grammatical or semantic class as the stimulus-words. Thus, not only do,

35. However, his main results were supported by group experiments with 73 women and 136 men students in his classes during a period of six years; the stimuli were given orally but the responses were written.

e.g., adjectives elicit adjectives, but, e.g., the name of a kind of animal elicits the name of another kind of animal. Reciprocal associations—in which *b* is the response to *a*, and vice versa—occurred especially with words of opposite meaning, and most especially when, e.g., *a→b* had occurred previously in the experiment.

6. Stimulus-words of different classes differ in familiarity (*Vertrautheit*), especially in the case of *nahegelegene Reizwörter* to which responses are *geläufig* 'facile'. The greater the familiarity, the greater is the number of symmetrical and automatic responses, and of same responses by different subjects; the shorter also is the reaction-time; thus responses to adjectives and concrete nouns were more facile than those to abstract nouns and verbs.[36]

7. Educated persons adjust more readily to the task and show a greater tendency to give high-frequency symmetrical responses with short reaction-times than do uneducated persons.

8. By repetitions of the same stimulus-words on different occasions, evidence was obtained of the variety of rival responses, a variety which was greater for the more familiar stimulus-words. Repetition of the same response may indicate either the strength of the association or the paucity of associations; the order of occurrence of different responses to the same stimulus-word is a function of their relative association strengths. Educated persons give a greater variety of responses in successive repetitions than do the uneducated.

9. In experiments with controlled associations, the greater the range of possible associates permitted by the assigned task, the longer is the reaction-time, but when the same associative response is given in controlled as in free association, the latter in most cases requires less time.

36. A number of studies have recently been made of the relation of the "familiarity," often measured by frequency in word-counts such as that of Thorndike-Lorge (1944), of stimulus-words to the nature or number of the responses which they elicit. Thus Lepley (1950) found that subjects produce more synonyms for stimulus-words which they rate as being familiar than for those which they rate as less familiar. Cofer and Shevitz (1952) found that when subjects were given ten minutes to write as many words as they could associate with the stimulus-word, more associates were given for the high- than for the low-frequency stimulus-words, a finding which seems in harmony

Wreschner, in his final theoretical discussion (pp. 577–599), rejects the explanations of association in terms of empirical contiguity or objective "similarity"; such theories "exclude from our ideational sequences all invention, discovery, and new combinations"; such sequences are not merely memory products but the results of "psychical reworking" of experiences. "Black is not always black"; it may on different occasions release the ideas of darkness, sorrow, a particular object, a color, a linguistic form, etc. "Here we see the yawning gulf between studies of memory for nonsense material and those of actual ideational sequences." The experimental results show how various may be the "psychical meaning" of stimulus- and response-words according to person and circumstances. A very interesting suggestion of Wreschner's (pp. 259ff.) is to the effect that the psychological analysis of associations requires the study, not of the associations themselves, but of the processes of memory-storage by which associations are established. He suggests also that a lexicon of associatively connected words could be the basis for many interesting studies, especially in the psychology of language.

Reinhold (1910) began the construction of such a lexicon by giving all of the responses of 300 school children to 46 stimulus-words, mostly common nouns. Most of the responses were coordinates. A year later he used the most frequent responses of the preceding experiment as stimuli and found reciprocal responses for all but 7 of the 46 words. In 1911, Dauber made further analyses of Reinhold's data. He demonstrated that many response-words occurred in response to a number—as many as 25—of different stimulus-words ("repeated associations"). This preference for certain response-words he regarded as not dependent upon the stimulus-words but as the same sort as the responses obtained when subjects were asked to write "any word"; of the words thus written, 57 percent were written by more than one subject. Dauber found that the greater the frequency of a word in Kaeding's (1898) dictionary of frequencies of occurrence of words in German—mostly formal—texts, the more often did it occur as a repeated association. Words which were most frequent in the language were among the most frequent associative responses.

with that of Zipf (1945) and of Thorndike (1948) that there is a relation between word-frequency and number of dictionary meanings.

Wreschner, who had taken as the measure of a stimulus-word's familiarity the associative reaction-time, had arrived at the dubious result that the number of different responses to the same stimulus-word is the greater, the less familiar the stimulus-word. Dauber, taking the entries in Kaeding's frequency-in-the-language dictionary as measures of familiarity, found that these were positively related to the number of different responses made to the respective stimulus-words; thus the greater the frequency with which a word occurs in speech, the greater is the number of its possible associates; also, the less is the frequency of its most frequent associate. Dauber found that as the subjects were increased in number, from 30 to 300, the percentage of frequent associates increased; this finding he attributed to the fact that there is a progressive decrease in the number of possible, but not yet made, responses. Clang-associations—in which the response is phonemically similar to the stimulus—occurred mostly in "isolated" responses, i.e., those given by only one subject. "That of all reactions only 3.5 to 4% were clang-associations demonstrates that a resemblance purely in sound between stimulus and response has no essential significance." Finally, Dauber performed association experiments with monosyllabic nonsense-syllables as stimuli; in free association, 81 percent of the responses were meaningful; with instructions to respond with nonsense-syllables, 32 percent were nevertheless meaningful. Many responses were shared by two or more subjects. Phonetic resemblances between stimulus and response, rare with meaningful stimulus-words, were frequent with nonsense stimulus-words.

Classes and Frequencies of Associations

An unfortunate contribution of Trautscholdt had been a classification of associative responses which was adopted by Wundt and which influenced a number of subsequent classifications. The main division was into "outer" associations—those attributable to repetition and contiguity, among which were listed whole-part and part-whole—and "inner" associations—those attributable to semantic or logical relationships, among which were listed superordination, subordination, coordination, and causality.

Aschaffenburg (1895 et seqq.) classified associations as "immediate" or "mediated." Mediated or indirect associations are those in which one idea is linked with another indirectly through an intervening idea. From Jung (1918, pp. 29–33) I take the following examples (in which the first term is the stimulus-word, the second represents an intervening process, "conscious" or "unconscious," and the third term is the actual response-word; unconscious links may be retrospectively reported by the subject or inferred by the experimenter): *hay→grass→green, love→hate→gate, ride→right→wrong, milk→maid→rosy;* there may be two or more intervening terms between stimulus and response, e.g., *revenge→sweet→sugar →white.* Indirect associations are of course particularly likely to occur with those subjects in whom the stimulus-word arouses a visual picture for which a word must then be found; they are also likely to occur when the association first aroused is repressed because it is embarrassing or otherwise inappropriate. We would expect indirect associations to show lengthened reaction-times.

Classifications intended for diagnostic purposes and based in part on the responses of abnormal subjects are exemplified by those of Jung and Riklin (Jung, 1918) and of Wells (1911b). In these classifications particular importance is attached to "egocentric" or otherwise individually peculiar responses. These include (1) predication: defining, describing, explaining, or making a sentence with the stimulus-word, e.g., *flower→ pretty, paper→for writing, angry→I am not;* (2) responses which are proper names or which interpret the stimulus as a proper name; (3) personal pronouns as responses; (4) repetitions of stimulus-word or of previous response-words, or responses related to previous stimulus- or response-words (perseveration); (5) meaningless responses; (6) *yes* or *no* as responses; e.g., *drink→no, sin→never, good→yes;* (7) misunderstanding of stimulus-word; (8) failure to respond. Such responses, which Wells found to constitute in different subjects from 2 to 60 percent of the totals, are of chief clinical interest, as suggesting peculiarities of personality or attitude or the presence of emotionally disturbing "complexes." Another class of responses may be of interest as particularly characteristic of certain subjects; this includes word-completion, compounding, or inflection—e.g., *table→cloth, play→ground, find→found—*

and rhyme and assonance—e.g., *tease→sneeze, fate→fat*. In contrast with the above two classes are the responses which are common to many subjects because they represent commonly shared language habits and, usually, obvious semantic relationships; here are included such relationships as synonymity, antonymity, membership in the same class, part-whole and whole-part, species-genus and genus-species.

Thorndike (1932) concluded, from a survey of associative responses, that 95 percent of responses in free association are evoked directly—as word-response to word-stimulus—on the basis of past experiential contiguities in hearing, reading, speaking, and writing; in only 5 percent is there first an association of things or qualities which must then be named.

There has been a good deal of dissatisfaction with the various schemes of classification of word-associations. It has been objected that they rest upon logical rather than psychological foundations, or that they classify the relations between objective data rather than the associative processes. A very troublesome difficulty has been that of the ambiguity of many responses in terms of the classifications. Thus it is not clear whether the association *man→animal* should be classed as supraordinate or coordinate, or whether the association *hand→foot* should be classed as coordinate, contrast, or similarity. Classification of response-words into grammatical categories may often be uncertain, especially in a language like English; is the response *desire* to the stimulus *wish* to be classed as a noun or as a verb? In applying the three-fold classification—egocentric, word-completion or rhyme, commonly shared language habit—we may find responses classifiable under either of the first two classes which are also "common to a large number of subjects," and which would be therefore of more linguistic than of clinical interest. Experimenters have often been troubled by the arbitrary and subjective nature of the judgments required, and different experimenters may disagree in the classification of the same response. As Woodworth (1938, pp. 351f.) has pointed out, it is not a matter of determining the correct scientific relationship, e.g., between *man* and *animal*, but of guessing the relationship implicit in the individual subject's response. Some have thought therefore to sort the associations on the basis of each subject's introspective reports, but such reports are often unreliable and in any case interfere with the experimental procedure.

From the point of view of individual differences, it would seem that we have here a situation analogous to that in "mental testing," where responses have to be classified, not on the basis of a priori categories of response, but in terms of the classes of individuals—classified on other grounds—who give the responses. Thus if there are differences in the responses given to the same stimulus-words, e.g., by children and by adults, it may be that some tolerably generalizing terms can be found to describe the juvenile and the adult responses, respectively. Similarly, if we have classified individuals as normal and neurotic, we may find differences in the word-associations of these classes which can conveniently be expressed by generalizing labels. The response classifications would therefore be ad hoc and not a priori; the purpose would be not to classify logical or grammatical relations between words but to describe any differences in word-associations which might be found to characterize different classes of human beings. On the other hand, if we are interested in the possibility that the associative relationships between words may throw light on the linguistic organization characteristic of the individuals of a speech-community—corresponding, presumably, to acquired patterns of cortical organization—then we will wish to examine those studies which have been concerned with the grammatical—morphological, syntactic, and semantic—relationships between stimulus- and response-words. But we shall also wish to examine the evidence, furnished by association studies, that the organization of language may include numerous and pervasive functional—semantic—categories which are not linguistic in the technical sense; i.e., are not marked by morphologic or syntactic features; it is perhaps functional categories of this sort which lurk behind the formal "logical" classifications—coordination, subordination, etc.

There is one way of classifying associative responses which is relatively objective. This consists in the construction of frequency tables, in which the associative responses made to each stimulus-word are classified according to the number of subjects who gave them. Such tables make possible the study of the most common associative interconnections among the words of a given speech-community, and may perhaps reveal some aspects of the organization both of the language habits and of the manual and emotional-motivational behavior integrated with the language habits.

They make possible also the identification of individuals who deviate from the usual verbal association habits.

The first frequency table[37] based on a large number of subjects was that of Kent and Rosanoff (1910; hereafter cited as K-R). They presented 100 familiar English words, mostly nouns and adjectives, orally to each of 1,000 "normal" subjects, mostly adults, of varying education and occupation. The test was given to each subject individually. The subject sat with his back to the experimenter and was instructed to respond to each stimulus-word by one word only, "the first word that occurs to you other than the stimulus-word." If a subject responded with a phrase or by repeating the stimulus-word or some grammatical variant of it, the stimulus-word was given again at the end of the list. For each of the 100 stimulus-words, a table was prepared showing the different responses made to that word, each response-word being preceded by the number of individuals (out of a total of 1,000) who gave that response. Thus to the stimulus-word *dark*, 427 subjects responded *light*, 221 *night*, 76 *black*, etc. Such frequencies will hereafter be referred to as measures of commonality of responses. Many response-words were of course given by only one individual; they have a "frequency" of 1. The purpose of Kent and Rosanoff was diagnostic; the title of the article in which these tables were presented was "A Study of Association in Insanity." The instructions for the use of the association test and frequency tables, as incorporated in Rosanoffs' *Manual of Psychiatry* (6th ed., 1927), state that "in the examination of a test record obtained by this method the first step is to compare it with the frequency tables and thereby distinguish the *common* reactions, which are to be found in the tables and which are for the most part normal, from *individual* reactions, which are not to be found in the tables and which include the great majority of those that are of pathological significance." However, response-words may occur which are inflectional variants of words in the tables (classed as doubtful responses); both common and individual responses may be non-specific (i.e., "so widely applicable

37. The idea of an "association lexicon" was first suggested by Marbe; the first attempt at such a lexicon was made by Marbe's pupil, Saling (1908); another "sample" was produced by Reinhold (1910). These studies were of school children. Saling reported six cases in which the responses were contaminations—i.e., mixtures of two words; e.g., *Herz→Scharz = Schmerz + Schatz*.

as to serve as more or less appropriate reactions to almost any of the stimulus words"; e.g., *man, article, large*; such words, if they occur repeatedly, may be "significant"); and many responses not found in the tables must nevertheless be considered "normal." Hence an appendix had to be provided in which, for each stimulus-word, were defined classes of response-words which were to be counted as normal. Thus the frequency tables by no means provide a mechanical means of arriving at clinical judgments; a good deal of more or less arbitrary judgment may be called for. (This is of course true of all clinical personality tests; it might almost be said that such tests merely furnish a relatively standardized situation in which the clinician can exercise his intuition, or obtain cues for further investigation.) Moreover, to define a "common" reaction as one that occurs at least once in a table and an "individual" reaction as one that does not occur at all seems quite arbitrary; a frequency of 1 in 1,000 seems hardly less uncommon than a frequency of 0. However, Kent and Rosanoff presented tables showing that whereas 1,000 "normal" adults gave 92 percent common reactions and 7 percent individual reactions, 247 "insane" adults gave 71 percent common reactions and 27 percent individual reactions. Woodworth (1938, p. 344) gives the following as average numbers of individual reactions for the list of 100 stimulus-words: normal persons with only common-school education, 5.2; college-educated subjects, 9.3; dementia praecox patients, 25 to 50. Instead of counting the number of individual reactions, we can of course count the number of high-frequency responses, if we can decide on a criterion of high frequency. We can, for each subject, take the average—or the median, as suggested by Woodworth, (1938, p. 344)—of the reference-population frequency values of the subject's responses to all of the stimulus-words.

The relative frequencies of the responses to the same stimulus-words have been found to vary with the age, intelligence, education, sex, and occupational status of the subjects, and with the historical-social-geographical setting of the population investigated. Whether they can be shown to vary with definable personality or clinical categories is still uncertain, as are those categories themselves.

Frequency norms for the K-R test were redetermined by a number of authors, sometimes under approximations to the original K-R conditions, sometimes with variations in stimulus-word order or in context, whereby the responses were found to vary; references to this literature may be found in Woodworth and Schlosberg (1954), Jung (1966), and Cramer (1968). In 1960, Jenkins and Russell published an account of the changes which had occurred in K-R word-association "norms" during the period 1910–1952; the chief comparison however was between the results of Schellenberg (1929) and the 1952 results of Russell and Jenkins (1954); in both of these studies the method consisted of a group test, with printed forms and written answers, the latter obtained from approximately 1,000 college students. Jenkins and Russell, contrary to Woodworth and Schlosberg (1954, p. 56), found reason to believe that the difference in method between the group-written and the individual-oral administrations had "negligible effect" on the frequency of primary, secondary, and tertiary responses. However, Palermo and Jenkins (1965), reporting on the associations of children, stated that "oral presentation of stimuli results in a greater frequency of contrast responses and a reduction in frequency of superordinate responses." Similarly, Entwisle and Forsyth (1963) found that in fifth-grade children commonality of responses was greater under individual-oral than under group-written administration; this was particularly true for children from homes of superior social status. The most striking differences between the 1930 and 1952 results reported by Jenkins and Russell (1960) were a considerable increase in 1952 in the frequency of primary—i.e., most frequent—responses, a decrease in popularity of abstract responses—specifically superordinates—and an increase in the frequency of "popular" responses—coordinates and "completions" such as *cheese→crackers, doctor→nurse*, or opposites such as *sickness→health*; many of these might be thought to result from frequent syntactic contiguity. Some changes in association could be identified as reflecting semantic changes of the stimulus-words. But the primary responses showed considerable stability over the period considered; 71 percent were identical in 1927 and 1952, but the frequencies of these primaries increased in 1952. The authors suggest the possibility that increased "homogeneity of our verbal culture" may have contributed to such changes, but place greater weight on changes in "test-taking attitudes" and such practice effects as had been demonstrated for word-associations by Wells (1911a). In 1960, Jenkins and Palermo (1965) repeated the group tests of 1927 and 1952 and found again "that the relative frequencies of the primary responses to particular stimuli tend to remain constant over time," while "a small set of relatively weak responses" varied. However, "the hypothesis of increasing frequency of popular responses over time must be regarded with some suspicion," and "the 1942 norm [Wilson, 1942] which was individual-oral, has the highest frequency of primary responses yet observed," whereas the other tests compared were group tests with printed forms and written answers. The question, which will be raised again in the section on associative reaction-time, of whether the measures obtained in a group test are equivalent to the measures obtained by repeated tests of individuals, was investigated by Jenkins, Russell, and Foss (cited as in preparation by Jung, 1966), who reported that comparisons across individuals in a given trial gave results similar to those resulting from comparisons across trials for a given individual.

Palermo and Jenkins (1965) compared the associations of children reported by Woodrow and Lowell (1916) with those obtained in 1960–1961 by Palermo and Jenkins. They found an increase in the percentages of same-form-class and contrast responses, and remark, "Since the changes observed in the responses of the children over this time span are all in the direction of changes which appear with increases in age (Palermo, 1963), one interpretation of these data would be that children today are linguistically more sophisticated." Wheat (1931) orally presented 25 stimulus-words, selected at random from the 500 most commonly used words in the English language, to groups of school children—total, 1,323—in grades 4 to 8—modal ages 9 to 11—who wrote their associates. He found that the number of "common" responses—defined as those which could statistically be expected to appear in another sample of the same size, in terms of the reliabilities of percentages—increased with age from 43.8 to 62.5 percent. Koff (1965), comparing the associations of children 9 to 12 years of age obtained by Woodrow and Lowell in 1916 with those of children of ages 8 to 12 which he obtained in 1963, found that the associations of the latter were much more like those of adults, particularly in a large increase in opposites, which of course was also an increase in commonality. Like Jenkins and Russell (1960) in their discussion of the increase in frequency of primary responses in adult associations, Koff suggested the possibility that the changes in children's associations might be attributable to "the cumulative effects of 'mass culture' on associations over time."

Skinner (1937), inspired by Zipf's "discovery" of the linear relationship between word-frequency and word-frequency-rank, plotted the frequencies of K-R responses against the rank-order of their frequencies on logarithmic paper and found here also a linear relationship, but with a deviation in "the relatively low value for the word[s] occurring most frequently"; this deviation was "contributed almost entirely by the group with the lowest frequency in Rank 1. It is significant that this group contains nearly all the abstract stimulus-words in the set (e.g., *religion, justice*) and many terms with no sharply defined referents (e.g., *comfort, sickness, hungry*). There are no single strong associations for words of this sort." Later (Cook and Skinner, 1939), a study of Schellenberg's (1929) data led to the conclusion that "the [Thorndike] commonness of a stimulus-word [within the limits of the Schellenberg list] has no statistically significant relation to the frequency of its first associated word." On the other hand, Cofer and Shevitz (1952), having instructed subjects to write as many associates as possible in ten minutes after hearing and seeing a stimulus-word, found that "there is a relationship between [Thorndike-Lorge] frequency count and number of associations given to stimulus-words of varying frequency." They suggested as a formulation for further research that "word-frequency (common or individual) is related to degrees of response availability, such that to a high-frequency stimulus-word there is a greater availability of both the stimulus-word as response and of verbal responses related to it than is the case with low-frequency words." They mentioned the findings of others that there is a relationship between word-frequency count and the number of meanings words have according to dictionaries; also that subjects produce more synonyms to stimulus-words that they rate as being familiar than they produce to words that they rate as less familiar. In studies using any population frequency-count there is always of course the question of the extent to which this count corresponds to the familiarity values of individuals.

Controlled Association

Most of the experimental work has used the technique of free association, but the controlled association technique is almost as old. It must be obvious to any psychologist that even "free" associations are only relatively free, since they occur under both experimenter's and self-instruction, and like other responses depend upon set, mood, etc. "In ordinary life," observes Woodworth (1938, p. 342) "we do not often respond to an isolated word by simply saying another word. Many persons unfamiliar with the psychologist and his peculiar ways cannot believe that he wants nothing more definite. They suspect him of seeking to discover how well they understand the stimulus words and set themselves, more or less intentionally, to give 'sensible' answers." They may also set themselves to give moral answers, as I found (Esper, 1918) when I obtained the associations of a number of uneducated adults; these men (university janitors), as I subsequently learned, could explain the experiment among themselves only as a test on which their continued employment might depend; thus, for example, the stimulus-word *drinking* elicited such unusual responses as *No!* and *Prohibition!* Calling out promptly a single, high-commonality response-word in response to a single stimulus-word is a game to which many educated persons can readily adjust themselves, but which is likely to be more difficult for the uneducated, as Wreschner (1907–1909) found. Jung and Riklin (Jung, 1918) point out that ordinarily when a single word is called out to someone it is a command or question; uneducated persons and persons in certain pathological states or of low intelligence are likely to try to show that they understand the word or that they have the proper attitude toward it; a common model is the schoolroom exercise: "make a sentence containing the word ———." This situation is exaggerated, as Wehrlin (1918) found, in the case of the feeble-minded; only sporadically and by dint of repeated and insistent instruction, whereby the freedom of association is lost, can the subject be induced to give single appropriate response-words; characteristic associations are: *Sunday →consists of a day on which one does nothing; schoolboy→when he goes to school; paper→you write upon it.*

When Koffka (1912) tried to secure genuinely free associations by instructing the subjects to maintain a passive attitude, to let the stimulus-word call up an image, and then to make a simple hand reaction, he found that the subjects nevertheless restricted the task by various individual self-instructions. Cason and Cason (1925), as a preliminary to the giving of the K-R test, used 12 practice words to determine how well each of the 100 subjects understood the instructions. "It was found that practically all subjects had some preconceived notion as to the particular kind of response desired by the experimenter. Even with the most careful instructions, the responses are not entirely uncontrolled or free." One might say, more generally, that aside from local muscle twitches, *no* animal responses escape the established and on-going processes of the central nervous system. Free associations are therefore simply those which are left to the control of unknown and varying intraorganic conditions of the individual subject. It is also true that even when the immediate "inner"—covert—association appears to be relatively free, it may be suppressed before overt vocalization can occur because of its unsuitability, some more conventional response being substituted. When Wells (1911a) said that "good" performance in a free association test depended upon freedom from hampering sets and obstructions, this could only have meant that if no unusual or very special set were present, a subject's responses might be expected to be in conformity with socially shared language habits.

The controlled-association experiments of Watt (1905) played an important role in the development of the concept of *set*. In the first decade of the present century a number of workers, particularly the group at Würzburg led by Külpe, were attempting to study, by introspective methods, the processes which occur in thinking. Watt used the controlled-association experiment for this purpose. His procedure was (1) to assign any one of six tasks (e.g., to name a concept related to the one named in the stimulus-word as part to whole, or as genus to species), (2) to present a short series of stimulus-words visually, (3) to take the reaction-times by means of a voice-key and a Hipp chronoscope, (4) after each single response to record the subject's introspective report. To increase the accuracy of these reports, Watt divided the processes to be observed into four periods: (1) the foreperiod, from the ready signal to the exposure of the stimulus-word, (2) the occurrence of the stimulus-word, (3) the period of the search for the reaction-word, (4) the occurrence of the reaction-word. On different occasions the subjects confined their observations to different ones of these periods. The reports showed that when the task was still new and unfamiliar, the foreperiod was occupied by conscious awareness of the required task in verbal, visual, or kinesthetic terms; the subject sought to define the relation, symbolize it by diagram or gesture, or find an example. When the stimulus-word appeared, the reaction sometimes followed "automatically," sometimes after an interval of waiting or searching, and sometimes after false reactions had been suggested and rejected. Definite consciousness of the task was usually confined to the foreperiod; it emerged again in the main period only when false reactions had to be rejected. When the same task had continued for a series of stimulus-words, the conscious awareness of the task faded out even from the foreperiod, but a preparatory set, a "mere feeling of readiness," remained which seemed to insure appropriate responses. As Woodworth (1938) says, "Watt's main result was the efficiency of the task-set or preparation, along with the fact that this preparation was completed during the foreperiod. It worked by *selecting in advance*. It did not select during the main period from among several responses called up by the stimulus word, but it limited the field of response in advance of the stimulus-word so that only responses conforming to the task were ordinarily called up." And Boring (1950) observes, "Every one had been expecting to find the key to thought in Watt's third period, the period of the search for the word that would satisfy the conditions, but it was the third period that presented inadequate content. Watt discovered that the thought-process would run itself off at the presentation of the stimulus-word, provided the task or *Aufgabe* had been adequately accepted by the observer in the preparatory period. This was really a remarkable result."

Loring (1918) called attention to the fact that "the free association method leads necessarily to a heterogeneous mixture of types of responses." The difficulty in classifying such responses "is avoided in the controlled word association method, where the stimulus words are uniform, and the response words, by virtue of the instruction to the subject are likewise uniform." A great deal of attention was given to the selection of a large stock of suitable stimulus-words; all one-, two-, and three-syllable adjectives, nouns, and verbs in a 300,000-word abridged dictionary were examined and tested, and those which were technical, unfamiliar, or vulgar were eliminated, as were homonyms belonging to the same grammatical category and words whose sounds were found to be difficult to discriminate in single-word oral presentation. The experiments consisted in presenting a list of adjectives with instructions to respond with nouns, a list of nouns with instructions to respond with adjectives, a list of transitive verbs with instructions to respond with noun objects, and a list of intransitive verbs with instructions to respond with noun subjects. Loring found that the reaction-time for the adjective-noun association was shorter than that for the noun-adjective, and that the verb-object association was shorter than that for the verb-subject association. She attributed these results to the influence of the "normal order for the English language" and suggested that different results for the adjective-noun relation might be obtained from speakers of the Romance languages, and for the verb-noun relation from German speakers.

Watt's type of research was continued by Messer (1906) and by May (1917). May presented both the task and the stimulus-word visually. He employed two ways of designating the task: (*a*) by exposing the name of the required relation (e.g., "give opposite of"); (*b*) by exposing a pair of words standing in the required relation (e.g., "above-below"). The task was usually changed for each successive stimulus-word. In one experiment, the subject controlled the length of the foreperiod; having perceived the task instruction, he exposed the stimulus-word when he was ready. Under this condition, the foreperiod was shortest when the subject reported relatively automatic types of preparation: either an immediate adjustment to the task, with no experience to report, or an "attitude of readiness" without imagery or other definite content. With practice the length of the foreperiod tended to decrease, as did also the amount of reported conscious experience. The reaction-time was also shortest when the introspective reports on the main period—the period from stimulus to response—indicated that the reaction process was automatic. The longest reaction-times occurred when wrong responses were suggested but inhibited.

Otto Selz (1913a, 1913b, 1920, 1922) investigated the problem of what it is that a set places in readiness. He carried out experiments in controlled association with a large variety of tasks, exposing the task-word and the stimulus-word simultaneously; e.g., *Superordinate? Tiger, Coordinte? Death*, etc. The introspective reports seemed to Selz to make untenable the "constellation theory" which had been held by James and Ebbinghaus; according to this theory, what the task-designation would arouse would be a large number of individual associations, not interrelated nor organized in any way. Thus in a controlled association task calling for opposites, the constellation theory would attribute the association *dark→ light* to the reinforcement by the stimulus-word of one of many associations which the task-set aroused. But, says Woodworth (1938, p. 797), "Why should not the response be, unhesitatingly, *night?* for *night* is a very familiar associate of *dark* and it is also a familiar opposite, the opposite of *day*." In reply, it might be said that such responses *do* occur! (Wilcocks, 1928;[38] Cofer, 1967b). Selz's solution of the problem was a further development of the "imageless thought" and especially the "determining tendency" of the Würzburg school. He rejected associationism, against which he polemized, and, under the joint influence of the Würzburgers and the gestaltists, he developed a "complex theory," according to which a given task sets in readiness a class of words-in-relation rather than a class of single words. For his more difficult tasks he devised the notion of "anticipatory schema," according to which the task and the stimulus-word are jointly integrated into a schema or frame with a gap which is to be filled—a "complex" or pattern which "tends toward completion." Selz distinguished between "reproductive" and "productive" thinking; in the latter "new mental products" are "creatively" achieved by means of "special mental processes." Humphrey (1951, pp. 142ff.) has criticized Selz's notion of creative thinking: "His is one more endeavor to show how novelty can be created by manipulation of standardized, pre-existing units"; having rejected the associational theory which had still been utilized by Ach and Watt, Selz tried to put the weight of explanation on the "determining tendency" as the energizing principle. In recent years, the

38. Wilcocks (1928) presented data and arguments against Selz's rejection of the "law of substitution" as an explanation of errors in controlled association. This "law" had been stated by Müller and Pilzecker thus: an idea *a* can be substituted in the association *ab* for the similar idea *á* ("active substitution"), or *a* reproduces, not *b* which is actually associated with it, but *b'* which is similar to *b* ("passive substitution").

notion of "novelty" and "creativeness" in linguistic syntax has been urged by a group of psycholinguists who similarly reject the mechanism of associative reproduction; though they seek to impart explanatory power to the concept by vague references to the brain, they, like Selz, make upon me the same impression as did the gestaltists—as people who state a problem with the air of having solved it (Esper, 1930, p. 335).

What is the relevance of the work of Selz to the problem of set in word-association experiments? There seems to be no doubt that in some controlled-association experiments a set may operate with great efficiency and automatically. The subjects are unable to report any conscious processes of searching or selecting, and their average reaction-times may be shorter than in free association. This mode of operation of set has been observed, as by Watt and by May, when the subjects have had some practice with a particular task-set, and when task and stimulus-words are familiar. In Selz's experiments, there was no foreperiod; tasks were presented simultaneously with stimulus-words; these can therefore hardly be called experiments on set. Watt had shown that where conscious preparation occurs, it occurs in the foreperiod. In Selz's experiments also, as Woodworth says, "the problems were intended to be fairly difficult and the instructions called for deliberation rather than speed." If we add the requirement of detailed introspection, it is clear that the conditions were very unfavorable to the operation of efficient and well-established sets. It may be that we can think of a continuum from simple controlled associations at one extreme up to complex trains of problem-solving at the other, as Watt and Selz seem to have assumed, but this is by no means certain. It is hard to see how introspective reports on problem-solving activity can give information relevant to the most automatic controlled associations. It may be that if we seek an explanation of the operation of set in the more automatic associations we shall find it only in at present non-existent neural physiology.

However, while the conditions of these experiments are not suitable for the study of the phenomenon of set as it appears in the more familiar types of controlled association, they do illustrate attempts to deal with a difficulty which has been repeatedly experienced in the application of traditional association theory. This difficulty arises from the atomistic nature of the traditional theory, the notion that what get "connected" are millions of individual "ideas" or "reflexes" or "stimuli-and-responses." As the cell theory and the neurone doctrine developed in the nineteenth century, these seemed to offer a parallel atomism; each "idea" resided in a brain cell; learning consisted in connecting up chains of individual neurones by "reduction of resistances" at synapses. As psychological research developed at an accelerating pace during the past half-century, this scheme seemed less and less adequate. It became increasingly obvious that behavior is a resultant not only of an environmental situation—which is not a mere additive totality of individual "stimuli"—but also of a total pattern of postural and visceral stimulation and of ongoing central nervous activity. Behavior—or consciousness—represents therefore an *integration*, and it is difficult to think of it in terms of simple isolated associations, concatenations of "reflexes," or activities of certain particular neurones. In addition, the alleged neural correlates of learning—the reductions of resistance, the wearing of paths, the connecting up of neurones—have no known physiological meaning. The dissatisfaction with atomistic associationism found notable expression in the monograph by Lashley (1929; see also Lashley, 1961), in which he reported the results of his studies on the effects of cortical extirpations on the learned performances of rats.

The problem of the physiological mechanism which selects responses is fundamental to the explanation of all word-associations, controlled and free alike. A special and enormously important manifestation of such selective processes is the sequence of words in linguistic utterances. In the days when he was still a Skinnerian behaviorist, Miller (1951, p. 186) expressed the relationship thus:

> Controlled associations are quite similar to the choice of successive words in speech. As we talk, the specific words we use are not chosen before we begin. They occur as needed, usually without any reportable searching. Established habits determine the choice of words as the response sequence moves from one set of verbal bonds to the next. In controlled association it is as though the subject had spoken all but the last three

words of "A word that is superordinate to ... is ... ." The occurrence of the reaction word is as natural and automatic as the occurrence of the word in a sentence.

The basic cause of both word-associations and sentence sequences is, according to Skinner (1957, pp. 75f.) [39] and the Miller of the 1950s (1951, pp. 185ff.), "contiguous usage"; words follow one another because they have occurred contiguously in the past; variation results from the fact that different persons have different histories of usage—"reinforcement" —and because the determinants are not merely single words but contexts —verbal and non-verbal. "It is not surprising," says Skinner, "that male and female college students tend to give different responses to such a stimulus word as *ring*, while medical students differ from students of law in their responses to such a stimulus word as *administer*." [40]

The effects of verbal context on word-association are illustrated by the sentence-completion test, in which one or more words, omitted from sentences, are to be supplied by the subject. In one variation of this (Selfridge, 1949, reported by Miller, 1951, pp. 187f.), subjects guessed at the successive words in a continuous passage; after each guess they were told the correct word and asked to guess the next. Some of the words were so determined by the context that all or almost all of the thirty-six subjects agreed upon the "correct" responses. Miller, with no foreboding of his coming conversion to the doctrine of syntactic novelty (1965), concluded that in both sentence-completion and word-association tests "the results show groups of words that function together," and that "these groupings, with minor individual variations, are common to all users of the language." Aborn, Rubenstein, and Sterling (1959) omitted one word from 1,380 sentences; they found that the length, distribution, and grammatical structure of context were all independently effective sources of constraint on words in sentences, and that the predictability of words belonging to a given class was inversely related to the size of that class.

39. I remind the reader that Skinner's views had been in informal circulation since the early 1930s and that they had been presented as lectures at Columbia and at Harvard in 1947; of the latter, several hundred copies had been circulated, and this version provided the psychological basis of Miller's book.

40. The reference is to experiments by Goodenough (1946) and by Foley and Macmillan (1943).

There have been attempts of another sort to study the effect on word-association of verbal context. Thus Howes and Osgood (1954) orally presented groups of subjects with sets of four words, with instructions to write a free association to the last word of each four-word set; stimulus-words of each set were selected so as to have "zero transitional probabilities." They reported that "the effect of a sequence of stimulus-words upon an associative response is an increasing function of the proportion of those stimulus-words having similar first-order associative effects on the response." Jenkins and Cofer (1957) presented, in printed form, compounds of adjective-plus-noun, to each of which the subjects were to respond by writing their association. They reported that "the results showed marked disparity in response distributions to the compounds, as compared to the norms for individual stimulus words, and there were also differences between types of compounds. The results support the importance of context as a factor in verbal behavior, but appear to be in conflict with predictions from information theory" (i.e., whereas information theory "would predict that context, imposing constraints on possible response alternatives, should produce a smaller variety of responses than that found for individual word stimuli," in this experiment "the compound stimuli produced a greater variety of response than do the individual word stimuli").

Cofer (1967a) summarized the studies, published in the preceding fifteen years, of contextual effects on word-association. Two methods had been used: (a) that of "compound stimuli," in which two or more stimuli are presented together and the subject is asked to respond either to the compound as a unit or to the last word in the set; (b) that of "priming," in which the subjects first learn either a list containing words which are known to be associates of subsequently given word-stimuli ("direct priming"), or a list of words which are known to elicit one of the associates of a subsequently given stimulus-word ("indirect priming"). The results of such experiments, while often showing contextual effects, have been variable, and Cofer mentions the suggestion, made by Cramer and others, that such effects depend upon "underlying associative structures or networks. That is, a response can be primed for a stimulus if the two belong in the same network, but not otherwise."

Textbooks have commonly contained the statement that the average reaction-time for controlled association is shorter than that for free association, and this seems reasonable insofar as a specific set means greater readiness of certain responses. However, an unqualified statement of this sort is unjustified; the task-set in controlled association may be unfamiliar and difficult, and so may be the stimulus-words. This is particularly true when the controlled-association experiment is used as a means of investigating thought-processes. Wreschner (1907–1909), using many difficult stimulus-words in his tests of controlled association, concluded that free association is quicker than controlled. May (1917) found no significant differences in median reaction-time. On the other hand, Cattell (1887) found that in general wholly restricted responses—e.g., *month-season, author-language*—gave shorter times than did partially restricted responses—e.g., *season-month, language-author*. Woodworth and Wells (1911) found that the time for a species-genus association—e.g., *horse-animal*—was reliably shorter than that for a genus-species association—e.g., *animal-horse*. Bills (1934, p. 353) suggested that "the more rigid the nature of the controlling set, the shorter the reaction time," and that "apparently the interference caused by the arousal of rival tendencies delays free association and is removed by a limitation in the number of possible responses allowed." Baker and Elliott (1948) attempted to answer the question raised by Woodworth (1938): "whether the *same response to the same stimulus* is quicker in free or controlled association"; they reported that for every one of their highly familiar stimulus-words the mean reaction-time was shorter in the controlled than in the free situation; unfortunately, defects in their procedure impair the reliability of their conclusion. Cofer (1967b) found "substantial similarities" between free- and controlled-association responses; "over half the CA responses occur in FA, and these responses account for a high proportion of the frequencies obtained in both CA and FA." A considerable number of "inappropriate" responses occurred under the controlled-association conditions, and these tended to be the high-frequency responses of free association; moreover, Cofer reported that Davidson (1965) had found that the associative strength—i.e., frequency—of the response to the stimulus in free association was predictive of the reaction-time in controlled association; "where controlled association is very quick . . . the appropriate response is also a high-frequency response in the FA hierarchy." [41]

The manner in which in a free-association experiment the context of the stimulus-words in a list can impose a "control" on responses has been demonstrated by Wynne, Gerjuoy, and Schifmann (1965): beginning a stimulus-word list with a series of words to which the most commonly given responses are antonyms increases the probability of antonym responses to words later in the series. The authors cite the researches of others who had found that "many Ss come into the testing situation with an already established response set to give antonym (and possibly also coordinate) associations and . . . this set is correlated with a tendency to give rapid and obvious responses." Moreover, it had been found that when subjects give associations under an extreme speed set, they give more antonym responses than they do under standard free-association instructions. Carroll, Kjeldergaard, and Carton (1962) found that subjects who in a free-association experiment respond mostly with opposites where possible also respond characteristically to "non-opposite-evoking" stimuli with contrast or coordinate responses. "A score based upon the number of opposites given to the opposite-evoking stimuli, both from the standpoint of consistency and stability (over a 16-month period), [is] more reliable than the primary responses to the 72 non-opposite-evoking stimuli or the commonality score (all K-R primary responses including most of the opposites)."

Cofer and Ford (1957) though it "reasonable to assume, when one sees, hears, thinks of, or speaks a specific word, that words closely related to that word (e.g., its synonyms) become more readily available and more likely to arise than do other words." They found however that when a stimulus-word was preceded by a synonym the association-time was lengthened, so that the synonym-context seemed to produce some sort of interference. It might be suggested that some of the interference was be-

41. Two features of Cofer's method should be noted: the controlled association stimuli were presented to groups, so that the responses had presumably to be written; and the subjects from whom the free associations were obtained were not Cofer's but those of Russell and Jenkins (1954). From a linguistic point of view, it is regrettable that so many word-association experiments have been conducted as group experiments, with written responses and often with printed stimulus-words.

tween two alternating tasks: pronouncing the synonyms and associating to the actual stimulus-words.

Associative Reaction-Times

The techniques used in measuring associative reaction-times have shown much variety. The experimenter may start a stopwatch as he speaks the stimulus-word and stop it when the subject starts to respond. Since the range of reaction-times encountered with, e.g., 100 untrained subjects may easily be 5 seconds—0.7 to 5 or more seconds—a unit of .2 second may seem fine enough, and the error of measurement to be expected with the use of a stopwatch may seem tolerable. But individuals may show much smaller ranges; practiced subjects show a decided decrease in median and dispersion; and the total distribution of association-times, whether of groups or of individuals, is likely to be heterogeneous, so that meaningful analysis will require the segregation of the data into a number of distributions, some of which may have ranges of only a few tenths of a second. The stopwatch can therefore hardly be justified for research purposes (cf. Dunlap, 1917). Loring (1918) remarks that "the watch method introduces into the total reaction time three reaction times instead of one"; she speaks also of "the unreliability of the Hipp chronoscope without considerable modification and standardization." The Dunlap chronoscope, which she used, is perhaps even more "temperamental." An instrument reading in units of 0.01 second, with a maximum error of 1 scale unit, would seem to be a reasonable minimum requirement for association work.

As previously mentioned, the highly accurate (when carefully calibrated) Hipp chronoscope reading in milliseconds was available to some of the earliest experimenters (Trautscholdt, 1882), as were also the lip-key and voice-key (Cattell, 1886, 1887). The experimenter's pronunciation of the stimulus-word may operate a lip- or voice-key and thus start the chronoscope, while the subject's response operates a similar key to stop the chronoscope. Assuming (*a*) that the clock motor runs at a constant rate and does not change its frequency—as may occur with the Hipp—or stop or start "hunting"—as may occur with the Dunlap, and (*b*) that the error of measurement due to the operation of the clutch mechanism which starts and stops the clock hand is sufficiently small, the chief sources of error in the apparently ideal two-voice-keys-and-chronoscope arrangement are (*a*) the accidental tripping of the voice-keys by a preliminary sound ("uh-") or by a room vibration, (*b*) the failure of some word-initials—particularly voiceless sibilants—to operate the voice-keys, (*c*) differences of word-length, particularly if words of three or more syllables occur (Loring, 1918).

An alternative method, first used by Cattell (1887), is to present the stimulus-words tachistoscopically; a contact device on the tachistoscope starts the chronoscope while the subject's actuation of a voice-key stops it. With this technique there may be, as compared with auditory presentation of stimulus-words, differences in the response words, and the median association-time is likely to be longer; such differences were cited by Marbe (1902) as the probable explanation for the divergence of Oertel's (1901b) results from those of Thumb and Marbe (1901; see also Menzerath, 1908b). In anticipation of later discussion, it may here be mentioned that the association experiment with oral presentation by an experimenter facing an individual subject seems to be a social situation quite different psychologically—and linguistically—from the experiment with visual presentation by a machine (cf. Ekdahl, 1929).

In some experiments the experimenter closes a reaction-key as he pronounces the stimulus-word and releases the key when the subject begins to respond (Esper, 1918), or actuates a switch as he gives the stimulus-word and again when the subject begins to respond (Schlosberg and Heineman, 1950). The amount of variability thus introduced depends largely on the degree of the experimenter's practice. But the experimenter, like the voice-key, is subject to the error of subject-produced preliminary noises. The variable error is probably increased if the experimenter looks at the subject and thus makes himself subject to visual cues. Like other reaction-times, association-times may be expected to vary in central tendency and dispersion with the length and variability of the foreperiod (the period between the ready signal and the stimulus-word).

The rationale of word-association research meets its severest tests in the statistical analysis of reaction-time distributions. We might take as the text of the following discussion T. L. Kelley's (1924, p. 44) dictum: "The most important single item of information to be known about a distribution is what it is a distribution of." The chief criticism which may be brought against many published distributions of association-times is lack of homogeneity. The kinds of heterogeneity may be conveniently illustrated by reference to a study by Schlosberg and Heineman (1950), hereafter abbreviated S&H.

1. There were 204 unpracticed experimenters (students of elementary psychology), who gave the first 50 words of the K-R (Kent-Rosanoff) list to their laboratory partners. Two gratuitous and irrelevant sources of heterogeneity were therefore (a) the fact that there were 204 different experimenters, and (b) the fact that these experimenters were unpracticed. Association reactions are very sensitive to variations in manner of presentation, personality traits of the experimenter, the relation between subject and experimenter, etc. There have been studies of such factors, but they were not under study in this experiment, and no information about them could be obtained by the plan of this experiment.

2. "There were about twice as many men as women in the group, but the self-chosen partners tended to be of the same sex." Cason and Cason (1925) found that the sex of the experimenter in their experiments influenced the reactions significantly. Since associative reactions have also been found to vary in certain ways with the sex of the subjects, there would seem to be no justification for including responses of both sexes in the same distribution.

3. The subjects were unpracticed. Woodworth (1938, pp. 358f.) refers to the work of Menzerath (1908b) and of Wells (1911c) who repeated the test on a series of days and found the average to go down from 1750 to 1200–1300 ms. "This result is rather remarkable, since new stimulus words were used on each succeeding day.... The gain in average speed was probably due to better adaptation to the experiment, greater freedom from inner obstruction, and the adoption of more facile and 'superficial' types of response." We may expect among the responses of unpracticed subjects a good many whose reaction-time depends upon special and even unique factors, and which would therefore be unlikely to

be of the sort which might portend analogical changes. There is likely to be great variability in individual self-instruction among unpracticed subjects, so that there is little justification for treating the scores obtained from such subjects as constituting a homogeneous population. Another factor that is likely to act dominantly is the subject's social relation to the experimenter; it might be said that at the beginning of the subject's laboratory experience the experimenter is in the foreground, but that with continuing experience the experimenter moves more and more into the background; the effects of this factor will vary with individual subjects and experimenters. We may therefore expect to find in reaction-time distributions obtained from practiced subjects a decrease in mean, scatter, and skewness.

4. In S&H's statistical analysis, the reactions to the 25 monosyllabic words in the first half of the K-R list were used. These stimulus-words are heterogeneous in several respects. (a) Some are adjectives, some nouns. It has been shown that associative reaction-times differ with the grammatical category of the stimulus-words. (b) In the absence of instructions, some of the words, at the moment of their presentation, belong to different categories for different subjects, e.g., *wish* is a noun for some, a verb for others. (c) Some words appear to belong to widely inclusive linguistic systems, others to relatively isolated systems; thus *slow* elicited from K-R's 1,000 subjects 204 different responses, while *sour* elicited only 91 different responses. (Other words of the K-R list, not used by S&H, show greater degrees of isolation, e.g., *mutton, needle, lamp, eagle, scissors.*) (d) Some of the words elicit responses of much higher commonality than do others; e.g., the most frequent response to *dark* is *light*, with a frequency of 427, whereas the most frequent response to *house* is *home*, with a frequency of 103. Since reaction-time has been found to vary with commonality of responses, this would be an important source of heterogeneity.

5. The chief purpose of S&H's study was to examine the relationship between association latency, i.e., reaction-time, and response commonality. Thumb and Marbe had published a table and graph which they described as showing "that with increasing *Geläufigkeit* ['readiness', 'ease',

'facility', 'familiarity'] of responses the association-times decrease, at first very rapidly, then progressively more slowly." The ordinates of the graph are reaction-times; the abscissae are frequencies. Actually, the coordinates were obtained by calculating the mean reaction-time for all responses which had the same commonality, regardless of the stimulus-words which elicited these responses. Since there were 8 subjects, the maximum possible commonality was 8, but the actual maximum was 7; that is, 7 subjects responded to *gross* with *klein* and to *leicht* with *schwer*, but the individualistic Herr Dr. Roos responded with *Goliath* and *Feder*, respectively. The plotted values therefore represent a confounding both of stimulus-words-and-responses and of individual subjects. For example, the mean reaction-time for the commonality value 3 results from averaging the latencies for the reactions *Mutter→Vater*, recorded for subjects Moritz, Schmidt, and Orth; *zehn→zwanzig*, recorded for subjects Schmidt, Ament, and Teichmann; etc. The relationship between commonality and latency described by Thumb and Marbe has come to be known as "Marbe's Law"; it has been "confirmed" by a number of other investigators (Woodworth and Schlosberg, 1954, pp. 61ff.).

S&H discuss their results in terms of the theoretical system of Hull and his associates. In this system there are said to be at least four measures of an "intervening variable" called *reaction potential*; these measures are amplitude, frequency, latency, and resistance to extinction. S&H perceive a need "to have some idea of the physiological mechanisms which make latency vary as some inverse function of reaction potential," and for "formulae expressing the relationship of latency to other measures of reaction potential." An estimate of the relationship between latency and frequency they think may be obtained from the relationship between reaction-time and response commonality in the association experiment. In a footnote they say, "In the free association experiment the construct being measured, associative strength, includes motivating as well as learning factors. It is thus analogous to response strength, reaction potential, or strength of the conditioned response, in contrast with strength of conditioning which is comparable to habit strength." In the theoretical interpretation of their results, S&H take as their model the development of electrical potential at synapses as a function of the time since onset of the stimulus; specifically, by way of illustration, they employ the negatively accelerated curve of this function obtained by Eccles from the ninth ventral root of the frog's spinal cord during stimulation of the ninth dorsal root. "In terms of the association experiment," they say, "the stimulus word releases excitation which builds up toward an asymptote at some 'center.' When the level of excitation reaches a threshold, the center will discharge, and the response will occur. If one assumes that the threshold varies in a normally distributed manner, it is possible to predict the distribution of associative reaction times." They found that prediction based on these assumptions gave a positively skewed distribution similar to the commonly accepted characteristic form of distribution of latency measurements. And finally, S&H say,

> As a byproduct of this analysis, the significance of communality is reasonably clear. Each stimulus word releases excitation to "centers" for many different response words. The first "center" in which net excitation reaches a threshold value will discharge, and the corresponding response word will occur. Thus communality (and percent frequency, in general) represents the number of times a particular response wins the race. All the factors which determine association time will influence this competition. Hence, communality will vary inversely with association time. The exact form of this relationship will depend on the competition a specific response meets with from other responses associated with the same stimulus word. For practical purposes, the relationship may be taken as linear.

This theoretical account of word-association, based upon a combination of reinforcement theory and neurophysiological theory, is interesting and may eventually turn out to have heuristic value, although at present the gulf between frog's spinal cord and human verbal organization appears truly formidable. But the crucial question to be raised here (and the reason for presenting the suggestions of S&H in this context) is whether the data of the association experiment, as gathered and analyzed by S&H, have any relevance to behavior theory.

In the first place, the locus of any construct such as "reaction potential" or "associative strength," or indeed of any relation or mechanism of behavior, must be in the individual nervous system. S&H say, "It is true that communality is not a measure of the response of one individual, but for a homogeneous population this objection is probably not serious." It appears to me that the objection is very serious indeed—particularly for psychologists who cherish the hope of someday establishing contact with the physiologists who are measuring the input and output of "centers." It is well known that individuals show wide differences in their tendencies to give unique or common responses, and in the distribution of their association times. Wallenhorst (1965) confirmed the finding of Moran, Mefferd, and Kimble (1964) and others that the associative responses of individuals may be under the control of self-imposed—"idiodynamic"—sets, e.g., antonym responses to adjectives, polar responses to verbs; moreover, subjects differ in their tendency toward "systematic perseveration" —i.e., the tendency to respond with words which had occurred earlier in the series—and this tendency varies, naturally, with the order in which the stimulus-words are presented. Moran (1966) concluded that "the commonality score of an individual subject . . . is a partial function of the individual's idiodynamic set and the set compatibility of the stimulus word list." He found that individuals "entered the word-association experiment with a definite [and highly consistent] tendency to give predominantly one class of associate, regardless of the stimulus words used. One group of such subjects tended to give synonym-superordinate, another to give contrast-coordinate, and the third to give 'functional' (e.g., FOOT, shoe) associates." A fourth group gave "predicate-type" responses —adjective-noun, noun-adjective. Such findings, Moran concludes, suggest that the commonality hierarchies of most words are "largely determined by the proportions of set 'types' in the normative sample. While the averaged frequencies shown in such tables may be of use in linguistics, they can be misleading as psycholinguistic indexes of 'association strength' of stimulus-response word pairs for persons who use the language." High commonality, says Moran, appears in the responses to certain stimulus-words of a sort which happen to occur in a large number in the K-R list, but which "are actually extremely rare in the English language. Most stimulus words evoke a wide variety of low-frequency associates."

Thus the relation between commonality and reaction-time based upon the combined responses of many subjects is not a continuous function; the various segments of the ostensible relation are dominantly determined by different subgroups of the heterogeneous population. There are of course important and interesting questions of individual differences— which are obscured by the pretence that a confounding of such differences reveals relations in an ideal individual; e.g., to what extent is uniqueness or commonality of response characteristic of individuals, and to what other behavior characteristics, including average association-time, may such differences be related? It would seem to be a statistical truism that if various individuals are to appear in a distribution or in a functional relationship, each individual should be represented by his average or other statistic and not by a population of scores intermingled with the score populations of other individuals; e.g., each individual might be represented in a graph by a coordinate point defined by his average commonality and his average association-time. But a functional relationship which exists only within an individual must be demonstrated in terms of the scores made by single individuals (cf. Mandler, 1963, p. 246). This has been attempted, for the relation between frequency and reaction-time, by Cason and Cason (1925); using the K-R words, they found for 28 subjects correlations ranging from —0.11 to —0.59. However, the frequency scores used were not those of the individual subjects but those published by K-R, and the association-times were measured by stopwatch; thus only the dubious association-times were measures of the individual subjects.

In the second place, the notion of a generalized relation between associative-response frequency and latency implies a continuous universe of verbal units whose probabilities of occurrence are represented at any time by the number of individuals of a large group who give these responses on given occasions. But perhaps there is better reason to assume that verbal response mechanisms are organized into somewhat discontinuous systems. The phenomena of controlled association strongly suggest such organization (cf. Loring, 1918, p. 370), and the normal highly selective—syntactically and semantically—occurrence of verbal units in speech depends upon such controlled-association organization. More generally, "set" would seem to be a universal selective factor in behavior; "free" behavior, in the sense of free association, occurring in accordance with some general probability function regardless of the past history and existing state of an individual nervous system, is hardly a recognizable phenomenon. Moreover, it is not a phenomenon which would be predicted from the work of the physiologists—e.g., Lorente de No—on central excitability states, according to which the firing of centers is not determined simply by intercurrent afferent volleys from any given sensory source but is dependent upon central excitatory and inhibitory states which in turn depend upon preceding and concurrent afferent and internuncial activity; there is evidence also—e.g., Morley and Stohlman (1969)—that such biological systems are subject to "intrinsic" oscillations (cf. Esper, 1968, pp. 193ff.). It is difficult to imagine a neutral state in which "associative strength as such" could be measured. I fear that the preceding discussion leads to the disconcerting conclusion that there can be no such thing as free association, that in the so-called free-association experiment the various subjects respond according to individually variable, experimentally uncontrolled momentary sets, so that the various responses are not comparable or functionally continuous either intra-individually or inter-individually. McGinnies (1950) found some evidence of a positive relationship between reaction-times and the individual subjects' personal values as "measured" by the Allport-Vernon scale (cf. Jenkins, 1960).

That the experimental conditions are not under reasonable control in free-association experiments is suggested by the association-time distributions, which usually show marked positive skewing. An extreme example of this is afforded by a distribution published by Williams (1937), in which the main distribution falls between the values of 1 and 5 seconds, approximately, but the tail is shown extending out to 30 seconds. The reaction of many experimenters to such distributions has been, not that the data were intolerably heterogeneous, the experimental controls inadequate, or the behavioral and statistical analysis insufficient, but that assumed continuous relationships were being obscured by the "raw" scores and that these relationships might be revealed by an appropriate "transformation" of the scores, preferably a transformation which would produce a distribution approximating the normal probability function. Thus Williams, finding that when log T-score is plotted against 1/time, a "very nearly linear" plot results, concludes that "the velocity of association in this type of test varies normally—within the restriction that the disturbing process varies proportionally with time." The "disturbing process" referred to is "emotional tension," which is assumed "to be present in all reactions, becoming increasingly great, however, in more than linear fashion with lengthened time." The experimental design, however, provides no measure of emotional tension, and the assumption that association-time is such a measure is gratuitous. As Wells (1911b) remarked long ago about association-times of 10 seconds and more, "terrible indeed must have been the emotional complexes stirred up in these associations if the time be directly proportional to the affective reaction. As a matter of fact, the group appears commonplace enough in everything but time, including such reactions as *fruit-apples, deep-ocean, rough-smooth, cabbage-leaves, city-town.* . . . Often by using a little 'summation,' repeating the stimulus word in a sharper tone, an entirely ordinary response is elicited with slight delay." In other words, what many of these long so-called association-times are measuring is non-experimental wool-gathering. It would seem that the burden of proof is on the experimenter if he wishes to maintain that "association" responses of 30 or 10 or even 5 seconds belong to the same experimental population or causal system as do responses of 1 or 2 seconds. This problem arose at the very beginning of word-association work; Cattell (1886) discussed "the method of deducing a correct average from the separate experiments":

Two methods have been employed: either all the reactions measured have been averaged together, or those times which the experimenter thought too long or too short have been altogether ignored. There are however serious objections to both of these methods. . . . I have used a different and, as far as I am aware, new method. . . . Either 13 or 26 reactions were made in a series; the average of these reactions was calculated, and the variation of each reaction from this average. Then the reaction having the largest variation was dropped, the average of the 12 or 25 reactions was calculated, and the reaction varying most from this average was again dropped. This process was continued until the 3 or 6 worst reactions had been dropped, I then having the 10 or 20 best reactions, and the variation of each of these from the average. (p. 229)

It should be observed that by this method many of the "corrected" averages were longer than the uncorrected. Interest has usually been directed more especially to the reaction-times which were "too long." Thus Lang (1943) suggested that a "too long reaction-time" be defined as any reaction-time longer than the shortest 10 percent of the reaction-times obtained from an individual on a given test. Jung (1918, p. 263) had recommended that all responses of an individual longer than that individual's median be regarded as "delayed." "In this way we deal pretty well with all the times delayed by emotion." Lang, whose interest, like that of Jung, was clinical, feared that some "complex indicators" would be missed by Jung's method. He gave the association test to "ten normal female uneducated Mental Hospital attendants" on ten occasions (on eight successive days, then after six weeks, and again after a further six weeks). He found about twice as many "complex indicators" associated with reaction-times above the median as were associated with those below the median, and this difference persisted through the ten repetitions, though the mean reaction-time decreased; the number of changes in response to the same stimuli showed a relationship to reaction-time similar to that shown by the complex indicators.

S&H found that when the association-times of their first 40 subjects were converted into logarithms they yielded an approximately normal distribution except at the extremes. When separate distributions were made of the log association-times for unique responses and for responses with a commonality of 76 percent—the extreme degrees of commonality in this experiment—it was found that the upper 10 percent of the unique responses were "too slow" while the lower 10 percent of the high-commonality responses were "too fast" (in comparison with a normal distribution). Similar distributions for seven intermediate degrees of commonality showed a gradual shift from one type of distortion to the other. S&H conclude that "it is a combination of these distortions that yields the distribution found for 1000 responses of mixed communality. Hence, one should not devote further attention to the heterogeneous distribution, for its exact form will depend on the original choice of stimulus words." But even if "one should not devote further attention to the heterogeneous distribution" because of the varying degrees of commonality, it would seem that the remaining sources of heterogeneity within the commonality classes would not be removed by the process of logarithmic transformation. For the various measures within each commonality class are still being determined by varying subgroups of individuals, under varying sets, responding with various words to varying subgroups of stimulus-words. I cannot agree with S&H that their results "indicate that one may legitimately perform many statistical operations on association times if they are first normalized by converting them into logarithms." Before resorting to this statistical sweeping-under-the-rug procedure, it might be well to experiment extensively on the effects of various sorts of experimental control on the distributions of association-times; e.g., Hall and Ugelow (1957) found that associative latencies were negatively related to frequencies of occurrence in the language of stimulus-words and to commonality of responses. Moreover, we need to remember that words, as units of language, always occur in contexts; if they can be said to have associative "frequencies," they have them within contextual systems, and these systems have their physiological loci in individual nervous systems. As for numerical transformations, Chapanis (1953) has pointed out that they have important consequences which "are generally ignored in most statistics textbooks written for psychologists."

The reason usually given for the skewing of reaction-time distributions seems to be that while physiological factors impose a lower limit there is no definite upper limit for reaction-times. While a fairly well-practiced subject may give most of his responses easily and promptly, some subjects will be caught on some stimulus-words in a moment of blankness or inattention, or some stimulus-words may produce a block or conflict, or initiate responses which have to be suppressed. As the seconds pass, the subject may become increasingly disturbed by the delay of his response, since the social situation in an association test is rather compulsive. At the high end of a distribution we may therefore expect to find a number of values which have been produced by special factors and which therefore do not belong to the general population of scores. On the other hand, we may find at the low end of the distribution some scores which are artifacts of measurement or of response; the subject may have preceded some of his responses with a preparatory "uh——" or in some other way tripped a voice-key, or if the experimenter is operating a manual key he may lag in pressing it when giving the stimulus-word or press it in anticipation of the response; the subject may also give a word which he had in readiness following the "ready" signal in anticipation of the stimulus-word or in response merely to the auditory signal of the initiation of the stimulus-word, i.e., without bothering to respond associatively. Some experimenters have arbitrarily rejected all responses which required more than some predetermined time, e.g., 5 seconds. It would perhaps be more justifiable to record all of the reaction-times and reject those which a subsequent analysis showed not to belong to the general population of scores. But is there a general or homogeneous population of scores? Are we justified, e.g., in throwing together the 5,000 responses made by 200 subjects to 25 different stimulus-words given by 200 different experimenters? Does the fact that logarithmic scaling of these scores gives an approximately "normal" distribution sufficiently encourage us to assume that all or almost all of these scores were determined by varying potencies of the same causal factors, acting independently and non-dominantly? Or would we be attempting here something analogous to our late unfortunate efforts to bind together different performances at different "stages" of learning into an "equation of the learning curve"? I am sufficiently dubious about this to be dubious also about drawing inferences from such distributions of association-times concerning hypothetical "excitation processes" in the cortices of individuals.

It is true that attempts have been made to relate the associative reaction-time of individuals to the controlled history of the previous stimulations of those individuals. Thus Wiggins (1957) had subjects learn paired-associate nonsense syllables, independently varying the frequency of given associates and the number of different associates paired with a given stimulus-syllable. He obtained results which suggested that "the fact that group-response frequencies are negatively related to group-response latencies may be a consequence of the fact that individuals' previous S-R histories with the words involved tend to be reflected in group norms." Unfortunately, his sophistication in experimental design was not matched by an equal linguistic sophistication; the syllables were presented visually, and they were phonemically ambiguous.

We have seen that the association studies of Thumb and Marbe at the turn of the century were an expression of a lively interaction between linguists and psychologists which found echoes in the literatures of both sciences. In linguistics, interest in the psychological processes of association which were presumed to underlie analogical assimilations was greatly stimulated by the importance which the neogrammarians had come to attach to analogy as a regularizing agent in language and, of course, as an explanation of exceptions to phonetic laws. In psychology, not a few eminent German scientists—e.g., Ebbinghaus and Marbe—had had university training in linguistics; moreover, a thorough training in Greek and Latin in the gymnasial years and lectures and reading in philology in the university were quite common features of German education. In America, these sources of shared interest were lacking. Thumb and Marbe have been cited—though not read—by numerous psychologists, but solely as the source of "Marbe's Law"; the problem of analogic change which interested Thumb and Marbe and which furnished the motivation for Esper's (1918) replication of their study has gained little attention. This is all the more the case now that American psychologists, under the influence of transformational-generative grammar, are concentrating on questions of synchronic linguistics and universal grammar.

The present lively interaction between psychologists and linguists can perhaps be said to date from the report which John B. Carroll made in 1950 to the Carnegie Corporation, entitled "A Survey of Linguistics and Related Disciplines," and which was published, in revised form, in 1953 as *The Study of Language.* This was the first systematic attempt in America and in recent time to relate psychological research, as practiced by psychologists, to linguistics, as known to professional linguists. In 1951 a summer research seminar in psychology and linguistics was held at Cornell University. In 1952 the Social Science Research Council set up a Committee on Linguistics and Psychology, which sponsored a seminar in psycholinguistics at Indiana University in the summer of 1953; the proceedings of this seminar, published under the editorship of Osgood and Sebeok (1954), contained a section on "Transitional Organization: Association Techniques" by James J. Jenkins. In this section, Jenkins presented the view of the significance of word-association for linguistics which he tentatively held on the basis of the research results then available:

> The general assumption being made here is that emission of any ante-cedent response increases the probability of occurrence of a hierarchy of interrelated subsequent responses. It is also assumed, of course, that these intraverbal connections arise in the same manner in which any skill se-quence arises, through repetition, contiguity, differential reinforcement. It should be recognized that this analysis does not lead immediately to a tool for breaking down contextual effects. Any utterance (especially a single word) may be thought of as belonging to a large number of response hierarchies, sound classes, form classes, sequence classes, frequency classes, etc. The analysis does suggest, however, experimental techniques for deal-ing with fragments of context in simple situations in which their specific influences may be more precisely studied. . . . [In controlled association, e.g., instructions to give opposites] it is as if a major portion of the response hierarchy were removed and only the specific subportion designated by dual class membership (related to stimulus word and opposition) were available. . . . (Jenkins, 1954, p. 113)
>
> Word associations may be interpreted as a result of relative distribu-tion of the stimuli and responses. The similarity between any two words can be conceived linguistically as the degree of similarity in distribution. However, it seems apparent that this similarity may be profitably divided into two classes, *paradigmatic* and *syntagmatic*. Two words are considered paradigmatically similar to the extent that they are substitutable in the identical frame . . . and syntagmatic to the extent that they follow one another in utterances. (Jenkins, 1954, p. 115)

Following a suggestion by Ervin (1957), Brown and Berko (1960) utilized the distinction between paradigmatic and syntagmatic associa-tions to demonstrate the differences between children's and adults' word-associations. (They used however the terms *homogeneous*="paradig-matic" and *heterogeneous*="syntagmatic.") They found not only that the proportion of paradigmatic associations increased with age but that in a "usage test" in which nonsense words were presented in various syn-tactic positions, the ability to create new sentences in which the nonsense words were "correctly" used according to the presented models also increased with age. These results were of course in accordance with the findings of various authors over the past half-century that educated adults tend more than do children and uneducated adults to give associates of the same grammatical and semantic class as the stimulus-words. However, Brown and Berko offer an interesting explanation for these observed changes with age: "*Bright* has more sentence contexts in common with *dark* than with such another adjective as *virtuous*. It is our general hypothesis that, as utilization of syntax develops in children, syntactic similarity in words becomes an increasingly important determinant of word association and that the developmental trend from [heterogeneous] responses toward [homogeneous] responses is a manifestation of this great step forward into syntactic operations." It will be noted that "paradigmatic" similarity cannot be defined exclusively in formal syntactic terms as "belonging to the same substitution-class." Using some illustrations of Jenkins, we find that the sentence-frame "I saw a ——" could be completed by almost any member of the form-class noun, but other frames could be suggested which would progressively narrow the choice, not with respect to grammatical category, but semantically; when we arrive at the frame "I like to sit in an easy ——" the choice is almost limited to *chair*. Syntagmatic similarity, on the other hand, "can be extended to include both words of the same as well as different form classes. . . . If we include the frame 'I bought a table and ——' we can establish a syntagmatic similarity between words of the same form class" (Jenkins, 1954, pp. 115f.). The organization which is reflected in word-association is thus not based solely on formal categories but is expressive also of semantic relationships.[42]

The Brown-Berko hypothesis was further applied to children's associations by Ervin (1961). She stated that "a paradigmatic response [in word-association]—that is, a response in the same grammatical class—

42. Cf. Deese (1965, p. 55): "A form class is a large but weak set of equivalences. As the equivalences become stronger . . . the sets become smaller, and we are more likely to describe the relation between the linguistic forms as one of meaning rather than grammar. The distinction, in the present context, between grammar and meaning is difficult to maintain in view of the great usefulness of regarding both grammatical and meaningful relationships among distributions of associations as arising from equivalences of frames in ordinary discourse."

might arise through similarity of referents, common affixes, or common past verbal contexts. . . . Two words may be said to be contextually similar to the degree that their past verbal environments overlap." She found that "there was a significant increase with age in the proportion of responses in the same grammatical class as the stimulus-word, with an earlier increase in words occurring more often in final position in sentences than in words typically medial in sentences." It had been predicted that "if a word occurs frequently in the final position of a sentence, it has relatively weak syntagmatic associations." (Ervin's estimates of the frequencies of syntactic sequences in children's speech were obtained from an analysis of the sequences in children's books.)

Entwisle, Forsyth, and Muuss (1964) presented high-frequency (Thorndike-Lorge, 1944) nouns, adjectives, and verbs to children 5, 6, 8, and 10 years of age. They found that commonality and number of paradigmatic responses increase rapidly with advancing age over the 5-to-10-year-old interval. They suggest that early "heterogeneous" responses (those not belonging to the same form-class as the stimulus-words) are not necessarily syntactic but may be "randomly selected," whereas "homogeneous" responses are more nearly equivalent to "paradigmatic" responses. Thus the shift with age and education might best be described as from non-paradigmatic to paradigmatic. The authors however suggest that there is an intermediate stage in which heterogeneous responses become increasingly syntactic.

The classification problem is important chiefly because a phase of syntactic responding suggests much more about the natural process of language acquisition than a phase of heterogeneous responding. A phase of syntactic responding suggests, among other things, that language may first be internalized in functional chunks that become dissected and differentiated with continued exposure and usage. The units of language comprehension may be phrases or larger parts of sentences, since obviously young children have no means of knowing what a word is defined to be, except by hearing it preceded and followed by various other sounds. This must be true especially for parts of speech other than nouns. (Entwisle et al., 1964, p. 21)

Nouns, the authors suggest, are the words which are most easily isolated by children and identified with referents. "With kindergarten children the number of noun responses is very high, irrespective of the form-class of the stimulus-word. . . . The amount of homogeneity for nouns increases only slightly from kindergarten to 5th grade." The authors consider their results to be consistent with Ervin's (1963) generalization: "low contextual variety following the stimulus word produced syntagmatic associates," and add, "This hypothesis is useful also in accounting for the fact that high-frequency adjectives apparently yield higher levels of paradigmatic responding than high-frequency nouns, for contextual variety must be greater for adjectives. The number of high-frequency adjectives in the English language is markedly less than the number of high-frequency nouns."

Though there was no historical connection, the study by Ervin (1963) might be said to be a modern attempt to answer the prime question raised by Thumb in the passage which I quoted above, pages 70–71: under what conditions do particular word- or form-associations arise? Ervin suggests that the "frequency of any particular response word for a high-frequency stimulus [may be predicted] as a function of four variables: its frequency as a substitute; its frequency just preceding the stimulus word in sentences; its frequency just following in sentences; and its relative frequency in single-word utterances." She summarized the prediction as a statement of multiple regression and attempted to find quantitative expressions of these variables and of their contributions to the prediction of associative responses. In experiments with young adults, Ervin, in addition to word-association tests, had subjects write sentences containing the stimulus-words and then write words which might be substituted for the key word in each sentence. She found that

for most stimulus words, the best predictor of associative frequency was the frequency with which the response could replace the stimulus in the same linguistic frames or contexts. . . . Common associative responses were most likely to be paradigmatic or substitution-responses when the variety of contexts in which the stimulus word is used was great. . . . For many words, contextual [i.e., syntactic contiguity] frequency was also a predictor of associative frequency, more often for the following context than for the preceding context. This asymmetry of contextual association appears to be a consequence of English syntactical structure rather than inherent in associative processes.

Ervin herself points out that her technique left open the question whether occurrence or substitution in sentences influences association, or the other way round, and there have been a variety of other alternative or dissenting opinions. Perhaps the leading dissenter—though he accepted Ervin's results in part—has been Deese (1965). Deese has taken the field against the law of contiguity, which, since ancient times, has been assumed to be the main principle of association. "The central thesis of this book," he says, "asserts that what is important about associations is not what follows what, but how sets of associations define structured patterns of relations among ideas." Cofer (1967c) remarks, "I think it is not easy to reject the principle of contiguity on the basis of the kind of evidence brought forth in this book," and it has seemed to me that Deese's adherence to his principle has resulted in a certain blindness; thus he says, "It is hard to think of the word *hot* as providing the principal or even a moderately frequent linguistic environment for the word *cold*," as though he had never heard of *hot and cold running water, to blow hot and cold*, etc., or, for opposites in general, such frequent collocations as *through thick and thin, here and there, young and old, in black and white,* etc. I am dubious also about the experimental technique used by Deese (and other leading experimenters); the stimulus-words were printed in a booklet, and the 100 or so subjects wrote their associates in a single group session; varied results have been reported in comparisons of this group visual-manual method with the individual aural-oral method; for association experiments relevant to analogical processes in language, however, the individual aural-oral method seems to me to be the method of choice (cf. Jenkins and Palermo, 1965; Palermo, 1963; and Entwisle and Forsyth, 1963). I am inclined to doubt also the relevance to the process of analogical change of association experiments performed with an array of stimulus-words chosen from word-frequency tables so as to constitute a scale from very frequently to very rarely used words; analogical changes would seem to require a high coincidence of primary associates among the members of a speech community; the results at hand do not suggest that infrequently used words have the individual-social properties requisite for analogy. And finally, it seems a regrettable limitation of the group method that no reaction-time measures are obtained; such measures are, as Thumb and Marbe believed, of considerable value in association studies related to analogical processes and might have resolved some of Deese's dubieties.

Deese's basic concept is that of the "associative meaning" of a word, defined as the distribution of the associative responses to the word; identical distributions for two words would define synonymy; the proportion of associative responses which words have in common gives the index of commonality. It is found that the indices of commonality of words belonging to a semantic set—e.g., names of animals—are greater than those of semantically unrelated words. Deese applies factor analysis to these relationships, and, as has so often happened, emerges from his laborious calculations with the semantic factors by which he had selected his sets of stimulus-words; thus little is gained. As Howes (1967) has said, "It is illusory to attribute greater objectivity to patterns just because they emerge from the mouth of a statistical meat-grinder." Deese argues that Ervin's explanation of the increase, with the age of children, of paradigmatic associations at the expense of syntagmatic associations—namely, the explanation that this results from the increasing variety of contexts—cannot be applied to the associations of adults, because he found no correlation in adults between syntagmatic associations and frequency of usage. But if, as several writers have suggested, verbal organization in adults becomes asymptotic, I cannot see the relevance of this objection; moreover, the inclusion in the tests of rarely used words perhaps takes us outside the system of ordinary oral language in which occur the "normal"— i.e., socially shared—processes of linguistic organization. Deese's argument is further confused by his use of the term *syntagmatic* to refer to associations which, he claims, cannot be supposed to result from syntactic contiguities, and which are therefore "like the paradigmatic associates" although they do not belong to the same form-class as the stimulus-word. Deese's argument that associative relations result, typically, not from word-contiguities, but from relations of "meaningfulness"—either because of semantic "equivalence" of words, expressed by their possible use in similar syntactic positions, or because of their belonging to a semantic complex which can include words of different form-classes—this argument is chiefly illustrated by results obtained with noun and adjective stimulus-words. The intended emphasis is on the organizing function of the human individual in contrast to the influence of random environmental contiguities. It might be suggested, however, that animal—including human —viability depends to a considerable extent on stimulus-response contiguities enforced by the environment, and that the concept of learning— now in ill-repute in cognitive circles—is very appropriate in dealing with behavioral matching to environmental contiguities, particularly in anticipatory adjustments to events by means of responses to signal-cues (cf. Esper, 1964, p. 177).

Of nouns, Deese says that they "do not have associations which readily appear in the immediate environment of the stimulus."

> This character of nouns makes a strong case for the stimulus-equivalence model for the development of associations. . . . It is possible that adults have so thoroughly learned the grammatical (sentence position) property of nouns that, without any intervening steps, nouns come to yield nouns, even though only the thinnest of experiential threads may bind a new noun to some old ones. . . . (Deese, 1965, p. 110)

Not all of the responses to any given noun are nouns of the same type as the stimulus. Often they do not fit the linguistic distribution of the nominal stimulus. For example, the noun *basket* elicits *paper, bread, food,* and *waste* in high frequency. Or, again, *bedtime* elicits *sleep* and *music.* The rare word, *academician,* yields, among other nominal associates, *academy, school,* and *diploma.* Therefore, while we may characterize the majority of responses to nouns as nouns, the responses are not always the same kinds of nouns as the stimuli, and often they may be fitted into common environments only in unusual and awkward constructions.

The implications of this fact are several and important. For one thing, it becomes immediately obvious that we cannot completely describe the paradigmatic associates to nouns within a supraordinate, subordinate, co-ordinate scheme. For another, it is certain that grouping nouns on the basis of their associative intersections does not sort these nouns according to the nature of the events and objects to which they refer. An *academician* and a *school* certainly cannot be said to be similar in their natures, though they clearly "belong together." It would seem that some nouns are thought of not only in connection with other concepts which share descriptive attributes but with concepts that are merely present with or related to the noun in question. Furthermore, it is at least a reasonable hypothesis that such words would more likely occur at different positions within the same sentences than as substitutes for one another within the same sentence. (Deese, 1965, p. 144)

While Deese had found no correlation between frequency of syntagmatic associates and frequency of usage for nouns, he found a significant negative correlation for adjectives; that is, the associates of the frequently used common adjectives were predominantly paradigmatic—either synonyms or antonyms, whereas "to some extent, the meaning of rare adjectives derives from the meaning of underlying roots borrowed from other form-classes, mainly from the class of nouns, and that condition accounts for the syntagmatic distributions to rare adjectives." In a study limited to common adjectives, Deese found that the paradigmatic associates were overwhelmingly opposites, whereas low-frequency adjectives commonly yield synonymic associates and very uncommon adjectives most often yield syntagmatic associates. Of the 278 common adjectives used by Deese, he found that 78, related semantically in pairs as polar opposites, were reciprocally related in association—i.e., each elicited the other as its primary associate.

As to the "cause" of associations, Deese states, as his general principle, "associative intersections are the outcome of shared contexts—of partial equivalences." But he finds it necessary to qualify this proposition: he points out that there may be associative relations between words which, though they belong to the same grammatical form-class, "have fundamentally different functions in sentences," and between others which do not belong to the same form-class but belong to the same small semantic class or sequential collocation. And rather surprisingly, he states (p. 140), "There is, then, considerable evidence for the correspondence between associative patterns and the contextual patterns of underlying sentences. The referential meaning of the contrasting members of pairs must be the outcome of some contingencies between events in the natural world and these words." Thus it appears that Deese has not succeeded in wholly exorcising the ancient principle of contiguity.

I think that we now have before us the general nature of the findings and hypotheses which have resulted from experimental work on word-association, or at least—for the literature has become vast and includes much that is of dubious quality—we have as much as is relevant to the problem of linguistic analogy. We must ask, what sort of word-associations are likely to be correlated with analogical changes and why are they so correlated? Between word-associations and analogical changes it does not seem to me to be likely that there is a causal connection—that word-associations cause analogical changes. Rather, it seems likely that word-associations are products of the same tendencies as give rise to the "associative interferences" of analogical change, blending, and contamination. Long ago I presented this view of the matter as follows:

> It has been sufficiently demonstrated in earlier studies that in English, as well as in other languages, certain words will elicit the same associations on the part of from 60 to 90 per cent. of any sufficiently large group of individuals, with very short average reaction-times. It is also known that these words have been involved in considerable analogic change in the histories of the various languages. And thus, in conformity with the psychological doctrines current in nineteenth century linguistics, the analogical changes have been causally attributed to the associations. If a word *a* is strongly associated with a word *b* (so runs the explanation), then the *idea* of *a* not only tends to arouse the corresponding articulation but also the *idea* of *b*, the latter tending also to arouse a corresponding articulation. The result will frequently be an *Entgleisung*, a "derailment," the articulation of *b* beginning before that of *a* has been completed. Or, to put the matter in more modern physiological terms, if the sound and articulation of a word *a* have become conditioned stimuli tending strongly to elicit word *b*, then the beginning of the articulation of *a* may activate the *b* mechanism so strongly that an interference of responses results.
>
> There are serious weaknesses in this explanation. Chief among these is the fact that though certain associations are found to be almost universal at the present time, and very constant and prompt in most individuals, they yet show very little tendency to produce mixtures of articulation. And, on the other hand, very many of the momentary *lapsūs linguae* which have been reported by various writers do not involve words between which

strong or common associations can be demonstrated. Secondly, it is extremely doubtful whether, if a verbal mechanism *b* must first be aroused by another verbal mechanism *a*, it can be set in operation so quickly as to interfere with the articulation of *a*. And, finally, it seems highly unlikely that whenever a situation calls out, e.g., the verbal response *black*, this word should automatically drag forth the word *white*, regardless of the nature of the stimulating situation [and the history and internal state of the individual].

These deficiencies in the traditional explanation seem to me to proceed from an almost total neglect of the relationship of verbal responses to the stimulus situations [including the total verbal context] which elicit them, and of the fundamental question of how the verbal associations themselves come to be established.

Why do certain words associatively elicit specific other words? The explanation offered by one of Thumb's critics was that the subjects *auf Schulbänken gesessen haben*. And, indeed, this would seem to indicate one type of situation in which verbal associations might well be established. For so far as our knowledge of the conditions of learning goes, if a sound-sequence or articulation *a* is to elicit an articulation *b*, then *a* and *b* must have occurred simultaneously or successively a certain number of times. Obviously, in the rote memorizing of grammatical paradigms, arithmetic tables, etc., such conditions are met, and this must account for much of the uniformity which we find in the associations of most [educated] individuals. But linguistic change did not begin with the foundation of schools, nor is it absent among unschooled populations today. And I have not found the associations of uneducated individuals or young children to differ much from those of the educated, *when the stimulus-words are chosen from the more universal and common stock of the language.*

The more general principle would be that the stimuli resulting from one verbal response become capable of eliciting a specific other response whenever there is a frequent occurrence of environmental situations which tend to elicit both responses simultaneously or successively. An environmental situation might elicit such multiple responses either because it contains *both* of the objects [or features] *a* and *b*, each of which tends to elicit its own specific response, or because it contains an object *a* which tends to elicit not only its own specific response but also the response specific to another (absent) object [or feature] *b*. . . . For the specificity of stimulus objects and of responses is a relative matter; every object in the world has some characteristics in common with other objects, and may on occasion elicit the verbal responses which are relatively specific to these other objects. Experimenters who work with "nonsense" material know how impossible it is to obtain any pattern, however fantastic, which does not set off some conventional verbalization. Thus when we say that a certain response is the specific response to an object [or situation], we are really stating a statistical probability: given numerous occurrences of this object, this response is the one which will occur most frequently.

The above formulation would mean a reversal of the traditional explanation; it is not the associations which cause the variations in response, but the tendency to variability is responsible for the associations. Thus both mixtures of articulation and verbal associations proceed from a common cause: the tendency of certain stimulus-objects to elicit multiple responses. It will be true, of course, that if we find a word *a* closely associated with a word *b* on the part of many individuals, this may serve as evidence that certain stimulus situations have had a strong tendency to elicit simultaneously or successively the two responses, and that under certain additional conditions this may result in mixtures of articulation. But, as has been pointed out above, mixtures of articulation may occur between words which are not at all strongly associated; a certain stimulus situation occurs which for the first time in the individual's history activates two particular verbal mechanisms simultaneously, and a "contamination" may result in the absence of any demonstrable previous association. A verbal association therefore tells us at most what verbal mechanisms have tended to be simultaneously activated most frequently in the past. But it does not tell us under what conditions such simultaneous activation will take the form of contamination or analogic change. (Esper, 1933, pp. 375–377)

Experimental results published in recent years require some amplification of the account given above. We have already seen that the "contiguity" which results in word-associations may be at one or more removes: i.e., that two words which have not actually occurred in contiguity may nevertheless become associatively connected by their having occurred in the same position in sentence-frames and thus having become members of a "substitution class." (Cf. Glucksberg and Cohen, 1965, who demonstrated this tendency in nonsense material.) But such associations do not depend merely on similarity of syntactic position; there must also be, in addition, some rather narrowly defined semantic similarity or contrast. Moreover, as Jenkins (1960) has shown, associations vary both with contextual stimuli and conditions and also with the intraverbal habits of individuals—there are "low-commonality" subjects (such as Thumb and Marbe's "Dr. Roos") who produce "a wide range of responses of relatively low strength which appear to shift and change from time to time"; we shall see that I also found reason, in a different sort of experiment, to postulate individual differences in the likelihood of contributions to analogic processes.

The concept of mediation has been prominent in discussions of the origin of word-associations (Jenkins, 1959, 1963, 1964). The simplest mediation paradigm, that for "chaining," is symbolized: Learn A→B, then learn B→C, then be tested for A→C. In the experiments, these symbols have commonly represented verbal units, e.g., nonsense syllables, and hence both stimuli and responses have been verbal. It has been found that not only do the stimuli become attached to their responses, but by "backward association" the original responses become stimuli for responses which were originally their stimuli. Moreover, in order for two items to become associated, it is not necessary for them to be experienced in direct contiguity; it is enough if they have both been experienced in contiguity with a third item. Jenkins (1964) has translated these relations into linguistic examples which reveal that the paradigm is that of linguistic analogy, and also that of the acquisition of form-classes:

> Baby cry
> Johnny cry
> Baby eat
> Johnny eat

No matter how these are initially learned, they should have a common outcome. *Baby* and *Johnny* should fall into one class and *cry* and *eat* into another with an ordering rule or contingency between the classes. Given now *Mary cry*, we would not be at all surprised to obtain *Mary eat* with external stimulus support. We expect that the structuring which seems to be a direct consequence of the mediating activities of learning sequences would be further supported by physical or functional stimulus generalizations which are extralinguistic, i.e., existing out in the referential world. The fact that there are semantic correlates of many grammatical classes (even though the correlations are not perfect) obviously simplifies the formation of equivalence structures.

143

At another level we might anticipate structures such as:

Where is the doggie?
Where is the kitty?
There is the doggie.
There is the kitty.

It would take a great deal of time to elaborate all that might be learned in a series such as this but immediately the equivalence of the *doggie* and *kitty* terms and the development of a relationship between *Where* and *There* is apparent. (Phrase structure and intonation pattern contingencies may also be extracted.) If *Here is the doggie* is now introduced, we may safely infer the possibility of *Here is the kitty* and expect a linkage of *Here* to the *Where, There* cluster which is emerging. (Jenkins, 1964, pp. 94f.)

Chapter 6

STUDIES WITH MINIATURE
LINGUISTIC SYSTEMS

Toward the end of Chapter 4, I quoted Thumb's suggestion that it might be profitable to try "to produce analogy-formations experimentally . . . in artificial sound-formations." In 1921–1922 I attempted to carry out this suggestion by means of "miniature linguistic systems" (MLS) (Esper, 1925). In my first studies, there were four nonsense figures in the four colors red, green, blue, and yellow, for which the subjects were orally and individually taught nonsense names in successive learning trials and on which they were tested in recognition trials; each subject appeared on seven days distributed over a period of two months. Two of the sixteen shape-color combinations were omitted in the learning trials but included in the recognition trials. Three degrees of correlation between the figures and the names were provided in different experiments with different sets of subjects.

In Experiment I, the names consisted of two elements which were exactly correlated with the factors of color and shape in the figures, and which conformed to English speech habits of word-order and syllable division—e.g., *nas-deg* = red + shape 3. Under these conditions, learning was very rapid and there was practically no forgetting thirty days after the last learning; the names of the two figures omitted from the learning series were learned, by analogy with the other names and figures, at about the same rate as the names of the other figures; there were very few cases of associative interference, and no definite tendencies toward the development of further linguistic categories.

In Experiment II, the names consisted of two elements which were exactly correlated with the factors of shape and color in the figures but which deviated from English speech habits in word-order and syllable division—e.g., *nu-gdet* = shape 1 + green. Under these conditions, learning was slow and incomplete; the names of the two figures omitted from the learning series were learned but slightly; there were numerous cases of associative interference; there was a general tendency to modify the non-English syllable division in accordance with English speech habits, and this tendency took the form of assimilating the words within each shape category to a particular word of that category—e.g., *nu-gdet* > *nul-det*, *nu-mbow* > *nul-bow*, after *nu-lgen*; there was a tendency to assimilate the syllable for shape 1 to that for shape 2—e.g., *nulgen* > *nojlgen*, after *dojlgen*—so that there would arise a further linguistic category which would include shapes 1 and 2, the difference between the two being marked by the initial consonant—e.g., *nojlgen* : *dojlgen*.

In Experiment III, the names showed no correlation whatever with the factors of color and shape of the figures. Under these conditions, learning was very slow and incomplete; the responses to the two figures omitted from the learning series—for naming which the material of the experiment provided no analogies—were the names of figures either of the same shape but different color or of the same color but different shape; there were very few cases of associative interference, but those which occurred showed a slight tendency toward the assimilation of the words of each shape category to each other. The most significant conclusions to be drawn from these experiments might seem to be (1) that analogical changes are most likely to occur when semantic similarity is matched with phonemic sequences which are similar but which, in terms of the speakers' speech habits, are irregular; the tendency of analogic change is to smooth out irregularities; (2) that within a category, assimilations are mostly to a particular form of that category; and (3) that when a related set of categories is represented by a phonemically regular pattern of forms, novel stimulus-patterns assignable to these categories elicit appropriate analogical responses without additional learning.

The conditions of experiments such as those described above are of course enormously simplified in comparison with those prevailing in natural languages; I subsequently made a number of attempts to introduce variables such as would be present in actual language behavior; viz., (1) social transmission, (2) high degrees of overlearning, (3) vocal-manual-visual interaction.

In an experiment of 1924 the effects of social transmission were essayed (Esper, 1966). The visual stimulus-objects were four nonsense shapes, each occurring in the colors red and green. Phonetically different names were assigned to these figures, so that the linguistic system was initially a totally suppletive one. I taught these names to the first subject and each subject thereafter taught his successor. I quote my summary of results:

> This experiment has demonstrated that, when a miniature linguistic system characterized by semantic but not by morphologic categories is transmitted from person to person in a long series of individuals, morphologic categories tend to develop in correspondence with the semantic categories. However, in the absence of initial phonetic similarities (which can serve, so to speak, as "morphologic catalysts"), analogical changes leading to morphological categorization seem to depend upon prior phonetic changes, which in an artificial system such as that of this system consist of dialectal variations, extra-experimental interferences, and the various sorts of intra-verbal effects: assimilation, dissimilation, metathesis, anaptyxis, etc. And finally, the record of this experiment illustrates . . . the very unequal parts played by different individuals in these linguistic processes. The variations which result in linguistic systematization seem to be the work chiefly of certain occasional individuals. (Esper, 1966)

In 1925–1926 I observed the responses of twelve persons during a period of some eight months (Esper, 1933). The sixteen nonsense figures varied as to shape (A, B, C, D) and size (1, 2, 3, 4). The phonetic forms of the names assigned to the figures were uncorrelated with the categories of shape and size; i.e., the "system" was totally suppletive. During an initial learning period of about four months the subjects appeared five times per week; thereafter (Period II) they appeared three times per week. Figures A1, B2, C3, and D4 were omitted during the learning period but included during Period II. On three occasions during the learning period and on three occasions during Period II, reaction-times to the figures and association-times to their names were taken; on these occasions reaction-times to familiar objects and association-times to common English words were also taken. I quote the "tentative principles" which the results of the experiment suggested:

1. Instability of verbal reactions results when stimulus-objects, because of common features, tend to activate not only the response most specific to them but also the responses relatively specific to other objects ("multiple responses").

2. This instability is revealed by frequent occurrences of the simultaneous or successive activation by one stimulus-object of two or more response mechanisms, and, where this tendency is strong, by lengthened reaction-time in the verbal response to the object.

3. This simultaneous activation of two or more response mechanisms may result in an interconnection between them, so that the sound or articulation corresponding to the one elicits the other.

4. Verbal associations are possible *results* and indicators, not *causes*, of "multiple response" tendencies such as are exemplified by contamination and analogic change.

5. A very strong verbal association $a \rightarrow b$, when the reverse association $b \rightarrow a$ is weak, may indicate an instability of the response b in relation to its stimulus-object B, rather than an instability of a in relation to its stimulus-object A.

6. When a stimulus-object B, whose name is b, tends to be confused with *two* other objects A and C in about equal degree, the stimulus-response unit $B \rightarrow b$ may be very unstable, but the name b will elicit extremely variable associations, with long association-times.

7. When to a group of named objects there are added new, unnamed objects resembling the others in such an attribute as shape, there will be a temporary increase in the instability of the entire system, but a tendency ensues toward a new equilibrium.... [If we represent the names of the various sizes of any shape category by the letters a, b, c, then we may represent the equilibrium which such a system tends to approach by the pattern *abbc*; that is, if for four sizes only three names are available, such shifts occur as to give sizes 1 and 4 distinctive names, while sizes 2 and 3 elicit a common name. Further, responses a and c will have shorter reaction-times and be more stable than will the b responses. These relationships hold regardless of which of the four sizes was absent during the original learning of the names.]

8. Decided individual differences were found in the manner and degree of verbal organization. Those individuals whose reaction-times are shortest tend to make the most frequent *overt* multiple or variable responses in naming stimulus-objects, but long reaction-times may indicate frequent *implicit* responses of this type, which show their effect in the associative connections between the words. In general, those individuals whose verbal associations show the greatest commonality with those of the group, the greatest constancy, and shortest associative reaction-time show the most consistent and ready tendencies toward organization of the verbal material, especially when this organization involves shiftings and changes in a system of stimulus-response units to restore a disturbed equilibrium. These facts very definitely suggest that the various individuals of a speech community would participate in very different degrees in the initiation of semantic and analogic change. [This conclusion is supported by the following rank-difference correlations: nonsense association-time vs. nonsense association commonality, −0.69; time vs. scatter, 0.85; reaction-times for English naming of familiar objects vs. those for naming the nonsense figures, 0.52; English association-times vs. nonsense association-times, 0.94; English vs. nonsense commonality, 0.84; English vs. nonsense associative scatter, 0.82.]

In 1926–1927 I made a first attempt (as yet unpublished[43]) to study the verbal organization which would arise when pairs of well-trained subjects interacted verbally and manually in response to the visual and aural nonsense stimuli of a miniature linguistic system. In each pair of subjects, one responded verbally to a visual object, thereby aurally stimulating his fellow, who then responded by a hand movement which again stimulated the first subject with the visual object. In 1927–1928, Wolfle (1928) made another attempt to assess the influence of manual responses on verbal organization; his subjects having been trained in an MLS of nine visual figures—in three shapes and three sizes—and their nonsense names, they were then trained to accompany their verbal responses with pressures on two push buttons, of which one designated the shape and the other the size of the figure; verbal and manual reaction-times and verbal associates

---

43. Unfortunately, upon completion of this experiment, which had continued for seven months, I left the University of Illinois for the University of Washington, where I became submerged in a heavy teaching load. In the leisure—and waning strength—of old age, I still had hopes—now extinguished—of publishing this experiment.

and association-times were taken. Wolfle found that "the manual habits set up by the push buttons apparently influenced the linguistic habits only in isolated cases." But, "given the number of errors during learning, the number of repetitions before the figure is named correctly, the reaction time to the figure, and the associations of the figure, not only the occurrence, but the type, of variant response that will be undergone by that figure may be predicted with some accuracy." Stevenson (1929), using the same apparatus and materials as had Wolfle, introduced in the post-learning period three figures of sizes intermediate between the smallest and the medium-sized figures of the learning period, and similarly, three figures of sizes intermediate between the medium-sized and the largest figures. Contrary to expectation, these "new" figures did not induce any predictable contaminations; the responses to these figures were predominantly the names of the regular figures nearest in size, except that the new figures half-way between the regular figures elicited mostly the names of the next larger figures of the same shape. The intercorrelations between reaction-time, association-time, associative scatter, number of errors, etc. showed great individual differences.

The first—and still one of the very few—linguists to take account, in his discussion of analogy, of the laboratory studies of miniature linguistic systems was Gustav Stern (1931, republished 1962, pp. 207–210). Stern used the first two of Esper's (1925) experiments to illustrate his "combinative" type of analogy, a type which he defined as "the naming of a previously unknown—at least momentarily unknown—combination of a basic [= material] and a relational meaning, or of two basic meanings, each meaning being expressed by its own name, except in cases where the relational meaning is left unexpressed, or is expressed by word-order." Stern considered my experiments as having elucidated "the psychic process underlying combinative analogy":

> We have now to explain how it was possible in the first experiment, which is most closely parallel to actual linguistic conditions, to supply the names of the unlearned figures almost as quickly and correctly as those of the other figures.
> It is clearly a case of formation of categories and general concepts. The observers are presented with certain factors running unchanged through a

series of varying concomitants. In such cases, as is well known, the permanent factor may be isolated from its varying surroundings and apprehended as a unit capable of being variously combined with other elements. In this case, the elements are the syllable *nas-* and the quality of redness, the syllable *-kop* and a certain shape, and so on. This shape, and the quality of redness, are then presented to the observer in a new combination, and on condition that the concomitance of the two factors with their respective names has been presented a sufficient number of times, so that they automatically accompany each other in our mind, there will be no difficulty for the observer to analyze the new figure into its elements, and to name it according to the "language system" of the "Morgavian" dialect, although he has never seen the figure before, and has never heard the name he is making up. (p. 209)

Stern bases an objection to Paul's "group theory" on the difference in the results of Esper's (1925) first two experiments:

Why is the process of analogy and learning so much slower in the second case? Taken as totals, the words of the second "language" are not more difficult than those of the first, and the grouping ought therefore to proceed just as easily, with formation of "Proportionengruppen." We should, on Paul's theory, expect the results to be about the same in both experiments. On the other hand, if we adopt the isolation-and-combination theory, we base it on the isolation of elements in the compound words, as names of corresponding elements in the referents. Such isolation requires a word as support. The word is the centre round which the notion crystallizes, and without a name the formation of a general notion is scarcely possible in ordinary circumstances. Now, in the second experiment, the compounds were formed in such a manner that the second element began with a consonant group that cannot be pronounced initially in English: *-zg, -mb*, etc. This difficulty retarded the isolation of the phonetic elements, the names, and so the formation of the general notion; the analogical process would therefore take more time to arrive at a satisfactory result. (p. 212)

Stern rejects Paul's insistence "that an analogical formation is equivalent to the solution of a proportional equation, so that at least three members must be known," and quotes Delacroix (1924, p. 250): "L'analogie linguistique ne consiste aucunement à calculer la quatrième proportionnelle. . . . Il n'y a pas de raisonnement dans l'analogie linguistique; tout au plus l'action de esprit qui continue spontanément un mouvement antérieur." But Stern rejects Delacroix's statement that analogy is the effect of the existence of a system of forms, and that the analogical form issues under the pressure of the form system. Analogy presupposes and imitates patterns, "but the effective factor, the causa movens, is the necessity of filling the functions of speech, and the formal system provides only the pattern or norm for the analogical creation. We find again that the striving to adapt speech to a better fulfilment of its functions is the driving power in the development" (p. 211). Stern points out that when analogical formations occur soon after the end of the second year of life, it is unlikely that the child produces them by the process of solving a proportional analogy.

Besides "combinative analogy," Stern distinguishes "correlative analogy," which consists "in the naming of a referent with a word that is evoked owing to its semantic correlation to another, known word, in the same, or in another, language." Opposites, such as Lat. *gravis—levis* illustrate such relations; synonyms might also be thus associated, but "if a pair of synonyms are confused by a speaker, this does not show that the two words were previously associated with each other, but only that both are associated with the referent that the speaker wants to denote, so that the thought of the referent may call up either word" (p. 226). Throughout his discussion of analogy, Stern is concerned with the notion of "groups," which "are taken to mean only groups that are apprehended as such by linguistic feeling." The basis of his discussion is thus a *Reflexionspsychologie*, which of course he is able to support by numerous linguistic examples. Stern's third type of analogy is "phonetic associative interference," consisting in the semantic influence of one word on another, owing to phonetic similarity. Such contaminations are likely to occur only when the words affected are very unfamiliar, as when nonsense or foreign words are assimilated to familiar words.

In general, I think that Stern's views are concordant with experimental findings, but I would suggest that there is no real psychological difference between his three types. The basic process consists in situations—i.e., environmental, physiological, and syntactic contexts—tending to arouse two different verbal responses, which may or may not have been previously associated. As Stern points out, logicians and linguists may be able to diagram many analogies as proportional equations, but it is absurd to suppose that such operations are implied by analogical changes in language. Nor is Stern's "isolation-and-combination" process more than an "as if" description. Except for those who are willing to rely on introspection or intuition, the actual process involved, whose description would constitute an "explanation," would be physiological, and such explanations are not yet available. In the meantime, all that we can properly say is that under certain circumstances two verbal responses are evoked simultaneously or in quick succession so that a mixture of articulations occurs of the sort which typically increases the regularity of a language. (Stern mentions the German term *Systemzwang* 'systematizing- or leveling-tendency'.) From this point of view I see no operational differences among the terms *analogical change, contamination, blending, crossing, telescoping,* etc. I agree with Stern and with Thumb and Marbe (1901, p. 82) that such changes, while they require models, do not necessarily require a group of models; a word may be—and I would add, usually is—influenced analogically, and is predominantly associated with, a single, or at most a small number, of other words; on a given occasion, the influence is that of a particular other word.

Wolfle (1932) replicated, with variations, the experiments of Esper (1925, 1933). Thus he found that a linguistic system completely correlated with the features of the referents and consistent with English speech habits was learned quickly; there were in the post-learning period few variants (mixtures), and these were very imperfectly correlated with the results of association tests; there was no tendency for associations to become more fixed. But in an experiment in which six of the names were altered phonemically or in syllable order from the system to which the other ten names conformed, learning was slow, associations became more fixed, and though the most frequent associations were not consistently in accord with the most frequent errors (= mistakes consisting in the names of other figures), they did predict the most frequent contaminations, and these contaminations were of the sort which increased the regularity of the system. Since the associations and the general distribution of errors were very similar in the two "languages," whereas the type of error (substitution vs. contamination) differed, Wolfle concluded "that while association may be a necessary antecedent of analogic change, it is not a sufficient cause. Whether or not a given association will result in actual change seems to be a function also of the nature of the names involved and of their systematic relation to the structure of the language." I have given above my reasons for doubting that word-association should be regarded as in any sense a cause of analogic change.

Wolfle (1933) compared the stability of first and second syllables in the dissyllabic names used in his previous (1932) and in Esper's (1925) experiments. In both cases he found that, regardless of the semantic order —size-form vs. form-size or color-shape vs. shape-color—the first syllable was more subject to analogic change than was the second syllable. In what degree syllable stress—on second syllable in Wolfle's experiments, with minimal stress difference in Experiment I and on second syllable in Experiment II of Esper—was a factor in these results is uncertain.

For some thirty years no notice appears to have been taken by psychologists of the experiments with the MLS technique.[44] Carroll (1953)

44. The long isolation of these experiments from the main body of the literature of verbal behavior was perhaps due in part to the lack of interest in and understanding of the problems of historical—particularly of systematizing—changes in language, as these were perceived by Thumb and Marbe. Moreover, the technique introduced by Esper required experimental programs, with a small number of individual subjects, of much longer duration than was customary; the data could not be collected wholesale from large groups within a few weeks. However, much relevant research was being done in the period beginning with Hull's (1920) study of the evolution of concepts and continuing in the work of his pupils, especially Eleanor Gibson (1940), whose concepts of discrimination, differentiation, and generalization are applicable to the MLS experiments; like Gibson, Yum (1931) and Gagné (1950) taught nonsense names for nonsense figures. Lenneberg (1957) performed experiments in which the subjects learned nonsense names for colors, the referential relations of names to hues being distorted from the distributions of occurrence in English in varying degrees in the different experiments. He found that "if the reference relationships in a nonsense language are identical with those in the S's native tongue, the learning task is relatively easy; but distortions in these relationships make the task harder." The extensive literature of concept attainment is of course also relevant (cf. Bourne, 1968). Hawkins (1964), working with young children, found that they could learn to abstract and respond selectively to various components of stimulus compounds when more than one name has been associated with a compound. Steiner and Sobel (1968) present evidence that when verbal responses to compound stimuli are taught, an association is established between the components of the compound stimulus, and they discuss a number

154

in his influential *Study of Language* made passing mention of the "interesting experiments" of Esper and Wolfle, and in the same year Arnold Horowitz (1955) adopted the technique for his Harvard doctoral dissertation, the main results of which, together with the results of additional experiments, he published six years later (Horowitz and Jackson, 1959). He concerned himself specifically with the difference in speed of learning which Esper (1925) had found between subjects who learned nonsense words conforming to English speech habits and those who learned words which did not so conform. He concluded that "of the possible causes of Esper's results, phonetic symbolism, particular grouping of nonsense syllables, particular referent dimensions, and morpheme order produced no effects in these experiments. The only variable causing a significant difference was whether or not the Miniature Linguistic System learned contained syllables of non-English structure." However, in neither purpose nor method were the Horowitz experiments replications of those of Esper. The main purpose of the Esper experiments had been to compare the tendencies toward contaminations and analogical formations induced by an MLS which was systematic and in conformity with English speech habits with an MLS which, though systematic, violated English speech habits. That the second Esper experiment involved two different departures from English speech habits might be regarded as a failure in fractionation, but it was not important in relation to the purpose of the experiments, whose results showed that a system which is perfectly regular, structurally and semantically, can be quickly learned and readily extended analogically, with few contaminations; whereas a system whose structure violates the speech habits of speakers tends strongly to become "regularized" and thus induces many contaminations and, in advance of such regularization, permits hardly any analogical extensions. Because of the purpose of my experiments, the events of the learning period were of interest only as providing the conditions and the preparation for the responses of the post-learning period—in particular, any analogical processes indicating a systematic reorganization of the verbal material. Hence the

---

of experiments by others on the learning of the components of compound stimuli. In none of the studies mentioned in this note was the research using the MLS technique mentioned.

extensive overlearning—over a period of two months in my experiments of 1925 and over a period of seven to eight months in those of 1933. Horowitz's experiments were strictly learning experiments—to three correct trials; he gives no deviant responses, and though at the end he gave five figures previously omitted but systematically related to the twenty learned figures, he apparently found nothing of interest in the responses to these in relation to his various conditions. Horowitz (1967) again reported MLS experiments in which stimulus and response features were varied in relation to each other. The stimulus features were size, color, and shape; the linguistic responses were dissyllables of which one syllable referred to one of the stimulus variables and the other syllable was composed of initial and final consonants referring to a second stimulus variable and a medial vowel referring to the third variable. The dependent variable was the number of repetitions required to reach a criterion of three successive correct trials. Ease of learning was found to depend mostly on the structure of the names; these experiments thus confirm the results, with respect to learning, both of Lenneberg and of Esper and Wolfle; difficulties of interpretation however arose from the use of syllables in which medial vowels varied independently of consonants and in which both of these varied independently in stimulus reference. In a paper which Horowitz read at a symposium on "The Miniature Linguistic System: Its Relation to Psychology and Linguistics," on the occasion of the American Psychological Association meetings in 1968, he gave a summarized account of the statistical results of studies of "Variables in the Learning of a Classical Esper Miniature Linguistic System," from which he concluded that "I am more than ever convinced that it is an ideal empirical testing ground for theoretical developments involving organizational factors in behavior, all the way from ... Osgood's elaborated S-R mediationalism to sophisticated demonology à la Chomsky or Selfridge."

The chairman of the symposium mentioned above was James Jenkins, whose interest in language dated from the early 1950s. In 1953 he had participated in the summer seminar sponsored by the Committee on Linguistics and Psychology of the Social Science Research Council. At this time neither he nor the linguist Leonard Newmark had become aware of the work with the MLS technique, as is evidenced by their jointly written section on "An Experimental Analogue for Studying Language Learning" (Osgood and Sebeok, 1954, pp. 135–139):

> One very basic question which might be asked is whether we could build up 'use by analogy' in our experimental model. Suppose in one sequence of learning trials we presented units singly at first and then in later stages began using the units in context. Suppose unit one were rewarded in context one and unit two also rewarded in context one. A new context might be introduced and again both units rewarded when they appear in the context, and so forth. Then, if unit one were presented in context 'X,' would the subject tend to encode unit two in that wholly new context? This learning-by-analogy is often assumed in descriptions of language processes but has rarely been attacked experimentally. If this can be demonstrated, then another very interesting question arises—will unit one evoke unit two in an association test? Here we could have a control over the paradigmatic class which is not at all possible in 'natural language.'

The MLS experiments are also not mentioned in Diebold's purported survey of "Psycholinguistic Research 1954–1964," which is appended to the 1965 republication of Osgood and Sebeok.

By the early 1960s, however, Jenkins had discovered the MLS experiments, used them as models in his theoretical discussions of mediation processes, and sponsored a number of doctoral dissertations which made use of the method. This work may be said to have been introduced by a paper given in 1961 which was published in 1964 (Jenkins and Palermo, 1964). The concern here was with the role of mediation processes in the acquisition of grammar. The authors, discussing Esper's 1925 Experiment I, make a statement very similar to that of Stern quoted above:"It would appear here that we must be prepared to deal both with the matter of analysis of the stimulus and segmentation of the response as well as a combination rule." In Experiment II, on the other hand, "the difference is that one response is familiarly divided and ordered and one is not"; here we recall Stern's statement that "the isolation of elements requires a word as support," whereas the un-English consonant group "retarded the isolation of the phonetic elements, the names, and so the formation of the general notion." Jenkins and Palermo, however, go on to apply their concept of mediation: "When any red figure is presented, we assume that the implicit naming response 'red' is made by the subject. At the same time the experimenter says 'nas——' and the subject echoes 'nas——.' This sequence sets up a virtually perfect chain from the color of the object to the implicit response and from the stimuli produced by the implicit response to the overt response itself." Similarly for the responses to the shapes. The authors "assume that [the subjects] are actively trying to link their own linguistic responses (which are implicit here) to the artificial responses the experimenter requires. Simple contingencies of implicit and explicit responses will account for the remainder of the experiment." I also had assumed that English speech habits would influence the acquisition of these systems, but I doubt that the mediation paradigm suggested by Jenkins and Palermo should be regarded as universally applicable; as we know, there is very great diversity in the learning methods of different individuals,[45] and I rather think that, e.g., the color red could itself very well serve as the "mediator" whereby the morpheme-class *nas* was formed; i.e., the contingency was between the color and the response. Moreover, very similar results have been obtained—as in my 1933 experiments—when great pains have been taken to construct nonsense figures and names for which, in pretesting, hardly anyone could find an association.[46]

Every discussion of analogical change is likely to include examples

45. Thus, in maze-learning experiments, it is usually a minority of the subjects who verbalize; indeed, many are unable to describe any method which they used.

46. The authors remark, "Finally, we should note that, despite the experimenter, the subjects in this portion of the experiment have learned a system," and that what they did "from Esper's point of view was exactly the opposite of what was occurring." The authors thus seem to assume that my purpose in these experiments was to conduct a learning or intelligence test, whereas the actual purpose was to study the *variant* responses—especially those which, though they would be called "errors" in a learning experiment, were of the nature of analogical changes and thus were in the direction of increased regularity in the system. In producing variant responses the subjects were therefore doing what I was interested in their doing, rather than dismaying me by their "errors." The stereotypes of the psychological laboratory and the "synchronic" preoccupations of many contemporary linguists have prevented other writers from perceiving that the experiments of Thumb and Marbe and of myself were directed at the *historical* processes of linguistic change. It was because my interest in conventional learning was secondary to my interest in post-learning analogical processes that I provided a great deal of overlearning—in my later experiments, over a period of seven months. These are matters which Jenkins and Palermo clearly recognized in their discussion of my 1933 experiments; here however they again introduced their hypothetical intervening implicit verbal processes as "mediators."

from the language learning of children, who are great analogizers; moreover, analogical extensions and contaminations throughout the lives of individuals are inevitable processes in the "creative" use of language—of "new but appropriate" forms of utterance. We thus come in contact with the contemporary literature of transformational-generative grammar, which however concentrates its interest, not on analogizing individual speakers, but upon a hypothesized ideal speaker who exemplifies, not actual "empirical" utterances, but "rules of linguistic competence," by virtue of which he can endlessly create novel sentences. The literature dealing with these matters is highly polemical and likely to cause confusion among psychologists.[47] What the role of an experimental—hence "empirical"—psychologist could be as a convert to Chomsky's (e.g., 1967) intuitive-logical-hereditarian theory of abstract linguistic "competence" is far from clear to me. As far as I can see, a psychologist would—as psychologist—have to deal, not with Saussure's *langue* but with *parole*, the *speech* of individuals in verbal, environmental, and physiological contexts. As Dixon (1965, p. 86) points out, "In fact [Chomsky] never considers external meanings; and pays little attention to internal meanings within sentences (he deals entirely with sentences—these are never considered as being embedded in a text, but as having distinct existence as self-contained entities): his linguistics is mostly concerned with formalizing previous ideas of linguistics in terms of logical rules, and making explicit various intuitions about language patterns." The "chunks" of speech which Dixon recorded can hardly be described as Chomskyan "well-formed sentences," and yet they are actual utterances, for the understanding of which knowledge of context is essential. The gestalt psychologists of language—e.g., Pillsbury and Meader (1928)—reduced everything to the Parmenidean slogan "All is One," and the Chomskyan psycholinguists reduce everything to the Heraclitean slogan "All is Rule." In either case, the resulting "scientific" activity seems to consist mostly in picking up and displaying choice examples. A psychologist might well be baffled by the metaphoric nature and vague topographic reference of Chomskyan linguistics. The basic rules are said to reside in deep structures, which are the products of logical analysis of sentences deemed to

47. For a critical review by a linguist, see Hall (1969).

be well-formed, but which are also localized as otherwise unknown brain mechanisms and as equally unknown components of the germ plasm. Other theories in psychology have of course also made references to the brain, but never, I think, to the accompaniment of expressed contempt for empirical data.

These logical hypothetical constructs are not only of dubious value for psychology but, in the view of some linguists (Grunig, 1965, 1966; Hall, 1968b, 1969; Herdan, 1965, 1968; Hockett, 1968; Lamb, 1967; Uhlenbeck, 1963, 1967), unsatisfactory for linguistics; thus,

> At present, the out-look for linguistics in America is unsettled. If (in an anonymous English observer's metaphor) Chomsky's *streltsy* succeed in disorganizing the American camp entirely, or if (to change the metaphor) his "Boxer rebellion" succeeds in driving out the "foreign devils" of objectivity and data-based study of reality, we shall be dragged back and down to a Renaissance and Baroque level of aprioristic speculation in theory, affording new support to our (never really banished) absolutist authoritarianism in practice. Perhaps it is not unreasonable to hope, however, that what is of value in Chomskyan procedures (the revival and systematization of I-P formulations, applied to those linguistic phenomena for which they are appropriate, in theoretical exposition and in practical language-teaching) can be salvaged and integrated into our general approach to language. The rest—aprioristic rationalism and all its consequences, such as the "innateness-hypothesis" and the establishment of "rule-governed behavior" as a goal—must be returned as quickly as possible to the limbo of outworn dogmas, and linguistics must return to its basis in observation of humans' activities in relation to their culture, if it is to continue developing as a science. (Hall, 1969, p. 227)

The above digression was prompted by the announcement by Jenkins (1968a) of his conversion to Chomskyanism. This psychologist, however, who has made many valuable contributions to the theoretical and experimental literature of psychology, has not found it necessary to adopt the attitude characteristic of the Chomskyans, which Hall (1969) describes as "arrogant and insolent, in personal contact and in print, towards anyone whom they considered in error"; Jenkins has continued to write judiciously and has not abandoned the methods and data of experimental psychology. In his 1968 paper, he described the effect of Chomskyanism on psychology in terms which—though he arrives at a different conclusion —parallel Hall's description of the effect on linguistics.

> There is a wealth of evidence that the established theoretical positions in psychology are currently under serious attack. This is dramatically demonstrated in Dixon and Horton's book, *Verbal Behavior and General Behavior Theory* (1968). The conference reported in that book was to have been a straightforward attempt to relate the experimental and theoretical work in verbal behavior research to general learning theory, the dominant theoretical area of American psychology. Instead of a quiet scholarly exploration, however, the result was more like a pitched battle. Traditional associative learning theory was attacked violently; defectors from the established positions gave testimony to new faiths; and revolutionary credos were shouted at conference table and dinner table alike. (Jenkins, 1968)

This effect on the progress of linguistics and of psychology—one writer speaks of "bloodletting"—cannot be dismissed, as Chomsky (1968) suggests, as merely the result of his critics' ignorance or stupidity; Rebecca Posner (1968) expresses a reaction which is shared by others and which is of considerable importance to the development of linguistics: "What provokes my reaction is not so much the content of Chomsky's article (indeed, as he himself reiterates, in the bored tone he adopts, much of it is 'obvious') but the manner in which it is presented." This reaction, however illogical it may seem, shares with its provocation the blame for the neglect of important considerations and for the loss of that friendly interstimulation among scholars which is so powerful a motivating force in the development of any science.

In view of the above, I find pleasant the equitable tone in which Jenkins and Palermo (1964) sought to bridge the gap between "transformationalism" and the body of psychological research—particularly that dealing with the acquisition of linguistic structure by children.

> Given that the child has a set of classes which he can arrange in functional sentences or utterances, all of the processes which led him to this point will similarly lead him to extend his behavior repertoire to other

forms of ordering. Similarly, as he learns new sentence forms, he begins almost immediately on the learning of transformation rules. At this level of sophistication, we encounter trouble again. If the child were a complete grammarian, we could let him name the classes and proceed to learn the transformation rules by rote, but this is obviously ridiculous. Not only does he not have names for the categories he is supposed to label, but the linguists are still attempting to state explicitly the transformation rules he is supposed to learn. . . . We applaud and respect the efforts of grammarians to create a grammar without reference to meaning, and we feel that such proposals call attention to the syntactic contribution to the formation of classes which we feel is highly significant. We must, however, remember that there are semantic correlates of the major classes and that the main business of language is wrapped up in function and reference. From a psychological point of view it seems to us highly unlikely that transformations are generated without semantic support. We can facilitate the application of our mediation models by providing that the new forms (which are to be the transforms) are first learned instance by instance as independent constructions, and that the equivalences between such forms and the basic or kernel forms are identified and mediated semantically. (Jenkins and Palermo, 1964, pp. 164f.)

In a 1965 paper, Jenkins begins, as have so many others, with Lashley's remark that for the sequential nature of language "there have been almost no attempts to develop physiological theories," and beside this observation he places Chomsky's pronouncement against "finite-state" models of language. From these propositions he draws the conclusion that "an approach through associational psychology cannot *by its very nature* be adequate to account for language phenomena."[48] But Lashley had demanded a physiological theory, and since no such theory has yet received physiological validation, Lashley's statements remain speculative, although we may readily grant that in language we see "patterned structural relationships," a fact which has been known to linguists for a very long time. As for Chomsky's dictum about finite-state models, this seems still to be moot in linguistics (Reich, 1969). Neither argument seems to me to justify any prescription as to psychological method or theory.

But apart from these contemporary theoretical difficulties, experi-

48. Wickelgren (1969) presents arguments to show "that Lashley's rejection of associative theories was premature."

mental psychology has a number of very interesting problems on which to work, and these problems Jenkins proceeds to discuss. He points to the systematic nature of the speech of young children, i.e., their tendency to morphological and syntactic analogy. He then enters upon a discussion of the psychological status of analogy, which, as he points out, has been neglected by psychologists. The experiments of Esper, he says, have either been ignored or interpreted in simple stimulus-response terms, whereas an ordering principle is obviously involved. The psychologist must begin with the process of class formation. "If a class may be treated as a stimulus and as a response, the problems of sequence learning and varied arrangement can be handled at least approximately with more traditional theoretical notions. Given the formation of classes, attention can then be turned to the problems of learning the 'rules of combination' which govern acceptable sequences in the language." He then applies his mediation model, whereby "Esper's system, then, affords a simple grammar which (as the subjects demonstrated) may be learned on the basis of an incomplete sample of the utterances and applied with accuracy to the new instances when they arise on the test trials. It is at the same time an instance of our mediation model." That is, "a sequence of learning such as A–B, C–B, A–D, C–D consists simultaneously of a stimulus-classing and response-classing operation. . . . It might also be referred to simply as a miniature grammar." He concludes that, "in general, studies in the Esper tradition seem to me to be most fruitful here. Studies that manipulate *systems* of responses seem to afford insights into the mechanisms that may underlie grammar and afford convenient tests of the generality of the system when missing cells are evaluated."

In an invited address before the Division of Experimental Psychology of the American Psychological Association in 1966, Jenkins discussed the role of experimentation in psycholinguistics. Here he proceeded from the assumption that there had been a "linguistic revolution [which] is only beginning to be consolidated in its parent field" and that "we are only at the stage of fighting in the streets in the derived field of psycholinguistics." The "new linguistics" became "more mentalistic" and insisted that psychology had little to contribute to either linguistics proper or to the psychology of language. The product of the "new grammar" is a "logic machine" which "generates sentences" conforming to rules; "this device is neither a speaker nor a hearer," and the rules are no longer considered to be "summaries of data." "They are, rather, ways in which 'ideal data' might be produced. The linguist tests his device and its subcomponents against examples he can think of, revises his rules, consults his friends, or informants, tries again, etc." At this point, I think that it would be wise for the experimental psychologist to tiptoe quietly away; he has no techniques for studying disembodied logic machines which have no biological locus and no environmental context. Jenkins however declares that "once the competency system exists, it provides a point of departure for a thorough-going psychological model, an automaton which represents the rules and processes of the competency system in a functioning, purposeful, real time, psychologically limited machine." And yet, Jenkins later points out that "the competency model is a purely logical structure and the competence that is represented in our subjects is, as is the case in any other pure construct, unavailable to us." It is not clear to me why psychologists should take the Chomskyan logical structure as a starting point or basic assumption. The adoption of this a priori system carries with it doctrinaire rejection of the experimental results and empirical generalizations of psychologists, who are perceived as members of a primitive outgroup. Thus Lenneberg (1967, p. 350) celebrates the new insights to which he has contributed by contrasting them with ancient error (to which he too, in his unregenerate youth, had once contributed):

> The first experiment on the effects of certain language habits on memory and recognition was carried out by Brown and Lenneberg (1954). Until that time investigators had attempted to manipulate language variables by quite ephemeral conditions such as teaching subjects nonsense names for nonsense objects . . . but the semantic structure of the subjects' native language was neither known to the experimenter nor utilized as a variable in the experiment.

The reader who remembers the first part of the present chapter will note that the portion of Lenneberg's statement following the ellipsis points above is contrary to fact. A less negative view of experimentation with miniature linguistic systems was expressed in 1966 by Jenkins:

Such experiments furnish important data with reference to the acquisition and employment of a system (a relatively new question to ask in contemporary psychology) and serve as a meeting ground for the psycholinguists and the psychologists of other persuasions.... [They] reflect a concern for the development of a systematic set of behaviors which will permit *productivity*, that is, which will allow the subject to produce a novel response that is appropriate to the circumstances in which he finds himself. Because the whole notion of novel but appropriate responses seems to smack of non-science or even free-will to ears carefully tuned to modern psychological terms, the experiments seem distant from the main stream of American psychology. Because the experiments are simple and well-controlled, however, they are amenable to careful study and fine-grained experimentation in the laboratory, a redeeming feature that brings them back into contact with the main stream.... If the system is unstable in one of several ways, the subjects will stabilize it over a period of time, presumably tapping the processes which on a larger scale produce some of the language changes we know. (Jenkins, 1966)

In his paper on psychological theory, Jenkins (1968a) presented his view that the Chomskyan transformational-generative grammar had produced a "revolution" not only in linguistics but also in psychology. He accepted the notion that the structure of speech—of what people say—is a "surface structure" which represents a deep structure. The Chomskyan linguist presented examples which "showed the importance of abstract terms and levels of representation between the final surface representation and the deepest underlying representation." Jenkins also accepted Chomsky's notion of "ambiguous sentences," in which "the stimulus is *in some degree* two different things"—a statement which is sensible only if we are logicians for whom a sentence has no context. I am surprised that a veteran experimentalist should attach such importance to concepts which are wholly metaphorical and which are in actuality only classifications, without explanatory power, of selected sentences. These classifications would attain explanatory power if it could be shown that they correspond to demonstrable neural mechanisms; they do not do so by being called "deep structures" or "mechanisms"; they remain merely one sort of classification which one group of linguistic logicians has made.[49] They

49. Cf. Hall (1969, p. 203): "In reality, a so-called 'deep structure' is only a

might also gain significance if it could be shown that they are correlated with historical development, but the Chomskyan linguists have not shown much interest in the histories of languages. I suppose that it is Chomsky's Saussurean abstraction *competence* which leads Jenkins to make a distinction between "what the subject *does do*" and *"what he can do"*; he remarks, "A very simple thing to do is to ask him." We know very well that performance varies with instruction and with set and self-instruction; any such change or any of many other changes which we can make in conditions we will expect to result in some change in performance, and I suppose that we might attach to the totality of such possible variety in response the abstract term *competence,* or we might apply a scale of some sort to the responses and regard the response which satisfies our design as the demonstration of competence. Jenkins himself points out that "particularly with problems concerning the linguistic system where so much of the subject's skill and knowledge is below the level of awareness, the questions of what constitutes appropriate and adequate instruction are thorny ones." We are here touching upon a feature of Chomskyan doctrine which should make that doctrine unacceptable to those whose aim is to create an empirically based science; compare the statement of Hall (1969):

> To justify the theory of grammaticality, especially when (as has often been the case) the linguist acts as his own informant, transformation-generative theorists have exalted the native speaker's "intuition" as the only valid source of knowledge. Chomsky has repeatedly declared that the aim of grammar should be to formulate "what a speaker knows about his language." This use of the word *know* exemplifies a prime characteristic of Chomsky's, like Plato's, treatment of terms—what Hockett has aptly termed "Tarzan thinking," swinging (without acknowledging it) from one meaning to another by means of a polysemic morpheme, in this case *know* "have analytical knowledge of" and "have the ability to, even outside awareness." It is well established that ordinary naive speakers know very little, in the first of these two senses, about what they actually do

---

gloss or paraphrase of an actual utterance, i.e., a restatement of the meaning of the utterance being analyzed. . . . The distinction between 'surface' and 'deep' structures should be given up, since no such contrast exists: there are only structures and their meanings."

166

when they use their language; and what little analytical cognition they have is often wrong, especially if they have gone to school and have been indoctrinated with their society's folk-lore on linguistic matters. (Hall, 1969, pp. 216f.)

There are other terms of deceptive promise which Jenkins has taken over from Chomskyan doctrine. Thus it has long been known that speakers can recombine morphemes, words, and prhases previously learned in accordance with previously learned syntactic patterns. We can call such recombinations "novel" or "creative" or "productive," but we do not thereby explain these processes. In the MLS experiments, the subjects, having learned to respond with dissyllabic names to shapes of various colors or sizes, could recombine the morphemes to correspond to previously unseen stimulus combinations, and they did this even without awareness that the combinations were novel. "Productiveness" is a description of this process; it is not a psychological explanation; we are not thus led to understand the phenomenon. I do not see how we can at present advance much beyond the "isolation-and-combination" account which I have quoted from Stern; "productiveness" is an empirical generalization, not an explanation or theory. The same can be said about the emphasis on rules; the behavior of a subject who responds to a new stimulus-combination with an appropriate morpheme-combination may be described as behavior according to a rule; this is also an empirical generalization by the linguist. If what we want is understanding or explanation, we will have to go to physiology. But the Chomskyan linguists, though they assert that their "mechanisms" are "brain mechanisms" (Katz, 1964), indignantly deny that they claim any competence in neurophysiology (Blumenthal, 1970). The psycholinguist who has attempted to provide a "biological foundation" for language concludes that "in general, it is not possible to assign any specific neuroanatomic structure to the capacity for language" (Lenneberg, 1967, p. 72), and his discussion is anatomical rather than physiological. And so too with the doctrine of linguistic "innateness," which is as little explanatory as psychologists found, painfully, the doctrine of instincts to be. The relation of Chomskyan theory to what psychologists have known as science is conveyed in Hall's (1969, p. 221) quotation from Fodor and Garrett (1966): "A grammar is

167

simply an axiomatic representation of an infinite set of structural descriptions, and the internal evidence in favour of the structural descriptions modern grammars generate is so strong that it is difficult to imagine their succumbing to any purely experimental disconfirmation" (p. 152). As Hall says, "If any statement is immune to experimental disconfirmation (e.g., one concerning an angel or a unicorn), it is, by its very nature, not scientific but theological; and any method based on such statements is anti-scientific." [50]

Jenkins (1969) surveys the approaches to language of Wundt, Paul, Watson, Allport, Skinner, Mowrer, Jenkins, and others. He gives brief but fair and informed accounts of each of these, but to all but the last he seems to be bidding a regretful farewell as he turns his face toward the "deep linguistic conception of language," though it is "as yet not well-integrated into the psychological framework." "While Skinner goes into laboratory psychology in a search for a solution," the new orientation rejects associationistic psychology and insists on "productive rules." "The approach of the linguist is not by any means that of the psychologist but the linguist's work may be used for a description of the sentences in the language that the psychologist has to explain." It may indeed, but so may the work of other linguists; the definite-articled "the linguist" stands here only for Chomsky and his disciples, and I think it unwise for psychologists to dedicate themselves to a doctrine which includes not only the systematic—"rule-governed"—nature of language (which is not a new discovery) but also a great deal of pseudo-psychology, pseudo-genetics, and crypto-physiology, as well as a pretentious "philosophy of science." As Jenkins says, "Very little is known about the acquisition of the rules of language"—too little, I would add, to assign any part of it to the germ plasm!

Our main interest in this book is the process by which rule-governed

50. On rules in the history of linguistics see Hall, 1969, pp. 206ff.; on intuition in linguistics, pp. 216ff.; for the fact that "the entire terminology of transformation-generative grammar is taken from the manipulation of written representations" rather than from speech, p. 214. Anyone who is disposed to take the Chomskyan doctrine as the new revelation or "Copernican revolution" in linguistics should read Hall's entire article, as well as his *An Essay on Language* (1968b), and Hockett's (1967) monograph.

linguistic morphology arises, so that the fact that a linguistic system is more quickly learned if it is already systematic in structure and in reference is of less interest than the fact that the more systematic it is the more readily is its system extended to new compounds of its components. This latter fact has been demonstrated by Foss (1968) in a series of ingenious experiments. His test results, as he says, "corroborate those of the original Esper (1925) experiment" and suggest the hypothesis "that Ss discover systematicity, not necessarily consciously, and utilize it in further behavior." But Foss is quite right in stating two qualifications of this empirically derived generalization: "The S may not always take advantage of, or discover, possible systematic covariations," and "of course, what needs to be clarified is the nature of the mechanism that discovers such systematicity as may be represented in the stimuli, and how and under what conditions the device extends the systematicity to new inputs." I would prefer, however, not to use the reifying terms *device* and *mechanism* in discussions of empirical generalizations about behavior; they suggest a reference to a still non-existent neurophysiology.

Palermo and Eberhart (1968) performed MLS experiments whose conditions and results were similar to those which Ervin (1964) had reported for the learning by children of the past tense of verbs and the plurals of nouns. Ervin had found that in children tense inflection begins with the more frequently used irregular verbs; then, when there has been a beginning of the acquisition of regular forms, these tend to be generalized to the previously used irregular verbs. Similar overgeneralizations were noted in the use of plurals. In the Palermo and Eberhart experiments, performance on stimulus-response pairs omitted from the learning presentations lagged behind until all or part of the matrix had been learned, whereupon performance on the omitted pairs became indistinguishable from that on the pairs which had been presented—a result similar to that which had been obtained by Esper and by Foss. In the Palermo and Eberhart Experiment III, in which two stimulus-response pairs were omitted and two irregular—with respect to the system of the 4×4 matrix—pairs were presented, the latter being presented twice during each learning trial, "the more frequently encountered irregular forms were learned first, followed by the acquisition of the regularized forms presented less frequently but in larger numbers, and finally, errors on the irregular forms occurred which reflected the regularized system." There was thus a striking analogy to Ervin's observations of children's acquisition of past-tense inflection.

F. J. Smith (1967) used a 4×4 matrix—four shapes in four colors, systematically correlated with two-syllable nonsense names—of which he taught one (control) group the diagonal items only, and two other groups one or four off-diagonal items, respectively, in addition; a fourth group saw the diagonal items and was told the grammatical rule. Half of the subjects were shown the shape and the color dimensions separately, paired with their one-syllable names. Half of the subjects were tested on their ability to give the names of all the items of the matrix (encoding), while the other half were asked to describe the color-shape stimulus-objects in response to their names (decoding). Only twelve learning trials were given. In their responses to items of the matrix never seen during learning, the control group did most poorly, the group who had seen one off-diagonal item and the group given the rule did about the same and significantly better than the control group, and the group who had seen four off-diagonal items did significantly better than the other two-component groups. But the subjects who had learned one-syllable responses to one-dimensional stimuli did significantly better than subjects who had learned two-syllable words paired with two-dimensional stimuli. Decoding performance was significantly better than encoding performance. The author concluded "that MLS learning, and language learning in general, is better typified as the acquisition of 'rules'" than as a process of stimulus-response learning.

Kirk Smith and Martin Braine have performed a formidable number of paired-associate experiments which they have recently reviewed (Smith and Braine, 1970). Though Smith (1967) initiated this program as "an attempt to dissect and understand the processes operating in the miniature linguistic system [which Esper] described in 1925,"[51] he and Braine have applied the term *miniature linguistic system* to a technique different from that of previous experimenters; they have applied it to sets of letters, nonsense syllables, melodies, and other items for which the subjects were not taught names but on which they were given recall and recognition

51. Kirk Smith, personal communication, January 9, 1970.

tests. The systems used by Smith and Braine were therefore, as they say, "semantically empty." In this they appear to have been influenced by the linguistics of Chomsky, whom they seem to have accepted as their chief authority in linguistics. Uhlenbeck (1967, pp. 314 f.) remarks, "Because of the tendency of transformational theory to account for many essentially semantic and cognitive phenomena in a syntactic way, it has artificially created problems which for other approaches are less difficult or even non-existent. . . . Because of its rationalistic and logical bias, transformational theory tends to present language as a huge, completely rigid system of rules of great complexity." Kirk Smith (1968) speaks of "the dazzling complexity of the rules of our own language," beside which an assumption of "simple associative rules" and "a primitive notion of similarity" is "at best an unwarranted assumption" and at worst "an insult to man's intellectual capacities." Within the limitations of their method, the authors have demonstrated the ability of their subjects to respond in accordance with rules—either rules provided in the material by the experimenter or rules imposed on the material by the subjects. In accordance with a present-day tendency, they are hesitant to speak of the acquisition of such behavior as "learning" rather than as "cognition," and they are pretty well convinced that the rules cannot be acquired by associative learning. They are however dubious about linguistic rules being carried in the germ plasm. While they make no claim that their experiments simulate first-language learning, they believe that data on the learning of artificial languages can throw light on natural language learning. They modify their purely syntactic analysis by the recognition that selectional restrictions in English sentence frames may be determined by the semantic rather than the syntactic structure of the language, as argued by McCawley (1968) and demonstrated by Lakoff (1968). In spite of the Chomskyan influence, the bias of Smith and Braine is obviously empirical rather than rational or logical.

My definition of an MLS had been that given by Foss (1968): "sets of stimuli that vary along certain dimensions (such as shape, size, position, or color) and a set of [verbal] responses to be made to these stimuli." This was in accordance with my conception of a natural language as a system in which certain sounds are coordinated with certain meanings. My purpose in using the MLS technique was that which had been suggested by Thumb: to attempt to reproduce artificially in the laboratory the sort of linguistic—analogical—changes which had been found to take place in the histories of languages. On pages 80–81 above I have quoted Thumb's suggestion, as I did in my 1925 monograph, where I followed it with these statements:

> When the problem is approached in this manner, however, its scope becomes ultimately much broader than the original question of the conditions under which analogic changes take place in the historic languages. It becomes a problem of how language reactions become organized into the systems which we call grammatical categories, and how the component reactions of these systems come to be marked by common elements; in other words, under what conditions the 'associations' which have been held to be responsible for linguistic assimilation are themselves established.
>
> A limitation of such an investigation is at once evident: we can experiment only with subjects who are already possessed of a highly complex and firmly fixed set of language habits; a 'primitive man' or isolated infants are unfortunately not to be obtained for experimental purposes. This limitation, however, is rather general in psychological experimentation. We can at least expect that the manner in which artificial linguistic material becomes organized into categories will bear a definite relationship to the tendencies inherent in the speech-habits of the subjects, and that a comparison of the results gained from subjects of widely different language habits may reveal certain uniformities and general laws according to which the organization of language habits takes place. (Esper, 1925, pp. 7–8)

My purpose was realized: it was found that if subjects are taught a systematic language, they readily extend its patterns—even without knowledge that they are doing so—to new stimulus objects (new in the sense that they are recombinations of previously learned components). If they are taught suppletive languages, they impose a system on its forms. Such changes were found to be reflected in word-association tests. I therefore agree with Smith that the phenomena observed in MLS experiments may usefully be compared with those observed in natural languages. As to the status of rules, I also agree with Smith that they are abstractions, and even that, while they are not represented in the subject's "verbalizations of what he is doing," they serve as "descriptions of what the S invents and imposes upon his behavior in rule use." But there I would stop. The next step would be into the nervous system; at present we had better be satisfied with empirical generalizations about behavior and about the ways in which it changes and becomes organized in systems.

Chapter 7

ANALOGY IN MODERN LINGUISTICS

Modern structural linguistics, of which Ferdinand de Saussure (1857–1913) was a founder, was, in its "psychology," a development of the psychologism of Humboldt, Herbart, and Steinthal. This psychologism (= mentalism) proceeded from the assumption that the psychological principles of human cultural processes, including those of language, could be discovered by means of introspective operations on cultural products. Wilhelm von Humboldt (1767–1835) had described language as the external expression of an "interior form," and as "a specific emanation of the spirit of a particular nation"; changes in language were expressions of the forward movement of the human spirit. Heymann Steinthal (1823–1899) was instrumental in inducing linguists to substitute psychology for logic in their classifications and explanations; his psychology was that of Herbart, in which "ideas" appear as a continual succession of mental processes which may be either compatible and mutually facilitating or incompatible and mutually inhibiting—the system being thus mentalistic, analytic, and associationistic. Steinthal introduced the distinction between the individual speech act and the language of the community. The philosopher-psychologist Wilhelm Wundt (1832–1920) had, in the early years of our century, a considerable influence on some linguists, and some present-day "psycholinguists" have undertaken to rehabilitate him. Another "psychologist of language," Anton Marty (1847–1914), has had a more restricted influence. Steinthal, Wundt, and Marty differed among one another in ways which they considered so important as to warrant extensive polemics, but as far as this history is concerned, it will suffice to say that their doctrines were mentalistic, subjectivistic, and non-experimental; to them could be applied the term with which Wundt described the writings of others: *Reflexionspsychologie*, "die . . . die subjektive logische Reflexion über die Tatsachen und die so gewonnenen Begriffe in die Tatsachen selber hineinträgt."[52]

To return now to Saussure: He derived his main tenets from the Polish scholar Baudouin de Courtenay (1845–1929): the distinctions between the speech-acts of the individual, *parole*, and the language system existing in the speech consciousness of all the members of a linguistic community, *langue* (a distinction which had been introduced by Steinthal); between the contemporary state of a language and its historical development; and between the conservative and innovative tendencies in language. Saussure's *Cours* (1916)[53] illustrates very transparently the sort of linguistics which results when the linguist freely and intuitively psychologizes and expresses his generalizations and definitions in the terms of traditional philosophy. Thus, referring to the neogrammarians, he says,

> The new school, using a more realistic approach than had its predecessor, fought the terminology of the comparative school, and especially the illogical metaphors that it used. . . . One must not go too far, however, and a compromise is in order. Certain metaphors are indispensable. To require that only words that correspond to the facts of speech be used is to pretend that these facts no longer perplex us. This is by no means true, and in some instances I shall not hesitate to use one of the expressions condemned at that time. (p. 5n.)

In accordance with this refusal to limit himself to the facts of language, Saussure proceeds in terms of traditional psychophysical dualism. He describes a linguistic "sign" as an entity consisting of two intimately united psychological elements, a concept and a sound-image. "Suppose that two people, A and B, are conversing with each other":

52. Most of the present-day psycholinguists are following in the Humboldt-Steinthal-Wundt tradition; their leader, who has declared against empiricism and in favor of rationalism, intuitionism, introspection, and mentalism, traces his views to Descartes and the Port Royal grammarians (Chomsky, 1966); in this he seems to have misread his references; cf. Hall (1969, p. 207n.). Percival (1968) has reported himself unable to verify Chomsky's attribution of linguistic invention to Descartes. See Aarsleff (1970), who declares that Chomsky's version of history is "fundamentally false."

53. References are to the English translation by W. Baskin (1959).

Suppose that the opening of the circuit is in A's brain, where mental facts (concepts) are associated with representations of the linguistic sounds (sound-images) that are used for their expression. A given concept unlocks a corresponding sound-image in the brain; this purely *psychological* phenomenon is followed in turn by a *physiological* process: the brain transmits an impulse corresponding to the image to the organs used in producing sounds. Then the sound waves travel from the mouth of A to the ear of B: a purely *physical* process. Next, the circuit continues in B, but the order is reversed: from the ear to the brain, the physiological transmission of the sound-image; in the brain, the psychological association of the image with the corresponding concept. (pp. 11f.)

Concepts and sound-images are thus "in the brain," but they are not physiological; nevertheless they can initiate and be initiated by physiological processes. These are certainly not "facts of speech," nor generalizations from the data studied by linguists; they are also not facts or generalizations of any other science; so far as science is concerned, the above propositions are semantically empty.

Saussure attributes to analogy "all normal, nonphonetic modifications of the external side of words"; it thus restores regularity—patterning—to a system which tends to become disturbed by phonetic changes. "An analogical form is a form made on the model of one or more other forms in accordance with a rule."

> The nominative form of Latin *honor*, for instance, is analogical. Speakers first said *honos : honosem*, then through rhotacization of the [intervocalic] *s*, *honos : honorem*. This duality was eliminated by the new form *honor*, created on the pattern of *orator : oratorem*, etc., through a process which subsequently will be set up as a proportion:
>
> $$oratorem \, : \, orator \, = \, honorem \, : \, x$$
> $$x \, = \, honor$$
>
> Thus analogy, to offset the diversifying action of a phonetic change . . . again unified the forms and restored regularity. (p. 161)

Saussure points out that the action of analogy is capricious: "beside [German] *Kranz : Kränze*, etc., stand *Tag : Tage*, *Salz : Salze*, etc., which for one reason or another have resisted analogy. Thus we cannot say beforehand how far imitation of a model will go or which types will bring it about. The most numerous forms do not necessarily unleash analogy." Moreover, "two or three words often suffice to create a general form such as an inflectional ending." Saussure assumes that *honor* and *honos* "coexisted for a time and were used interchangeably," but the less regular form then fell into disuse and disappeared; "analogical innovation and the elimination of the older form are two distinct things.... So little does analogy have the characteristic of replacing one form by another that it often produces forms which replace nothing at all." Thus on the model of Fr. *pension* : *pensionnaire*, etc., somebody might "create" *repressionnaire*, 'one who favors repression'. Analogical *change* is an illusion, "since formations classed as changes (like *honor*) are basically the same as those I call creations (like *repressionnaire*)." Analogy is "psychological," "grammatical," and dependent on meaning. Its creative end result "belongs at first only to speaking. It is the chance product of an isolated speaker." But it "must be preceded by an unconscious comparison of the materials deposited in the storehouse of language, where productive forms are arranged according to their syntagmatic and associative relations." Thus the creative acts of individual speech (*parole*) presuppose the system of institutional language (*langue*). This system is organized according to two kinds of relations, syntagmatic and associative. Syntagmatic relations may be pictured as linear ribbons, whose sequences may be relatively free, as in the sentences of *parole*, but are in large part bound, as in complex words and idiomatic phrases (syntagms). Associative relations for, e.g., a compound or complex word, may be pictured as several converging series of forms which have an element in common with the syntagm. "When a Frenchman says *marchons!* '(let's) walk!' he thinks unconsciously of diverse groups of associations that converge on the syntagm *marchons!*" (p. 130). Analogy has a conservative as well as an innovative role; a form which is integrated in a system, in which its elements are supported by other forms organized in parallel series, may remain stable for centuries.

What is the significance of Saussurean doctrine for the psychology of language—in particular, for the study of analogical processes? It must be said, in the first place, that very much of this doctrine is the product of armchair psychologizing; the statements about mental concepts and images "in the brain," about "unconscious thinking" of associated forms, about a "system existing in the consciousness of individuals," have no basis in scientific psychology. The sharp distinction between speech and language—which according to Godel (1957) Saussure actually recognized as untenable in practice—has been taken over by contemporary psycholinguists as the distinction between competence and performance. It seems surprising that psychologists, trained in statistics, should have failed to recognize that *langue* or "competence" is a linguist's abstraction,[54] a generalization or "average" (though contaminated by uncontrolled introspection and normative judgments) from the study of the speech of individuals—often the speech of the linguist himself, regarded as ideal—and that the primary data—the speech of individuals—show individual, temporal, and situational variations whose study is an essential part of the psychologist's—and, one might suppose, of the linguist's—task; particularly is this so in the study of analogical formations. Anyone who has performed experiments such as I have described in Chapters 4, 5, and 6 will have been impressed with the extent of individual differences; the results of my own experiments (1933, 1966) have suggested that "the variations

---

54. Cf. Waterman (1963, p. 64): "A *langue* is not spoken by anybody, but is a composite body of linguistic phenomena derived as it were from the personal dialects (*paroles*) of all native speakers. It is in essence a social phenomenon, having reality only as a social institution." The notion of *langue* or "competence" might well suggest to psychologists the unhappy parallel of the "group-mind fallacy" (cf. LaPiere and Farnsworth, 1942, pp. 52, 299, 394), which, initiated by Hegel, found expression in Humboldt's "spirit of a nation." (It was also a central feature of the sociology of Emil Durkheim, a contemporary of Saussure's, who described the group mind as impersonal and superior to the individual minds for which it acts as a directive force.) Saussure's *langue* too was an abstraction which tended to be reified. On p. 14 he says: "Language is not a function of the speaker. . . . Language is concrete, no less so than speaking. . . . Linguistic signs, though basically psychological, are not abstractions." When Saussure says that the associations "which added together constitute language" are "realities that have their seat in the brain," one seems to be invited to imagine a group brain, although he more frequently implies a collective consciousness. All of this nonsense is the result of refusing to admit that the linguist is discussing either generalizations of his own creation or else proposed methodology. When Saussure, on the one hand, declares that *langue* is "exclusively psychological," and on the other, says that it "exists in the form of a sum of impressions deposited in the brain of each member of a community" (pp. 18f.), he is talking, not as a linguist, but as an amateur physiological psychologist. Similarly, our contemporary mentalists, while denying that they espouse a mind-body dualism—and also that they claim to have any competence in neurophysiology—nevertheless localize their mental structures in "the" brain.

178

which result in linguistic systematization seem to be the work chiefly of certain occasional individuals," whose reaction and association characteristics differ from those of others.

The other sharp distinction, that between "synchronic" (descriptive) and "diachronic" (historical) linguistics, also seems unfortunate for the study of analogy. If we accept the proposition that there is no intrinsic psychological difference between analogical re-creation by an individual of forms already current in a language though not previously used or heard by the speaker and analogical creation of wholly new forms, then there can be no justification, in principle, for separating the processes. When someone has learned a number of linguistic units and the rules of their combination, a large part of his speech will be analogical, its combinations based on models. ("Forms are preserved because they are constantly renewed by analogy.") As Saussure said, analogy is both innovative and conservative; in either case, it depends on the relation of a form to the system of the language. But the notion that there exists at a given instant of time a uniform system from which processes of change and variation can be excluded is another of those linguistic fictions which, since they are contrary to reality, can obstruct the proper study of language; it is essentially the same notion as that of prescriptive grammar, from which linguists have in the past sought to free themselves. As long as a language is spoken, change is an inevitable process, and local and individual variation an inescapable fact; analogical processes are an essential feature both of daily speech and of historical extension and change; in either case, they arise in the *parole* of individuals. The rigidity ascribed to *langue* and "competence" is illustrated by Saussure's (pp. 88f., 110) analogy of the game of chess. Lyons (1968, p. 50), while accepting the chess analogy, concedes that in its application to language it involves "some degree of 'idealization'" and adds, "From the *microscopic*, as distinct from the *macroscopic*, point of view it is impossible to draw a sharp distinction between diachronic 'change' and synchronic 'variation.'" Leroy (1967, pp. 55f.) speaks of *langue* as "an abstract system that is a social phenomenon"; it seems to me to be rather a noumenon, a creation of the linguist which would be justifiable if it were presented as such. But I can see no justification for Saussure's statement that "the opposition between the two points of view—the synchronic and the diachronic—is absolute and admits of no compromise." These dichotomies have not, I think, been helpful in linguistics; they have resulted, for example, in linguists who deal in universals on the basis of very limited comparative and historical knowledge.

Rulon Wells (1947), in his critique of Saussure, points out the contradictions which result from Saussure's treatment of analogy. Saussure declared that linguistic change is mostly phonetic change and that every linguistic change is "isolated"—i.e., external to the synchronic system. But, asks Wells, if speakers manifest their understanding of the system by analogical creation, isn't analogy a change of the system which is inspired by the system itself? To which Saussure replies that analogy is not change at all, but a synchronic fact, and that a distinction must be made between (1) conscious comparison of the relation between the productive forms (a state belonging to *langue*), and (2) the result suggested by the comparison (which belongs to *parole* and is "the chance product of an isolated speaker"). Wells observes,

The fact is that de Saussure's idea of a system is radically vitiated by an ambiguity. *In his parlance, 'système' has two meanings: (1) state and (2) stable state, that is, equilibrium.* His argument that linguistic changes always arise externally is wholly dependent upon the switch from one of these senses to another. Every language during a sufficiently short span of time is necessarily a system in the first sense; but when de Saussure says that a system never originates a change, he can only mean an equilibrium, as he himself calls it. . . . Another way of expressing de Saussure's ambiguity is that in effect he assumed the effects of every linguistic change to be instantaneous. His idea seems to have been that linguistic change is like a car going uphill: it stops as soon as it is no longer actively propelled. (p. 23)
Can one, by an inductive study of antecedent and consequent states, establish that given states lead to given changes, regardless of the external buffets or supports to which they are subjected? Or can one make such predictions by taking into account the prior history of the system? . . . When it becomes predictive not only of the past but also of the future, linguistics will have attained the inner circle of science. In admitting that "on ne peut pas dire d'avance jusqu'où s'étendra l'imitation d'un modèle,

ni quels sont les types destinés à la provoquer," de Saussure shows that linguistics has not yet achieved this triumph. (p. 24)

Leonard Bloomfield (1887–1949) was, like Saussure, a pupil of the great Leipzig neogrammarians, and in that tradition he described a rigorously scientific linguistics as being concerned with the formal aspects of language: phonology, morphology, and syntax. But, like Saussure, he emphasized the distinction between descriptive or structural and historical linguistics. "In order to describe a language one needs no historical knowledge whatever; in fact, the observer who allows such knowledge to affect his description, is bound to distort his data" (1933, p. 19).[55] Accurate and unbiased descriptions, he said, were a prerequisite of historical-comparative studies. He declared that "the only useful generalizations about language are inductive generalizations. Features which we think ought to be universal may be absent from the very next language that becomes accessible" (p. 20). Thus Bloomfield advocated an empirical approach to languages and opposed introspective, intuitive, and mentalistic methods. When he presented in his second chapter a behavioristic or mechanistic approach to linguistics, he did this, it has seemed to me, as a means of sweeping out of linguistics all of the traditional verbiage about forms as expressions of ideas and the other mentalistic embroideries of linguistic literature, in conformity with Delbrück's dictum that "we can pursue the study of language without reference to any one psychological doctrine." Thus, when we examine his chapters on linguistic change, we find purely linguistic statements about linguistic forms, without pseudo-psychological or pseudo-physiological admixture. In appealing to introspective evidence, said Bloomfield, linguists must avoid the mistake of supposing "that language enables a person to observe things for which he has no sense-organs, such as the workings of his own nervous system." Hence, "to say, for instance, that combinations of words which are 'felt to be' compounds have only a single high stress (e.g., *blackbird* as opposed to *black bird*), is to tell exactly nothing, since we have no way of determining what the speakers may 'feel': the observer's task was to tell us, by some tangible criterion, or, if he found none, by a list, what combinations of

55. Quotations are from Bloomfield's *Language* (1933).

words are pronounced with a single high stress" (p. 38). Such figures of speech as "deep structure" and "surface structure," which have lately been in lively play among many linguists, would, I think, have been similarly rejected by Bloomfield.

Bloomfield (pp. 393ff.) presents the neogrammarian doctrine that exceptions to phonetic change—"residues"—are innovations which may be accounted for either as borrowings from other languages or dialects, or as analogic changes. In changes of the latter two sorts, fluctuation in the frequency of speech-forms is a factor; an innovation, if it is to prevail in general usage, must have gained in popularity since its first introduction, whereas a form for which the innovation has been substituted must have decreased in frequency of use, e.g., Old English plural [ky:] modern *cows*. We can observe some forms in "complementary fluctuation": e.g., *it's I* and *it's me* are rival forms, as at one time were *kine : cows*. "Where a speaker knows two rival forms, they differ in connotation, since he has heard them from different persons and under different circumstances." We may imagine a vast tally-sheet in which would be recorded each utterance made in a community during a certain period of time; we could then note the great differences in relative life-span of various forms: very brief for slangy witticisms to very long for the stable forms whose change becomes visible only when historical stages are compared. Progressive disuse of a form seems to result from semantic rather than formal factors; thus homonymy, especially with tabu-words or with very common words, has appeared to be a factor. Bloomfield suggests a process of social reinforcement very similar to Skinner's (1957, pp. 29f., 84f.): English *let* represents two Old English verbs with the meanings 'permit' and 'hinder', respectively. "A speaker who wanted his hearers to stop someone—say a child that was running into danger, or a thief—and cried *Let him!* might find his hearers standing aside to make way. Then he would have to add *Stop him!* or *Hold him!* After a few such experiences he would use one of the effective forms at the first trial" (p. 398). "The practical situation works in favor of words that call forth a good response" (p. 401).

The most powerful force of all in fluctuation works quite outside the linguist's reach: the speaker favors the forms which he has heard from certain other speakers who, for some reason of prestige, influence his habits of speech. . . . In the ideal diagram of density of communication we should have to distinguish the arrows that lead from each speaker to his hearers by gradations representing the prestige of the speaker with reference to each hearer. If we had a diagram with the arrows thus weighted, we could doubtless predict, to a large extent, the future frequencies of linguistic forms. (p. 403)

Regular forms—e.g., *roofs, hoofs, dwarfs*—frequently exist beside irregular complex forms—e.g., *rooves, hooves, dwarves*. In general, regular forms have an advantage over their rivals, but very common forms, such as the paradigm of the verb *be* and the personal pronouns, persist in spite of great irregularity. Since fluctuation depends on meaning, it is influenced by extralinguistic factors, such as the introduction or obsolescence of cultural objects or practices.

Of analogic change, Bloomfield, in his chapter on the subject, says that "ordinarily, linguists use this term to include both the original creation of the new form and its subsequent rivalry with the old form." But "we can distinguish only in theory between the actual innovation . . . and the subsequent rivalry between this new form and some older form. . . . It is safe to say that the factors which lead to the origination of a form are the same as those which favor the frequency of an existing form." When a new object is introduced, e.g., the radio, there is no rivalry; everybody may independently make the plural *radios*. Concerning models for analogical formations, Bloomfield says,

The independent utterance of a form like *dreamed* instead of dreamt [dremt], could be depicted by the diagram

scream : *screams* : *screaming* : *screamer* : *screamed* =
dream : *dreams* : *dreaming* : *dreamer* : x

Psychologists sometimes object to this formula, on the ground that the speaker is not capable of the reasoning which the proportional pattern implies. If this objection held good, linguists would be debarred from making almost any grammatical statement, since the normal speaker, who is not a linguist, does not describe his speech-habits, and, if we are foolish enough to ask him, fails utterly to make a correct formulation. . . . We have to remember at all times that the speaker, short of a highly specialized training, is incapable of describing his speech-habits. Our proportional formula of analogy and analogic change, like all other statements in linguistics, describes the action of the speaker and does not imply that the speaker himself could give a similar description. (p. 406) [56]

As to the immediate causes of analogic changes, Bloomfield says,

> We do not know why speakers sometimes utter new combinations instead of traditional forms, and why the new combinations sometimes rise in frequency. A form like *foots*, instead of *feet*, is occasionally uttered by children; we call it a "childish error" and expect the child soon to acquire the traditional habit. A grown person may say *foots* when he is tired or flustered, but he does not repeat the form and no one adopts it; we call it a "slip of the tongue." It seems that at any one stage of a language, certain features are relatively stable and others relatively unstable. . . . The most powerful factor is surely that of numbers and frequency. On the one hand, regular form-classes increase at the cost of smaller groups, and, on the other hand, irregular forms of very high frequency resist innovation. (p. 409)

An important condition of analogic creations, emphasized by Bloomfield, is the support afforded by various other forms within the system: "Thus, the use of [-z] with *cow* was probably favored by the existence of other plurals in [-aw-z], such as *sows, brows*. Similarity of meaning plays a part: *sows, heifers, ewes* will attract *cows*." Even a contamination such as Latin *gravis* > *grevis* 'heavy' which has been attributed to the influence of *levis* 'light' may have been assisted by *brevis* 'short'. The influence of other forms is not necessarily expressible in a strictly proportional equation. Thus an adaptive new-formation "resemble[s] an old form with some change in the direction of semantically related forms":

> For instance, of the two slang forms *actorine* 'actress' and *chorine* 'chorus-girl,' only the former can be described as the result of a proportional analogy (*Paul : Pauline = actor : x*). Now *chorine* seems to be based in some way on *actorine*, but the set *chorus : chorine* is not parallel with

56. This view may be contrasted with the repeated assertion of Chomsky that the aim of grammar should be the formulation of "what a speaker knows about his language," an assertion discussed by Hall (1969, pp. 216f.).

actor : actorine either in form or in meaning. . . . We can say only that many nouns have a suffix [-ijn], e.g., *chlorine, colleen;* that this suffix derives some women's names and especially the noun *actorine;* and that the *-us* of *chorus* is plainly suffixal, in view of the adjective *choral.* (p. 420)

After giving examples of the contaminations of numerals in the histories of Indo-European languages, Bloomfield remarks, "Psychologists have ascertained that under laboratory conditions, the stimulus of hearing a word like 'four' often leads to the utterance of a word like 'five'—but this, after all, does not account for contamination. There is perhaps more relevance in the fact that contaminative 'slips of the tongue' are not infrequent, e.g., 'I'll just *grun* (*go* plus *run*) over and get it.' " As an example of contaminative innovations in syntax, Bloomfield cites the type *I am friends with him,* which has been explained as due to contamination of *I am friendly with him* and *we are friends.*

In a paper on analogy whose subtitle was "Das Grundkapitel in der Psychologie der Sprache," Rogge (1925) presented a thesis which, though expressed in mentalistic terms, is rather similar to that which I suggested above in Chapters 5 and 6: "dass der Wortangleichung immer eine Sachangleichung vorausgeht." Analogical changes in language occur in accordance with perceived relationships between *things.* Rogge rejects Paul's classification of analogical formations into "material" and "formal," and Wundt's into "grammatical" and "conceptual." He rejects also the implied assumption that the manner in which a child learns his native language is like the unfortunate vocabulary-learning method of acquisition of a foreign language; true language-learning is not merely word-learning but, in large measure, it is thing-learning. Some analogical formations may be innovative and may give rise to a new morphological type, whereas others merely preserve or extend a traditional type; there is no essential difference, psychologically, between these two classes of analogical processes. Rogge declares that an analogical form can only be explained when the particular model, of related meaning, has been identified. Hence, when Paul sets up proportions such as *Tag : Tages : Tage =*
Arm : Armes : Arme = Fisch : Fisches : Fische, he implies psychological connections which have no reality. It is otherwise when we link *Tages,*

Jahres, Monats, etc.; *Armes, Beines, Fusses; Fisches, Frosches, Krebses.*
Paul's equation *animus : animi* = *senatus : x* is another unlikely example;
the true model for *senati* is *populi*; the contrast between ruler and ruled
was a familiar one, commonly expressed in syntactic collocations. In order
to achieve a true understanding of linguistic processes, the linguist must
free himself from paradigms and direct his attention to the individual
form and its psychological relations; every member of a paradigm is an
independent word with its own relationships.

Since in his view analogy always results from an association between
things, Rogge could not accept the notion of a general tendency toward
leveling or simplification; he quotes Brunot, "Enfin l'analogie simplifie et
embrouille à la fois." A speaker, as the result perhaps of a momentary in-
sight of a similarity between things, assimilates the names of the things
to one another, and a hearer tends to accept an innovation as if it were his
own. If the speaker uses unfamiliar words, the hearer may hear them as
familiar words, and there may thus result auditory assimilations, as in
"folk etymology." In semantic changes also the process results primarily
from an association between things which had not previously been perceived as similar; thus in "lighting a lamp" we no longer set fire to
anything.

In 1949, Kuryłowicz published a paper on "the nature of the processes called 'analogical,'" which he summarized as follows:

> A concrete grammatical system determines which analogical trans-
> formations are possible, but it is the social factor which decides whether
> and to what extent these possibilities are realized. The processes may be
> compared to rainwater which must follow a prepared path—gutters,
> sewers, conduits—*when it rains.* But rain is not inevitable. Likewise, fore-
> seen actions of analogy are not inevitable. Since linguistics must reckon
> with these two different factors, it can never foresee the changes to come.
> Besides the mutual dependence and the hierarchy of linguistic elements
> within a given system, linguistics has to deal with the historical contin-
> gency of the social structure. And while general linguistics tends rather
> toward analysis of the system as such, the concrete historical problems will
> find a satisfactory solution only if account is taken of the two factors
> simultaneously. (p. 174)

Among Kuryłowicz's examples is the following: in ancient Scandinavian, a phonetic change abolished the difference between second and third persons present singular of certain strong verbs; this leveling then spread to all verbs, strong and weak, with pronouns taking the place of the distinctive endings. Icelandic remained at this stage, but in Swedish the process continued through the preterite and subjunctive. "The same phonetic germ has thus had unequal morphological consequences in western and in eastern Scandinavian." The cause of this difference, he thinks, must be "exterior," i.e., independent of the given linguistic system; the extent of analogical action was greater in the east than in the west; it took longer in the west to overcome the greater social resistance.

In 1958, Mańczak, in an article "inspired by [that of] the eminent linguist" Kuryłowicz, presented a series of hypotheses concerning analogical processes which were mostly in contradiction to the formulae of Kuryłowicz, and for which he offered lists of examples—all, like those of Kuryłowicz, from Indo-European languages. He cautioned, however, that these hypotheses "do not cover even a half of all the analogical formations which are produced in the course of the development of languages. Although we cannot exclude the possibility that in the future other regularities will be discovered in this domain, we must remember that a considerable number of changes—perhaps even the larger number—should always be regarded as having a quite fortuitous character" (p. 404). This statement seems rather similar to Kuryłowicz's about "historical contingency"; one might say that each writer had presented a number of "gutters, sewers, and conduits" which had in the past conducted "rain"; that is, their formulae and hypotheses were empirical generalizations, not general laws with predictive power. Two further points made by Mańczak may be mentioned: he declared it to be, in many cases, "absolutely impossible" to apply the proportion $a : b = c : x$, and that in such cases a word may have been influenced by a single other word; and as against Kuryłowicz's rejection of frequency in favor of "sphere of employment," he showed that the latter is a function of the former.

Hockett, to whose study of tongue-slips (1967) I have already referred in Chapter 3, has given considerable attention to analogy. In his *Course*

(1958) he discusses (pp. 303–309) idiom formation, pointing out that while new idioms cannot be reliably predicted, each language favors certain patterns in their creation. "This favoritism is part of the design of the language at the time of observation, and is therefore properly reported in a descriptive study of the language." When a speaker produces a "novel" form, "the new utterance is a nonce-form, built from familiar material by familiar patterns." Such nonce-forms become idioms when their context is shared by hearers and when their structure or their linguistic or environmental context is striking. On pages 389–399 we read, "The mechanism of analogical creation is obviously that involved in most instances of idiom formation." As "minor mechanisms" of linguistic change are distinguished: *contamination*—"the reshaping of a word on the basis of constant association with some other word," but arguments that such a reshaping might come about analogically "are not convincing"; *metanalysis*—"folk etymology" also "cannot be purely analogical"; *slips of the tongue*—metathesis, haplology, assimilation, dissimilation. In a chapter on "Innovation and Survival" (pp. 393–401) Hockett distinguishes between the innovating event and the subsequent spread of the new feature. "There must have been one or more specific individuals who first— and independently, if there were several—uttered the analogical plural /bówkəs/ 'books' instead of using the inherited form /béjč/; before long, though, many people were saying /bówkəs/ through imitation of the innovators, or because they had never heard /béjč/." When such an innovation arises, the old and the new forms are for a time in competition. "Languages differ as to the sort of welcome they offer innovations of various kinds, and within a single language this seems to change, through successive periods of history, much as do fashions of dress or etiquette." *Analogical leveling* occurs when "a morphophonemically irregular form is replaced by a more regular one. Other things being equal, irregular forms of high frequency are less apt to be so replaced than are rarer ones."

Hockett further discusses analogy in two chapters on pages 425–436. Here he includes under analogical creation *back-formation* ("the peeling-out of a form shorter than that which previously was current"; e.g., the interpretation of singulars ending in /z/ or /s/ as plurals; thus *pea* and *cherry* are back-formations from older singulars ending in sibilants), and *recutting* ("where a form which historically has a morpheme boundary in one place is treated as though the boundary were elsewhere"; e.g., the German abstract suffix *-keit* is the result of the recutting of forms where the older suffix *-heit* was preceded by a stem ending in a velar stop). In "semantic change through analogy," Hockett says, "we have to take into consideration the practical situation or the emotional connotations as well as the speech forms themselves," e.g., the substitution of *home* for *house* by real-estate salesmen. *Blends* are said to result from conflict of analogies, when "a speaker follows two models at once," as in *smoke + fog > smog*.

In his 1967 paper, Hockett took as his point of departure Sigmund Freud's *Psychopathology of Everyday Life* on the assumption that "Freud's remarkable insights, properly supplemented and amplified, may tell us things about language that we have not known." Since Freud has been celebrated by many psychologists and literary men as the great pioneer of modern psychology,[57] this assumption was not unreasonable. Unfortunately, however, it leads into the perennial trap for linguists—the notion that an examination of samples of speech, or the recording of introspections—can enable a scientist to "read the speaker's mind;" the linguist may thus think to gain access to another sort of "deep structure." I have briefly discussed, in my *History* (1964, pp. 242f.), the irrationality of this approach, with a quotation from the memorable paper by the psychiatrist Bailey (1956). Freudian analysis is of course inconsistent with the objectivist tradition stemming from Leonard Bloomfield which I described in a subsequent book (1968, Ch. 9).

However, Hockett's main purpose I take to have been to present and support the proposition that slips of the tongue are a normal feature of linguistic behavior for which provision must be made in linguistic theory. A second proposition is that in many cases a blend might conceivably consist of various combinations of several forms, but that the blend which actually occurs may be favored by the phonemic identity of the blend.

57. Much as Chomsky has been hailed as the great revolutionary, not only of modern linguistics, but also of psycholinguistics.

Thus *yell* + *shout* might give *shell, yout, shoul,* etc., but the existence of the ordinary English word *shell* may favor this as a blend; moreover, *shell* is in accordance with the phonetic habits of English.

Much of Hockett's discussion deals with slips which result from momentary syntactic collocations or semantic conflicts of individuals on single occasions. Collocations may indeed give rise to linguistic changes, just as they may give rise to syntagmatic associations, but they must be frequently occurring sequences. Similarly, semantic conflicts must be of sufficiently frequent occurrence to produce word-associations; as I pointed out in Chapter 3, the association *avoid⇌afford* assumed by Hockett is very unlikely, and the published collections of lapses, such as that of Meringer and Mayer, consist mostly of momentary slips such as could hardly ever become current as linguistic innovations. So too with the haplologies, metatheses, assimilations, etc. which Hockett cites; these are in large part momentary slips and in any case are to be reckoned as phonetic rather than analogical phenomena.

In his 1968 monograph on *The State of the Art,* Hockett has performed the great service of thoroughly and carefully dissecting the view of language which Chomsky has foisted upon linguistics. This is important in the present discussion because the Chomskyans, in their attempt to abrogate almost all linguistics published between 1836 and 1955, have rejected the notion of analogical change[58]—along with such basic

58. The Chomskyans were at first wholly preoccupied with discovering the rules governing what were presumed to be wholly stable systems of linguistic "competence"; i.e., their concern was with a hypothesized, idealized, timeless, and invariable state of a language. Lately, however, they have extended their attention to linguistic change, and here too they have thought it necessary to eliminate concepts, such as that of analogy, which they associated with what they refer to as "taxonomic" linguistics, i.e., pre-Chomskyan linguistics. Thus Kiparsky (1968) gets rid of analogy by subsuming it under a concept of "simplification"; his treatment is confusing in that he seems to make no distinction between analogy and sound-change. King (1969), in attempting to bring historical linguistics under the schemata of generative grammar, also finds means of disposing of analogy, namely, by substituting processes of "simplification" and "changing of rules." King is chary of attributing explanatory power to these concepts, and he makes little attempt to relate them to psychological principles or research; he takes full advantage, however, of the Chomskyan speculative-intuitive method to hypothesize (p. 84) a "Language Acquisition Device" which is described as a "black box construct designed to cover the child's whole complex process of receiving the primary data of his language and developing from it the optimal (descriptively adequate) grammar for his language."

concepts of psychology as habit, skill, learning, reinforcement, and generalization. Hockett's main effort is to show that the basic assumption of the Chomskyans—that languages are rigid systems and that the grammar of a language is a well-defined system which can generate an infinite set of well-formed sentences—is contrary to fact. Hockett's discussion (pp. 62ff.) of the "Tarzan thinking" involved in the assertion that the user "knows" the grammar of his language—and that there is thus a body of knowledge which constitutes his "competence" and the grammar of the language—is, I think, definitive. "All this is old hat, and is exactly why linguists traditionally have chosen to speak of *habits* or *skills* rather than of knowledge." In commenting on Chomsky's assertion that probabilistic considerations pertain only to "performance," not to "competence," and that most actually used sentences are novel and spoken once only, Hockett observes, "One assumes that, in a situation in which various partly incompatible patterns are all apt, their interplay and the resolution of their incompatibilities can lead to a sentence that has not been said before. The probabilities may change, sometimes rather kaleidoscopically, but for any one speaker at any one moment they are an integral part of his language habits. Now, by definition, a probabilistic system is not well-defined." On page 73 Hockett says, "The basic assumption has to be that *if something is in fact said in a language, it is allowed by the patterns of that language*— even if we fail to 'understand' it or are unable to 'parse' it. . . . A string assembled by consciously violating the common patterns of the language, like Chomsky's (1957) *Colorless green ideas sleep furiously*, read forwards or backwards, is equally unimportant for linguistic purposes: it is fully explained when we understand how Chomsky produced it, and for what purposes." On pages 81ff. Hockett writes:

> some of Chomsky's students . . . are trying to invent historical linguistics all over again, and are repeating the mistakes of the first half of the nineteenth century. . . . One of my main reasons for having become suspicious of Chomsky's views, before I took the trouble really to study them carefully, was that they appeared to be in conflict with what has been discovered about linguistic change. . . . My conviction that analogy, borrowing, and sound change are the major mechanisms of linguistic change is not predicated on a blind faith in Brugmann, Leskien, and company.

Rather, my respect for them is based on the fact that, by paying honest attention to the evidence, even when it forced them to set their own personal predilections aside, they found that the evidence overwhelmingly supported the hypothesis—as, indeed, it still does.

On page 92 Hockett defines blending as a subform of analogy. "In many, perhaps most, speech situations, many different analogies are at work, each with its own degree of 'configurational pressure.' Some of them are incompatible, in the sense that following one precludes accurately following another." If only one analogy is followed, the result may be either a repetition of something previously said or heard, or it may be an innovation which is a simple analogy: e.g., a child's *swimmed* on the analogy of the regular verbs. But "if two (or perhaps more) incompatible analogies are followed—as best one can, with one tongue and one larynx— then the result is a blend. Hesitating between *sigh* : *sighed* :: *swim* : *x* and *sing* : *sang* :: *swim* : *x*, a child or a tired adult may come out with *swammed*, where both analogies are attested."

Two further matters discussed by Hockett require mention: namely, the nature of brain storage and the concept of "editing."

Any three forms, A, B, and C that have been registered as units by a speaker, provided there are shared features of sound and meaning between A and B and appropriately shared features of sound and meaning between A and C, may form the analogical basis for the coinage of a new form X, which is the solution of the proportion A : B :: C : X .... If one has a half dozen underlying pairs, A_1, B_1, A_2, B_2, . . . , A_6, B_6 and C shares appropriate material with A_1 through A_6 then the configurational pressure is greater. Doubtless the frequency of occurrence of the underlying forms also plays a part in determining the pressure. The great regular patterns of inflection and syntax of any language, such as the singular and plural of regular nouns in English, rest on such enormously large sets of underlying forms that we lose count.

This raises an important question. Even when we can be sure that a routine sentence we hear is in fact being coined for the occasion, we cannot know exactly what stock of already-familiar forms are supplying the bases for the various analogies, in the head of the speaker; and, whatever they may be, the stock of already-familiar forms in our own heads, on the basis of which we understand the new utterance (if we do), need not be at all the same. Is it possible that the brains of speakers and hearers coin and understand on the basis of "abstract patterns" of some sort, extracted over the months and years of language-learning and language-use from actual utterances of similar shapes? I do not know how we could test this hypothesis at present, but it does not seem unreasonable. To entertain it is not to propose, I believe, an additional independent mechanism of the generation of speech, but only to suggest that analogy may work indirectly, via abstraction, as well as directly with actual sets of stored whole utterances; also, we should then have the possibility that the abstract patterns might themselves give rise, via analogy and blending, to new abstract patterns. (pp. 94f.)

My comment on the above passage would be similar to my discussion, toward the end of Chapter 6, of the concepts of creativity and productivity in the recent writings of Jenkins. Both the statement of proportional equations and that of brain mechanisms imply knowledge which we do not have. If speakers make use of equations in coining analogies they must usually do so (i.e., processes must occur in their brains) with such lightning speed that they could seldom verify the processes introspectively, and of course no physiological techniques of such verification are available. That is, proportional statements may serve very well as conjectures concerning the probable sources within the language of given analogical formations, but they must not be taken as descriptions of actual processes in the brains of speakers.[59] I say this quite in agreement with a well-known passage in Bloomfield:

> Psychologists sometimes object to this formula, on the ground that the speaker is not capable of the reasoning which the proportional pattern implies. If this objection held good, linguists would be debarred from making almost any grammatical statement, since the normal speaker, who is not a linguist, does not describe his speech-habits, and, if we are foolish enough to ask him, fails utterly to make a correct formulation. Educated persons, who have had training in school grammar, overestimate their own ability in the way of formulating speech-habits, and, what is worse, forget

59. Hockett utters this same caution (1968, p. 96n.): "It is safer not to pretend that we know things about the brain that in fact we do not know." Such caution has not inhibited the Chomskyans from identifying their "underlying mechanism" with a brain mechanism which has "just the structure that the formulated theory attributes to it" (Katz, 1964, pp. 128f.).

that they owe this ability to a sophisticated philosophical tradition. They view it, instead, as a natural gift which they expect to find in all people, and feel free to deny the truth of any linguistic statement which the normal speaker is incapable of making. We have to remember at all times that the speaker, short of a highly specialized training, is incapable of describing his speech-habits. Our proportional formula of analogy and analogic change, like all other statements in linguistics, describes the action of the speaker and does not imply that the speaker himself could give a similar description. (Bloomfield, 1933, p. 406)

Sturtevant, however, offers a dissenting opinion:

There is, however, available a more fundamental answer to the psychologists quoted by Bloomfield; young children sometimes justify their employment of an unusual form by citing the formula upon which it is based. Jespersen [1922, p. 131] tells of a Danish child, who was corrected for using a strong preterit *nak* 'nodded' instead of the usual weak preterit *nikkede*, and who immediately retorted *stikker stak, nikker nak*. Bernard Bloch assures me that his three-year-old son has frequently defended himself by similar formulas, e.g., *sing sang, swing swang*. Of course children do not use a colon or a sign of equality or an *x* in stating analogic proportions, but they do sometimes state everything essential. (Sturtevant, 1947, p. 98)

It seems, however, unwise to generalize from such surprising utterances of certain children (particularly of linguists' children!) to analogical formations in general.

And now as to "editing": Hockett (1968, p. 92) lists "three fundamental mechanisms jointly responsible for a wide variety of instances, perhaps for all instances, of 'blunderful' or otherwise deviant new utterances: analogy, blending . . . , and editing." He states (pp. 98f.) that the act of speaking aloud is typically a two-stage process; there is an "inner stage" (primary generation) which is a "virtually unbroken inner flow of 'heard' speech, from which we make certain selections to be spoken aloud." This inner flow is "covertly edited" (one thinks of the Freudian "censor"), so that much in the inner flow is rejected before it can be overtly spoken. "Much more typically, what is actually said aloud includes various signs of overt editing." In his *Course* (1958) Hockett had said (p. 142):

> The succession of units produced by a speaker is governed constantly by the changing context, by the units already produced, and by his habits. These factors often supply conflicting directives, not only as to what unit to produce next, but also as to whether to keep on speaking or to stop. Consequently, speech is broken up by pauses, by hesitations, by interruptions, by repetitions, by sudden changes of direction. As hearers, we unconsciously edit out many of these overt manifestations of the hard work of utterance production.

The example of a transcription from a tape recording of a real conversation which Hockett gives on page 143 amply illustrates these statements; further evidence may be found in the transcriptions recorded by Dixon (1965). Such transcriptions are shocking reminders of the gulf which separates actual spoken language from the orderly systems of linguistics. One of the basic principles of linguistics has been that this science deals primarily with spoken language; but if this is true, the "spoken" language has been well edited, and indeed, Hockett (1958, p. 144) says that since paralinguistic phenomena "are not manifestations of the speaker's *linguistic* habits, it is proper to ignore them in the study of language, basing that study exclusively on edited speech."

There seem to me to be several objections which could be made with respect to the above suggestions of Hockett. First, with regard to the "inner stage," "primary generation," and "unbroken inner flow": Hockett (1967, p. 922) suggests that it is as though "the speaker first constructed a 'text' somewhere inside himself and then read it off, sometimes inaccurately." This notion of what one might call an "intraprompter," comparable to the teleprompter of television, seems to me, besides being unhappily reminiscent of Humboldtian "inner speech" and Chomskyan "deep structure," to describe processes which occur particularly and perhaps peculiarly in persons who lecture and write books; most people, I think, "just talk," and if they "get hung up" or "say the wrong thing," pause, or "hem and haw," or utter "autoclitics" until the stream resumes itself. (*Auto-*

clitic is a term taken from Skinner [1957]; it is defined as "behavior which is based upon or depends upon other verbal behavior"; it is thus the sort of commentary on or qualification of the rest of an utterance which Hockett calls "quotation" or "dequotation."[60] In the second place, it seems doubtful whether editing should be listed as a cause of deviant responses; rather, deviant responses may give rise to editing in some persons on some occasions; as Hockett points out, there are great individual differences in fluency. Editing may be said to occur when a speaker notices that he "has said something wrong," and since in such circumstances there may be a certain amount of emotional confusion, the attempt to correct the error may include a further error.

Winter (1970) has attempted to define the semantic relations which tend to give rise to analogical changes, paying special attention to the relations between numerals and between names of family relationships. He follows Hermann (1931) in attributing to Paul (1880–1920) the view "that, assuming that beside an A there is an A', a new B' can arise beside a B. For this, according to Paul, there need exist between A and B no definable relation." It is difficult to imagine that either Hermann or Winter has read Paul's Chapter 5 (1920, pp. 106–120). At any rate, it does not seem to me that Winter has added notably to our knowledge of the conditions which give rise to analogical changes.

In a paper presented in December 1969, Sarah Thomason presented

60. Skinner's two chapters on "self-editing" (pp. 369–402) show how this activity can be brought into relation with experimental psychology, and I think that linguistics would have benefited had linguists given careful attention to the entire book. But the name of Skinner is not to be found in the indexes of books by linguists—who have, however, given elaborate attention to the speculations, introspections, and intuitions of a logician. This is not to say that Skinner's book is the definitive account of verbal behavior which psychology can give, or that Skinner gave adequate attention to the works of linguists, but it is certainly the most thoroughgoing attempt which has yet been made to relate verbal behavior to other behavior and to environmental factors. Not the least of the disservices which Chomsky has done to linguistics is that of persuading the gullible that Skinner's work is not only negligible but also absurd, and that a logician can construct a superior psychology free of empirical data. Surely Dixon (1965) is right when he says in his Preface: "For an examination into the way language is used, in the daily round of living, it appears that consideration of correlations between language patterns and other behavioural or situational patterns is at least as important as a study of correlations wholly inside language."

"a preliminary outline of a proposed method for describing analogical changes."[61] She states that "an analysis of any analogical change should consist of two parts: a description of the basis for the comparison of the two forms or sets of forms, and a determination of the factor or factors motivating the direction of change." As "points of similarity" she lists "phonological, grammatical and semantic, and syntactic juxtaposition." She believes that "the classic sound-and-meaning resemblance is probably overestimated somewhat, but still it's rather unusual for a case of analogy to be based on one point of comparison alone"; as such an unusual case she cites dialectal /mawntiŋ/ 'mountain'←/mawntin/ etc., leveled after /goiŋ/ 'going'←/goin/ etc. I think however that it would be inadvisable to thus obscure the distinction between phonetic and analogic change; the leveling cited can be described in terms of conditional sound-change, and if we retain the sound-plus-meaning description of analogic change we maintain the relation to association studies.

As for the direction of analogical changes, Thomason lists the following "basic influences": (1) "If the choice of directions is between a simplifying or grammatically neutral change and one that would complicate a rule (or rules) of grammar, the change will be in the former direction"; (2) "All things being equal, forms or sets of forms that occur in greater numbers or with greater frequency will be analogical models rather than victims"; (3) There is "a tendency to add an extra formal marker to a given class of forms rather than to subtract one" (here she cites, e.g., such cases as the spread of the umlaut to German a-stem plurals); (4) social pressure, "when it is directly involved, is of overriding importance in determining the direction of change," but "it is impossible to recover information about social pressure in the great majority of the linguistic changes." Thomason states that any of the other three factors will overcome the effects of the second one listed above.

Thomason has demonstrated, I think, that careful study of historical and comparative records can yield useful generalizations about analogy.

---

61. In a letter of 6 August 1970 she informs me that she is continuing her study of analogical change: "dealing with the foundation of change—its relationship to the relative stability or instability of the portion of the grammar in which the change occurs."

Chapter 8

CONCLUSIONS: THE DEFINITION
AND USES OF THE TERM *ANALOGY*

We must first of all arrive at some notion of the kind of science which could most usefully employ the term *analogy*. It does not seem to me that either linguistics, as now practiced, or psychology, as now applied to language, is alone such a science. In linguistics we have found that scholars have not hesitated to invent "psychological" processes without troubling to study, or cite, the literature of experimental psychology, and lately some linguists have even ventured into the fields of biological genetics and neurophysiology, seemingly without awareness that these are vast fields of experimental research whose results impose restrictions on speculation. Moreover, linguists have tended to concentrate their attention on what they figuratively call "structure," i.e., intraverbal patterns within utterances, and have commonly left out of account the relations of utterances to other behavior and to the organic states and environmental conditions of speakers and hearers. As for psychology, its practitioners, at least in America, were, until recently, almost totally unaware of the literature of linguistics, but did not on that account refrain from theorizing about language. When some psychologists finally, in the 1950s, came in contact with linguists and their literature, the linguistic field, as seen by "psycholinguists," was about to be preempted by a special school of linguists who rejected most of the experimental and theoretical work of psychologists and persuaded their psychologist colleagues to accept nonexperimental speculative constructs which were declared to be superior to empirically derived generalizations. Since the subject-matter of this school was "idealized" utterances, and the goal was the construction of a hypothesized static "underlying system" or "competence" rather than generalizations empirically derived from large bodies of recorded actual utterances, analogy, which is a phenomenon mostly of ordinary unguarded speech—which does not by any means consist wholly of strings of well-formed sentences—was not considered an important or interesting phenomenon, nor was the concept considered useful.

However, there had been a continuing interest in psychology in word-association, at first without relation to linguistics. Woodworth's (1938) chapter on association was largely responsible for this continued interest, and particularly for the numerous citations of Thumb and Marbe by psychologists, who did not however trouble to read that monograph but contented themselves with repeating the finding of a negative relation between frequency and reaction-time. No attention was paid by these psychologists to the linguistic purposes and implications of the studies by Thumb and Marbe (1901), Thumb (1907a, 1909, 1910, 1911), and Esper (1918, 1925, 1933, 1935), until Jenkins (Jenkins and Palermo, 1964; Jenkins, 1965) called attention to them. Various other psychologists, under the influence of Jenkins, took up work with "miniature linguistic systems" (MLS); especially active with this method, both experimentally and theoretically, have been Braine (e.g., 1965a, 1965b, 1966) and Kirk Smith (e.g., Smith and Braine, 1970). But these workers, under the Chomskyan influence, inclined to describe the performance of subjects in such experiments as the discovery of rules. Here I think that some comments by Skinner (1966) are relevant:

> The behavior of one who speaks correctly by applying the rules of a grammar merely resembles the behavior of one who speaks correctly from long experience in a verbal community. The efficiency may be the same, but the controlling variables are different, and the behaviors are therefore different. Nothing which could be called following a plan or applying a rule is observed when behavior is a product of the contingencies alone. To say that "the child who learns a language has in some sense constructed the grammar for himself" (Chomsky, 1959) is as misleading as to say that a dog which has learned to catch a ball has in some sense constructed the relevant part of the science of mechanics. Rules can be extracted from the reinforcing contingencies in both cases, and once in existence they may be used as guides. The direct effect of the contingencies is of a different nature. (Skinner, 1966, p. 29)

Analogical formations can indeed be described by an observer as applications of rules, but the cases must be very rare in which the speaker has actually formulated rules—which he could state—and applied them in his speech. Rules are products, not of speakers, but of linguists or psycholinguists. In my MLS experiments, most of the subjects were not aware that figures not previously seen, but systematically related to the ones whose names had been learned, were being presented; nevertheless they responded analogically. In experiments in the learning of sequences of manual movements (button pressing), subjects, when asked how they had learned, characteristically had little to report; some had tried to assist themselves by a parallel learning of a covert verbal series, but others said, "It was just my fingers that learned." I think that as psychologists we delude ourselves when we accept the linguistic rules formulated by logicians as descriptions of what goes on in the heads of speakers when they learn or speak a language; neurophysiology has not as yet arrived at a stage where it could justify talk about brain mechanisms involved in such activity.

We are limited then to generalizations which summarize as concisely as possible the relations which we find in the speech of individuals, not only however within the speech itself but also between speech and other behavior, organic states, and environments. I do not think that we shall make much progress as long as we limit ourselves to purely intraverbal correlations. To make progress, linguists must make a closer acquaintance with experimental psychology, and psychologists must learn general linguistics—and not merely the doctrines of Chomsky. The fact that the Chomskyans declare their interest to be exclusively in Saussurean *langue* and regard *parole* as of inferior interest, and that in general they speak disparagingly of empirical science, would seem to mark them as unsuitable collaborators for those psychologists who regard psychology as a behavioral science.

And now, how shall we define analogy? I think that the literature of linguistics justifies us in beginning with a delimitation: Analogical changes are those which cannot be attributed either to borrowing or to purely phonetic factors. Under phonetic factors I mean to include both those which, though unknown, are operative in phonetic "laws," and those which are operative in momentary slips of the tongue resulting from anticipations, interferences, omissions, etc. among the articulations of a single utterance. True analogical formations may then be described as those which may occur when a syntactic or semantic context elicits a morph or morphs which, though previously learned in similar contexts, have not previously been uttered or heard by the speaker in this particular context, and which may or may not be conventional. Two different morphs may be elicited either consecutively, as in my first MLS experiment, or nearly simultaneously, as in contaminations or blends.

Such behavior may of course be described by saying that speakers apply rules or follow models or display creativeness or productivity, but at the risk of being accused of insulting human intelligence, I must declare my belief that sober science will be better served if we assume that an individual's behavior at a given time is a product of his past environmental-behavioral contingencies. Certainly, those who have been most vociferously denouncing this policy and proclaiming the mentalistic powers of the brain have very little knowledge either of the brain or of behavioral contingencies, and, I would add, no knowledge at all of actual speech, in which analogical formations occur, as distinguished from the "well-formed" sentences of linguistic logicians.

In such situations as were provided in my first MLS experiment, appropriate responses to the novel figures had actually been previously learned. When in the learning of a 4 × 4 matrix two combinations previously omitted are presented, responses have previously been attached to each of the features of the novel combination. That is, if two-morph "words" are learned in correlation with two-feature stimulus-patterns, the correlations between each morph and each stimulus-feature are also learned, so that new combinations of these seame features may be "appropriately" responded to (cf. also the cited experiments of F. J. Smith, 1967). This paradigm may be generalized to the universe of stimulus-response correlations: very few stimulus-patterns occur which do not bear some resemblance to previously experienced patterns, so that they tend in some degree to elicit responses made previously. In this generalization I of course mean to include the features of "displaced speech" (Bloomfield, 1933, pp. 141–143).

The relation of analogical formations to word-associations comes about through the fact that when a context tends to elicit several different forms, each form also acquires a tendency to elicit the others. The existence however of a word-association does not justify the prediction of an analogical change. In fact, "prediction" here expresses an unsuitable notion.[62] As Kuryłowicz and Mańczak have emphasized, there is always a factor of historical contingency in the causation of any analogical changes, or, as Thumb said, "other times, other analogical changes." On the other hand, it seems unwise to either posit or expect an analogical change if the forms in question could not be associatively linked by many individuals.

62. Rulon Wells (1951), like Hockett, took his departure from Freud, but declared that Freud's theory failed in one criterion of a theory, namely, prediction—e.g., of "concrete specific slips of the tongue"—because of "his neglect of the linguistic factor." But Wells admits that linguistic predictions have two limitations: "they are conditional and they are alternative"; i.e., they cannot predict "concrete, specific slips." The discussion is mostly of blends, but semantic factors, such as synonymity, are ruled out of the discussion as being "psychological"; the "linguistically relevant" factor is formal similarity, summarized in three laws: (1) "A slip of the tongue is practically always a phonetically possible [i.e., in the given language] noise"; (2) "If the two original words are rhythmically similar, a blend of them will, with high probability, rhythmically resemble both of them"; (3) "If the two original words contain the same sound in the same position, a blend of them will contain that sound in that position." Wells points out that "there is already evidence that certain people are more prone to one kind of slip of the tongue than to another," and declares that "the study of such tendencies is properly a collaborative job: the linguist furnishes the classification of slips of the tongue, and the psychoanalyst or other psychologist correlates the tendency to select this or that kind of slip with the personality type of the speaker."
On Wells's paper I would make the following comments: (1) The term *slips of the tongue* had better be abandoned in linguistics; it seems to lead to a confusion between momentary articulatory interferences within the utterances of individuals, and analogical formations resulting from semantic relations of the sort which also result in word-associations shared by many speakers. (2) Psychoanalysts are not psychologists and their methods are not accepted by experimental psychologists; they are dubious collaborators for linguists. (3) Linguists who wish to discuss analogy should be well versed in experimental psychology, and they should regard semantics as an essential part of their task. (4) The meaning of *prediction* in linguistics is far from clear. Certain general trends in a given language may be expected to continue—e.g., certain types of analogical change characteristic of a certain language at a certain period; we may also state a general "law" to the effect that semantic resemblances tend to become marked by phonetic resemblances, but actual changes involve unpredictable "initial conditions." A language is not, as the Chomskyans seem to assume, an isolated system, and a linguistics which limits itself to linguistic structure is not adequate to deal with such a phenomenon as analogical formations.

And finally, I call attention once more to my finding that some individuals are more prone than are others to produce analogical formations, and that these individuals differ from those others in associative and reaction characteristics. These differences would seem to be in harmony with the emphasis which some linguists have placed on the function of prestige and imitation in linguistic change.

The analogic change discussed in this book has been of the type which includes all those cases where words or groups of words, associated semantically or formally, become assimilated to each other in form; analogical changes of these sorts have therefore been called *morphological* and *functional*. Oertel (1901, pp. 154, 324ff.) distinguished a class of *semantic* change attributable to association, consisting of two subclasses: "(1) those in which the associative link is purely formal, as when homophones influence each other semantically, and (2) those cases in which the associative bond is semantic." The first subclass is illustrated by New England Anglo-German "Ich kann es nicht erfordern," where English *afford* has "infected" German *erfordern*; the second subclass is illustrated by German "Habt ihr keine Scheu und Schande," where *Schande* = *Scham* through the influence of Slavic *sramota*, which covers the meaning of both German words. Kroesch discusses "Analogy as a Factor in Semantic Change" in *Language*, 1926, 2, 35–45, giving many examples. The concept of "semantic analogy" has been critically discussed by Stern (1931, pp. 224–227).

REFERENCES

Aarsleff, H. The history of linguistics and Professor Chomsky. *Language*, 1970, 46, 570–585.

Abercrombie, D. Conversation and spoken prose. In *Studies in phonetics and linguistics*. London: Oxford University Press, 1965.

Aborn, M., Rubenstein, H., and Sterling, T. D. Sources of contextual constraint upon words in sentences. *Journal of Experimental Psychology*, 1959, 57, 171–180.

Arens, Hans. *Sprachwissenschaft: Der Gang ihrer Entwicklung von der Antike bis zur Gegenwart.* München: Karl Alber, 1955.

Aschaffenburg, G. Experimentelle Studien über Association. *Psychologische Arbeiten*, 1895, 1, 209–299; 1897, 2, 1–83; 1902, 4, 235–373.

Ascoli, G. J. Die Entstehung des griechischen Superlativssuffixes -tato-. [*Curtius'*] *Studien zur Griechischen und Lateinischen Grammatik*, 1876, 9, 339–360. Trans. by R. Merzdorf.

Bailey, P. The great psychiatric revolution. *American Journal of Psychiatry*, 1956, 113, 387–406.

Baker, L. M., and Elliott, D. N. Controlled and free association-times with identical stimulus- and response-words. *American Journal of Psychology*, 1948, 61, 535–539.

Bawden, H. H. A study of lapses. *Psychological Review Monograph Supplements*, 1900, 3, no. 4 (whole no. 14).

Benfey, T. *Geschichte der Sprachwissenschaft.* München: Cotta, 1868–1869.

Bills, A. G. *General experimental psychology.* New York: Longmans, Green, 1934.

Bloomfield, L. *Language.* New York: Holt, 1933.

Blumenthal, A. L. *Language and psychology.* New York: Wiley, 1970.

Boer, T. J. de. Zur gegenseitigen Wortassoziation. *Zeitschrift für Psychologie*, 1908, 48, 397–405.

Boomer, D. S., and Laver, J. D. Slips of the tongue. *British Journal of Disorders of Communication*, 1968, 3, 1–12.

Boring, E. G. *A history of experimental psychology.* 2nd ed. New York: Appleton-Century-Crofts, 1950.

Bourne, L. E., Jr. Concept attainment. In T. R. Dixon and D. L. Horton, eds., *Verbal behavior and general behavior theory.* Englewood Cliffs, N. J.: Prentice-Hall, 1968. Pp. 230–253.

Braine, M. D. S. The insufficiency of a finite state model for verbal reconstructive memory. *Psychonomic Science*, 1965, 2, 291–292. (a)

Braine, M. D. S. Inferring a grammar from responses. *Psychonomic Science*, 1965, 3, 241–242. (b)

Braine, M. D. S. Learning the positions of words relative to a marker element. *Journal of Experimental Psychology*, 1966, 72, 532–540.

Bredsdorff, J. H. *Om Aarsagerne til Sprogenes Forandringer* ("On the Causes of

Change in Language"). Printed as a Prospectus for the Public Examination in the Roskilde Cathedral School, 1821. Republished: Copenhagen: Vilhelm Thomsen, 1886. Republished: Copenhagen: Levin and Mandsgaard, 1933.

Brown, R., and Berko, J. Word association and the acquisition of grammar. *Child Development*, 1960, 31, 1–14.

Brugmann, K. Nasalis sonans in der indogermanischen Grundsprache. [*Curtius'*] *Studien zur Griechischen und Lateinischen Grammatik*, 1876, 9, 285–338.

Brugmann, K. Zur Geschichte der Nominalsuffixe -*as*-, -*jas*- und -*vas*-. [*Kuhn's*] *Zeitschrift für vergleichende Sprachforschung auf dem Gebiete der Indogermanischen Sprachen*, 1877, 24 (n.s. 4), 1–99.

Brugmann, K. *Zum heutigen Stand der Sprachwissenschaft*. Strassburg: Trübner, 1885.

Carroll, J. B. *The study of language: A survey of linguistics and related disciplines in America*. Cambridge, Mass.: Harvard University Press, 1953.

Carroll, J. B., Kjeldergaard, P. M., and Carton, A. S. Number of opposites versus number of primaries as a response measure in free-association tests. *Journal of Verbal Learning and Verbal Behavior*, 1962, 1, 22–30.

Cason, H., and Cason, E. B. Association tendencies and learning ability. *Journal of Experimental Psychology*, 1925, 8, 167–189.

Cattell, J. McK. The time taken up by cerebral operations. *Mind*, 1886, 11, 220–242; 377–387; 524–538.

Cattell, J. McK. Experiments on the association of ideas. *Mind*, 1887, 12, 68–74.

Cattell, J. McK., and Bryant, S. Mental association investigated by experiment. *Mind*, 1889, 14, 230–250.

Chapanis, A. Notes on an approximation method for fitting parabolic equations to experimental data. *Psychometrika*, 1953, 18, 327–336.

Chomsky, N. *Cartesian linguistics*. New York: Harper and Row, 1966.

Chomsky, N. The formal nature of language. In E. H. Lenneberg, *Biological foundations of language*. New York: Wiley, 1967. Pp. 397–442.

Chomsky, N. Reply. *Current Anthropology*, 1968, 9, 165–168.

Classen, J. *De grammaticae Graecae primordiis*. Bonn, 1829.

Cofer, C. N. Associative commonality and rated similarity of certain words from Haagen's list. *Psychological Reports*, 1957, 3, 603–606.

Cofer, C. N. Conditions for the use of verbal associations. *Psychological Bulletin*, 1967, 68, 1–12. (a)

Cofer, C. N. Some data on controlled association. *Journal of Verbal Learning and Verbal Behavior*, 1967, 6, 601–608. (b)

Cofer, C. N. [Review of] *The structure of associations in language and thought*, by J. Deese. *American Scientist*, 1967, 55, 228A–229A. (c)

Cofer, C. N., and Ford, T. J. Verbal context and free association-time. *American Journal of Psychology*, 1957, 70, 606–610.

Cofer, C. N., and Shevitz, R. Word-association as a function of word-frequency. *American Journal of Psychology*, 1952, 65, 75–79.

Colson, F. H. The analogist and anomalist controversy. *Classical Quarterly*, 1919, 13, 24–36.

Cook, S. W., and Skinner, B. F. Some factors influencing the distribution of associated words. *Psychological Record*, 1939, 3, 178–184.

Cook, T. H., Mefferd, R. B., and Wieland, B. A. The effects of idiodynamic set and stimulus characteristics on numerical homonym associates. *Psychological Reports*, 1965, 17, 583–589.

Cramer, P. *Word association*. New York: Academic Press, 1968.

Crane, H. W. A study in association reaction and reaction time. *Psychological Monographs*, 1915, 18, no. 4 (whole no. 80).

Curtius, G. Das dreisilbengesetz der griechischen und lateinischen betonung. [*Kuhn's*] *Zeitschrift für vergleichende Sprachforschung*, 1860, 9, 321–338.

Curtius, G. Bemerkungen über die Tragweite der Lautgesetze. *Berichte der Phil.-Hist. Klasse der kgl. Sächs. Gesellschaft der Wissenschaft*. Leipzig, 1870.

Curtius, G. *Zur Kritik der neuesten Sprachforschung*. Leipzig, 1885.

Dauber, J. Über bevorzugte Assoziationen und verwandte Phänomene. *Zeitschrift für Psychologie*, 1911, 59, 176–222.

Davidson, E. H. Some determinants of verbal association times. Doctoral dissertation, Pennsylvania State University, 1965.

Deese, J. *The structure of associations in language and thought*. Baltimore: Johns Hopkins Press, 1965.

Deese, J. *Psycholinguistics*. Boston: Allyn and Bacon, 1970.

Delacroix, H. *Le langage et la pensée*. Paris: Alcan, 1924.

Delbrück, B. *Einleitung in das Studium der indogermanischen Sprachen*. 5th ed. Leipzig: Breitkopf and Härtel, 1908.

Dixon, R. M. W. *What is language?* London: Longmans, 1965.

Dunlap, K. The stop-watch and the association test. *Psychobiology*, 1917, 1, 171–175.

Ebbinghaus, H. *Ueber das Gedächtnis*. 1885. (*Memory*, trans. H. A. Ruger and C. E. Bussenius. New York: Teachers College Press, 1913.)

Eberschweiler, A. Untersuchungen über die sprachliche Komponente der Assoziation. *Allgemeine Zeitschrift für Psychiatrie*, 1908, 65, 240–271.

Eccles, J. C. An electrical hypothesis of synaptic and neuromuscular transmission. *Annals of the New York Academy of Science*, 1946–1947, 47, 429–455.

Eccles, J. C. Acetylcholine and synaptic transmission in the spinal cord. *Journal of Neurophysiology*, 1947, 10, 197–204.

Ekdahl, A. G. The effect of attitude on free word-association time. *Genetic Psychology Monographs*, 1929, 5, 253–332.

Entwisle, D. R., and Forsyth, D. F. Word associations of children: effect of method of administration. *Psychological Reports*, 1963, 13, 291–299.

Entwisle, D. R., Forsyth, D. F., and Muuss, R. The syntactic-paradigmatic shift in children's word associations. *Journal of Verbal Learning and Verbal Behavior*, 1964, 3, 19–29.

Ervin, S. M. Grammar and classification. Paper read at the meeting of the American Psychological Association, New York, 1957.

Ervin, S. M. Changes with age in the verbal determinants of word-association. *American Journal of Psychology*, 1961, 74, 361–372.

Ervin, S. M. Correlates of associative frequency. *Journal of Verbal Learning and Verbal Behavior*, 1963, 1, 422–431.

Ervin, S. M. Imitation and structural change in children's language. In E. G. Lenneberg, ed., *New directions in the study of language*. Cambridge, Mass.: M.I.T. Press, 1964.

Esper, E. A. A contribution to the experimental study of analogy. *Psychological Review*, 1918, 25, 468–487.

Esper, E. A. A technique for the experimental investigation of associative interference in artificial linguistic material. *Language Monographs of the Linguistic Society of America*, 1925, 1.

Esper, E. A. [Review of] Pillsbury and Meader: *The psychology of language*. *Pedagogical Seminary and Journal of Genetic Psychology*, 1930, 37, 332–337.

Esper, E. A. Studies in linguistic behavior organization. *Journal of General Psychology*, 1933, 8, 346–381.

Esper, E. A. Language. In C. Murchison, ed., *A handbook of social psychology.* Worcester, Mass.: Clark University Press, 1935. Pp. 417–460.

Esper, E. A. *A history of psychology.* Philadelphia: Saunders, 1964.

Esper, E. A. Social transmission of an artificial language. *Language,* 1966, 42 (no. 3, pt. 1), 575–580.

Esper, E. A. *Mentalism and objectivism in linguistics.* New York: American Elsevier, 1968.

Fehling, Detlev. Varro und die grammatische Lehre von der Analogie und der Flexion. *Glotta,* 1956, 35, 214–270; 1958, 36, 48–100.

Flavell, J. H., Draguns, J., Feinberg, L. D., and Budin, W. A microgenetic approach to word association. *Journal of Abnormal and Social Psychology,* 1958, 57, 1–7.

Fodor, J., and Garrett, M. Some reflections on competence and performance. In J. Lyons and R. J. Wales, eds., *Psycholinguistics papers.* Edinburgh: Edinburgh University Press, 1966. Pp. 135–154.

Foley, J. P., and Macmillan, Z. L. Mediated generalization and the interpretation of verbal behavior: V. 'Free association' as related to differences in professional training. *Journal of Experimental Psychology,* 1943, 33, 299–310.

Foss, D. J. An analysis of learning in a miniature linguistic system. *Journal of Experimental Psychology,* 1968, 76, 450–459.

Friedrich, M. Ueber die Apperceptionsdauer bei einfachen und zusammengesetzten Vorstellungen. *Philosophischen Studien,* 1883, 1, 39–77.

Fröbes, J. *Lehrbuch der experimentellen Psychologie.* Vol. 2. 3rd ed. Freiburg in Breisgau: Herder, 1923.

Gagné, R. M. The effect of sequence of presentation of similar items on the learning of paired associates. *Journal of Experimental Psychology,* 1950, 40, 61–73.

Galton, F. Psychometric experiments. *Brain,* 1879–1880, 2, 149–162.

Gibson, E. J. A systematic application of the concepts of generalization and differentiation to verbal learning. *Psychological Review,* 1940, 47, 196–229.

Glucksberg, S., and Cohen, J. A. Acquisition of form-class membership by syntactic position: Paradigmatic associations to nonsense syllables. *Psychonomic Science,* 1965, 2, 313–314.

Godel, R. Les sources manuscrites du Cours de linguistique générale de F. de Saussure. *Société de publications romanes et françaises,* 1957, 61.

Goldstein, M. Some slips of the tongue. *Psychological Reports,* 1968, 22, 1009–1013.

Goodenough, F. L. Semantic choice and personality structure. *Science,* 1946, 104, 451–456.

Grunig, B. Les théories transformationnelles: Exposé critique. *La Linguistique,* 1965, pt. 1, 1–24; 1966, pt. 1, 31–101.

Guthrie, E. R. *The psychology of learning.* New York: Harper, 1935.

Hall, J. F., and Ugelow, A. Free association time as a function of word frequency. *Canadian Journal of Psychology,* 1957, 11, 29–32.

Hall, R. A., Jr. [Review of] R. M. W. Dixon's *What is language? Foundations of Language,* 1968, 4, 87–96. (a)

Hall, R. A., Jr. *An essay on language.* Philadelphia: Chilton, 1968. (b)

Hall, R. A., Jr. Some recent developments in American linguistics. *Neuphilologische Mitteilungen,* 1969, 70, 192–227.

Hawkins, A. S. Verbal identification of stimulus components in ambiguously named compounds. *Journal of Experimental Child Psychology,* 1964, 1, 227–240.

Henry, V. *Etude sur l'analogie.* Paris, 1883.

Herdan, G. The crisis in modern general linguistics. *La Linguistique,* 1965, pt. 2, 27–37.

Herdan, G. "Götzendämmerung" at M.I.T. *Zeitschrift für Phonetik, Sprachwissenschaft, und Kommunikationsforschung*, 1968, 21, 223–231.

Hermann, E. *Lautgesetz und Analogie.* Berlin: Weidmannsche Buchhandlung, 1931.

Herzog, E. [Review of] Thumb and Marbe, *Experimentelle Untersuchungen. Zeitschrift für französische Sprache und Literatur*, 1903, 25, 124–132.

Hobbes, T. *Leviathan.* London, 1651.

Hockett, C. F. *A course in modern linguistics.* New York: Macmillan, 1958.

Hockett, C. F. Where the tongue slips, there slip I. In *To honor Roman Jakobson: Essays on the occasion of his seventieth birthday.* The Hague: Mouton, 1967. Pp. 910–936.

Hockett, C. F. *The state of the art.* The Hague: Mouton, 1968.

Horowitz, A. E. The effects of variation in linguistic structure on the learning of miniature linguistic systems. Doctoral dissertation, Harvard University, 1955.

Horowitz, A. E. Experimental studies of the relation between language and cognition. Technical report, Hofstra University, 1967. (Under contract of the United States Office of Education.)

Horowitz, A. E. Variables in the learning of a classical Esper miniature linguistic system. Paper read at a symposium on The miniature linguistic system: Its relation to psychology and linguistics, at the meeting of the American Psychological Association, 1968.

Horowitz, A. E., and Jackson, H. M. Morpheme order and syllable structure in the learning of miniature linguistic systems. *Journal of Abnormal and Social Psychology*, 1959, 59, 387–392.

Howes, D. In search of meaning. [Review of] *The structure of associations in language and thought*, by J. Deese. *Contemporary Psychology*, 1967, 12, 548–549.

Howes, D., and Osgood, C. E. On the combination of associative probabilities in linguistic contexts. *American Journal of Psychology*, 1954, 67, 241–258.

Hull, C. L. Quantitative aspects of the evolution of concepts. *Psychological Monographs*, 1920, 28, no. 123.

Humboldt, W. v. Ueber das vergleichende Sprachstudium in Beziehung auf die verschiedenen Epochen der Sprachentwickelung. *Abhandlungen der Berliner Akademie der Wissenschaften, historischephilologische Klasse*, 1820–1821, 239–260. Reprinted, *Gesammelte Werke*, 3, 249ff.

Humboldt, W. v. *Ueber die Verschiedenheit des menschlichen Sprachbaues und ihren Einfluss auf die geistige Entwickelung des Menschengeschlechts.* Berlin, 1836. Facsimile reprint, Bonn: Dümmler, 1960.

Humphrey, G. *Thinking: An introduction to its experimental psychology.* New York: Wiley, 1951.

Jenkins, J. J. Transitional organization: Association techniques. In C. E. Osgood and T. S. Sebeok, eds., *Psycholinguistics.* Baltimore: Waverly Press, 1954. Pp. 112–118.

Jenkins, J. J. A study of mediated association. *University of Minnesota Studies in Verbal Behavior*, 1959, report no. 2.

Jenkins, J. J. Commonality of association as an indicator of more general patterns of verbal behavior. In T. S. Sebeok, ed., *Style in language.* New York: Wiley, 1960. Pp. 307–329.

Jenkins, J. J. Mediated associations: paradigms and situations. In C. N. Cofer and B. S. Musgrave, eds., *Verbal behavior and learning.* New York: McGraw-Hill, 1963. Pp. 210–245.

Jenkins, J. J. A mediational account of grammatical phenomena. *Journal of Communication*, 1964, 14, 86–97.

Jenkins, J. J. Mediation theory and grammatical behavior. In S. Rosenberg, ed., *Directions in psycholinguistics.* New York: Macmillan, 1965. Pp. 66–96.

Jenkins, J. J. The role of experimentation in psycholinguistics. Invited address,

American Psychological Association, Division 3, 1966. To be published in T. C. Bever and W. Weksel, eds., *The structure and psychology of language*, vol. 2. New York: Holt, Rinehart and Winston, 1970.

Jenkins, J. J. The nature of psychological theory. *Psychological Scene*, 1968, 2, 55–60. (a)

Jenkins, J. J. (Chm.) The miniature linguistic system: its relation to psychology and linguistics. Symposium, at the meeting of the American Psychological Association, San Francisco, 1968. (b)

Jenkins, J. J. The acquisition of language. In D. A. Goslin, ed., *Handbook of socialization theory and research*. New York: Rand McNally, 1969. Pp. 661–686.

Jenkins, J. J., and Palermo, D. S. Mediation processes and the acquisition of linguistic structure. In V. Bellugi and R. W. Brown, eds., *The acquisition of language*. Monographs of the Society for Research in Child Development, 1964, serial no. 92, 29, no. 1. Pp. 141–169.

Jenkins, J. J., and Palermo, D. S. Further data on changes in word-association norms. *Journal of Personality and Social Psychology*, 1965, 1, 303–309.

Jenkins, J. J., and Russell, W. A. Systematic changes in word association norms, 1910–1952. *Journal of Abnormal and Social Psychology*, 1960, 60, 293–304.

Jenkins, P. M., and Cofer, C. N. An exploratory study of discrete free association to compound verbal stimuli. *Psychological Reports*, 1957, 3, 599–602.

Jespersen, O. *Language: Its nature, development and origin*. New York: Holt, 1922.

Jung, C. G. *Studies in word-association*. Trans. M. D. Eder from the *Diagnostische Associationsstudien* published in 1904. London: Heinemann, 1918.

Jung, J. Experimental studies of factors affecting word associations. *Psychological Bulletin*, 1966, 66, 125–133.

Kaeding, F. W. *Häufigkeitswörterbuch der deutschen Sprache*. Steglitz bei Berlin, 1898.

Katz, J. J. Mentalism in linguistics. *Language*, 1964, 40, 124–137.

Kelley, T. L. *Statistical method*. New York: Macmillan, 1924.

Kent, G. H., and Rosanoff, A. J. A study of association in insanity. *American Journal of Insanity*, 1910, 67, 37–96, 317–390.

King, R. D. *Historical linguistics and generative grammar*. Englewood Cliffs, N. J.: Prentice-Hall, 1969.

Kiparsky, P. Linguistic universals and linguistic change. In E. Bach and R. T. Harms, eds., *Universals in linguistic theory*. New York: Holt, Rinehart and Winston, 1968. Pp. 171–202.

Koff, R. H. Systematic changes in children's word-association norms 1916–63. *Child Development*, 1965, 36, 299–305.

Koffka, K. *Zur Analyse der Vorstellungen und ihrer Gesetze*. 1912.

Kraepelin, E. Experimentelle Studien über Associationen. *Versammlung deutscher Naturforscher und Aertzte*, Freiburg in Breisgau, 1883.

Kuryłowicz, J. La nature des proces dits "analogique." *Acta linguistica*, 1949, 5, 15–37. References are to the republication in E. P. Hamp, F. W. Householder, and R. Austerlitz, eds., *Readings in Linguistics II*. Chicago: University of Chicago Press, 1966. Pp. 158–174.

Laffal, J. Response faults in word association as a function of response entropy. *Journal of Abnormal and Social Psychology*, 1955, 50, 265–270.

Lamb, S. [Review of Chomsky's] *The logical basis of linguistic theory* and *Aspects of the theory of syntax. American Anthropologist*, 1967, n.s. 69, 411–415.

Lang, J. B. Die "zu lange Reaktionszeit" beim Associationsexperiment. *Schweizerische Zeitschrift für Psychologie und ihre Anwendungen*, 1943, 2, 100–116.

Langendoen, D. T. A note on the linguistic theory of M. Terentius Varro. *Foundations of Language*, 1966, 2, 33–36.

LaPiere, R. T., and Farnsworth, P. R. *Social psychology*. 2nd ed. New York: McGraw-Hill, 1942.

Lashley, K. S. *Brain mechanisms and intelligence*. Chicago: University of Chicago Press, 1929.

Lashley, K. S. The problem of serial order in behavior. In Sol Saporta, ed., *Psycholinguistics*. New York: Holt, Rinehart and Winston, 1961. Pp. 180–198.

Lenneberg, E. H. A probabilistic approach to language learning. *Behavioral Science*, 1957, 2, 1–12.

Lenneberg, E. H. *Biological foundations of language*. New York: Wiley, 1967.

Lepley, W. M. An hypothesis concerning the generation and use of synonyms. *Journal of Experimental Psychology*, 1950, 40, 527–530.

Leroy, M. *Main trends in modern linguistics*. Trans. G. Price. Berkeley: University of California Press, 1967.

Lersch, L. *Die Sprachphilosophie der Alten*. Bonn, 1838–1841.

Leskien, A. *Die Deklination im Slavisch-Litauischen und Germanischen*. Leipzig, 1876. Republished: Leipzig: Zentral-Antiquariat der Deutschen Demokratischen Republik, 1963.

Loring, M. W. Methods of studying controlled word associations. *Psychobiology*, 1918, 1, 369–428.

Lyons, J. *Introduction to theoretical linguistics*. Cambridge: University Press, 1968.

McGinnies, E. Personal values as determinants of word association. *Journal of Abnormal and Social Psychology*, 1950, 45, 28–36.

Mańczak, W. Tendences générale des changements analogiques. *Lingua*, 1958, 7, 298–325, 387–420.

Mandler, G. Comments on Professor Jenkins's paper. In C. N. Cofer and B. S. Musgrave, eds., *Verbal behavior and learning*. New York: McGraw-Hill, 1963. Pp. 245–252.

Marbe, K. *Experimentell-psychologische Untersuchungen über das Urteil*. Leipzig: Engelmann, 1901.

Marbe, K. [Critique of] On the association of numerals, by H. Oertel. *American Journal of Psychology*, 1902, 13, 450–451.

Marbe, K. [Autobiography] In C. Murchison, ed., *History of Psychology in Autobiography*, vol. 3. Worcester, Mass.: Clark University Press, 1936. Pp. 181–213.

Marshall, J. C. "E. A. Esper: *Mentalism and objectivism: The sources of Leonard Bloomfield's psychology of language*." *Semiotica*, 1970, 2, 277–293.

May, M. A. The mechanism of controlled association. *Archives of Psychology*, 1917, 25, no. 39.

Mayer, A., and Orth, J. Zur qualitativen Untersuchung der Association. *Zeitschrift für Psychologie*, 1901, 26, 1–13.

Menzerath, P. Psychologische Untersuchung über die sprachliche Kontamination. *Zeitschrift für angewandte Psychologie*, 1908, 2, 280–290. (a)

Menzerath, P. Die Bedeutung der sprachlichen Geläufigkeit oder der formalen sprachlichen Beziehung für die Reproduction. *Zeitschrift für Psychologie*, 1908, 48, 1–95. (b)

Meringer, R., and Mayer, K. *Versprechen und Verlesen*. Stuttgart: Göschen, 1895.

Merzdorf, R. Vokalverkürzung vor Vokalen und quantitative metathesis im Ionischen. [Curtius'] *Studien zur Griechischen und Lateinischen Grammatik*, 1876, 9, 201–243.

Messer, A. Experimentell-psychologische Untersuchungen über das Denken. *Archiv für die gesamte Psychologie*, 1906, 8, 1–224.

Middleton, G. *An essay on analogy in syntax*. London: Longmans Green, 1892.

Miller, G. A. *Language and communication*. New York: McGraw-Hill, 1951.

Miller, G. A. Some preliminaries to psycholinguistics. *American Psychologist*, 1965, 20, 15–20.

Misteli, F. Lautgesetz und Analoge. *Zeitschrift für Völkerpsychologie und Sprachwissenschaft*, 1880, 12, 365–475; 12, 1–27.

Monboddo, Lord (James Burnet). *Dissertation on the origin and progress of language*. 1773.

Moran, L. J. Generality of word-association response sets. *Psychological Monographs*, 1966, 80, no. 4, 1–25.

Moran, L. J., Mefferd, R. B., and Kimble, J. P. Idiodynamic sets in word association. *Psychological Monographs*, 1964, 78, no. 2.

Morely, A., and Stohlman, F. Erythropoiesis in the dog: The periodic nature of the steady state. *Science*, 1959, 165, 1025–1028.

Münsterberg, H. Studien zur Associationslehre. *Beiträge zur experimentellen Psychologie*, 1892, 4, 1–39.

Nagel, F. Experimentelle Untersuchungen über Grundfragen der Assoziationslehre. *Archiv für die gesamte Psychologie*, 1912, 23, 156–253.

Oertel, H. *Lectures on the study of language*. New York: Scribner's, 1901. (a)

Oertel, H. On the association of numerals. *American Journal of Philology*, 1901, 22, 261–267. (b)

Osgood, C. E., and Sebeok, T. A., eds. *Psycholinguistics*. Indiana University Publications in Anthropology and Linguistics. Memoir 10 of the *International Journal of American Linguistics*. Baltimore: Waverly Press, 1954.

Osgood, C. E., and Sebeok, T. A., eds. *Psycholinguistics*. Bloomington: Indiana University Press, 1965.

Osthoff, H. *Das Verbum in der Nominalcomposition*. Jena, 1878.

Osthoff, H. *Das physiologische und psychologische Moment in der sprachlichen Formenbildung*. Berlin, 1879.

Osthoff, H., and Brugmann, K. *Morphologische Untersuchungen auf dem Gebiete der indogermanischen Sprachen. Erster Theil*. Leipzig: Hirzel, 1878.

Palermo, D. S. Word associations and children's verbal behavior. In L. P. Lipsitt and C. C. Spiker, eds., *Advances in child development and behavior*. New York: Academic Press, 1963.

Palermo, D. S., and Eberhart, V. L. On the learning of morphological rules: An experimental analogy. *Journal of Verbal Learning and Verbal Behavior*, 1968, 7, 337–344.

Palermo, D. S., and Jenkins, J. J. Changes in the word associations of fourth- and fifth-grade children from 1916 to 1961. *Journal of Verbal Learning and Verbal Behavior*, 1965, 4, 180–187.

Paul, H. Die Vokale der Flections- und Ableitungs-Silben in den aeltesten germanischen Dialekten. *Beiträge zur Geschichte der deutschen Sprache und Literatur*, 1877, 4, 315–475.

Paul, H. *Prinzipien der Sprachgeschichte*. Halle: Niemeyer, 1920. 1st ed., 1880. Quotations are from the 5th ed.

Pedersen, H. *Linguistic science in the nineteenth century*. Trans. J. W. Spargo. Cambridge, Mass.: Harvard University Press, 1931.

Percival, W. K. On the non-existence of Cartesian linguistics. Paper presented at the Annual Meeting of the Linguistic Society of America, December, 1968.

Peters, W. Ueber Aehnlichkeitsassoziation. *Zeitschrift für Psychologie*, 1910, 56, 161–206.

Pipping, H. Zur Theorie der Analogiebildung. *Mémoires de la Société Néo-Philologique à Helsingfors*, 1906, 4, 237–318.

Posner, R. Comments. *Current Anthropology*, 1968, 9, 131–132.

Reich, P. A. The finiteness of natural language. *Language*, 1969, 45, 831–843.

Reinhold, F. Beiträge zur Assoziationslehre auf Grund von Massenversuchen. *Zeitschrift für Psychologie*, 1910, 54, 183–214.

Robins, R. H. *A short history of linguis-*

tics. Bloomington: Indiana University Press, 1968.

Robinson, E. S. *Association theory today*. New York: Century, 1932.

Rogge, C. Die Analogie im Sprachleben, was sie ist und wie sie wirkt. *Archiv für die gesamte Psychologie*, 1925, 52, 441–468.

Russell, W. A., and Jenkins, J. J. The complete Minnesota norms for responses to 100 words from the Kent-Rosanoff word association test. Technical report no. 11, 1954. Contract N8–ONR–66216.

Saling, G. Assoziative Massenversuche. *Zeitschrift für Psychologie*, 1908, 49, 238–253.

Saussure, F. de. *Cours de linguistique générale*. Geneva, 1916. References are to the English translation by W. Baskin, *Course in general linguistics*. New York: Philosophical Library, 1959.

Schellenberg, P. E. A free association group test for college students. Doctoral dissertation. University of Minnesota, 1929.

Scherer, W. *Zur Geschichte der deutschen Sprache*. Berlin, 1868. References are to the "neuer Abdruck" of 1890.

Schlosberg, H., and Heineman, C. The relationship between two measures of response strength. *Journal of Experimental Psychology*, 1950, 40, 235–247.

Schmidt, F. Experimentelle Untersuchungen zur Associationslehre. *Zeitschrift für Psychologie*, 1902, 28, 65–95.

Schmidt, J. Gedächtnisrede auf Wilhelm Scherer, 1887. Citations are to the reprint in T. A. Sebeok, ed., *Portraits of linguists*. Bloomington: Indiana University Press, 1966. Pp. 474–489.

Scripture, E. W. *The elements of experimental phonetics*. New York: Scribner's, 1902.

Ščur, G. S. On the associative principle and field in linguistics. In G. Bolognesi et al., eds., *Studi Linguistici in onore di Vittore Pisani*, vol. 2. Brescia, Italy: Editrice Paideia, 1969. Pp. 937–962.

Selz, O. Die Gesetze der produktiven Tätigkeit. *Archiv für die gesamte Psychologie*, 1913, 27, 367–380. (a)

Selz, O. *Ueber die Gesetze des geordneten Denkverlaufs*. Stuttgart: Spemann, 1913. (b)

Selz, O. Komplextheorie und Konstellationstheorie. *Zeitschrift für Psychologie*, 1920, 83, 211–234.

Selz, O. *Zur Psychologie des produktiven Denkens und des Irrtums*. Bonn: Cohen, 1922.

Seymour, T. D. William Dwight Whitney. *American Journal of Philology*, 1894, 15, 271–298. References are to the reprint in T. A. Sebeok, ed., *Portraits of linguists*, vol. 1. Bloomington: Indiana University Press, 1966. Pp. 399–439.

Shepard, J. F., and Fogelsonger, H. M. Studies in association and inhibition. *Psychological Review*, 1913, 20, 290–311.

Sievers, E. *Grundzüge der Lautphysiologie zur Einführung in das Studium der Lautlehre der indogermanischen Sprachen*. Leipzig, 1876. Quotations are translated from Arens, pp. 292–299.

Skinner, B. F. The distribution of associated words. *Psychological Record*, 1937, 1, 71–76.

Skinner, B. F. *Verbal behavior*. New York: Appleton-Century-Crofts, 1957.

Skinner, B. F. Operant behavior. In W. K. Honig (Ed.), *Operant behavior: Areas of research and application*. New York: Appleton-Century-Crofts, 1966. Pp. 12–32.

Smith, F. J. *Rule learning in a miniature linguistic system*. Doctoral dissertation, University of Wisconsin. Ann Arbor, Mich.: University Microfilms, 1967. No. 67–17,024.

Smith, K. H. "Learning" miniature languages: Language acquisition, concept formation, or pattern perception? Paper presented at a symposium on The miniature linguistic system, at the meeting of the American Psychological Association, 1968.

Smith, K. H., and Braine, M. D. S. Miniature languages and the problem of language acquisition. In T. G. Bever and W. Weksel, eds., *The structure and psychology of language*, vol. 2. New York: Holt, Rinehart and Winston, 1970.

Smith, K. H., and Gough, P. B. Transformation rules in the learning of miniature linguistic systems. *Journal of Experimental Psychology*, 1969, 79, 276–282.

Steiner, T. E., and Sobel, R. Intercomponent association formation during paired-associate training with compound stimuli. *Journal of Experimental Psychology*, 1968, 77, 275–280.

Steinthal, H. *Abriss der Sprachwissenschaft. Erster Teil. Die Sprache im Allgemeinen*. Also with separate title: *Einleitung in die Psychologie und Sprachwissenschaft*. Berlin: 1871. References are to the 2nd ed., 1881.

Steinthal, H. Wie einer den Nagel auf den Kopf trifft. *Zeitschrift für Völkerpsychologie*, 1874, 8, 216–249.

Steinthal, H. *Geschichte der Sprachwissenschaft bei den Griechen und Römern*. 2nd ed. Vol. 1, 1890; vol. 2, 1891. References are to a photographically reproduced edition: Hildesheim: Georg Olms Verlagsbuchhandlung, 1961.

Stern, C., and Stern, W. *Die Kindersprache*. 3rd ed. Leipzig: Barth, 1922.

Stern, G. *Meaning and change of meaning*. Göteborg: Göteborgs Högskolas Arskrift, 1931, vol. 38. Republished: Indiana University Press, 1964. References are to the latter edition.

Stevenson, H. A study in associative interference. Master's thesis, University of Washington, 1929.

Sturtevant, E. H. *An introduction to linguistic science*. New Haven: Yale University Press, 1947. References are to the Yale paperbound, 1960.

Thomason, S. G. On the nature of analogical change. Paper read at the meeting of the Linguistic Society of America, December 1969.

Thorndike, E. L. The significance of responses in the free association test. *Journal of Applied Psychology*, 1932, 16, 247–253.

Thorndike, E. L. On the frequency of semantic changes in modern English. *Journal of General Psychology*, 1948, 39, 23–27.

Thorndike, E. L., and Lorge, I. *The teacher's word book of 30,000 words*. New York: Teachers College Press, 1944.

Thumb, A. Psychologische Studien über die sprachlichen Analogiebildungen. *Indogermanische Forschungen*, 1907, 22, 1–55. (a)

Thumb, A. Die experimentelle Psychologie im Dienste der Sprachwissenschaft. *Sitzungsberichte der Gesellschaft zur Beförderung der gesamten Naturwissenschaften zu Marburg*, 1907, no. 2. (b)

Thumb, A. Assoziationsversuche in Dienste der Sprachwissenschaft. *Berichte des III. Kongresses für Experimentellen Psychologie*, 1909.

Thumb, A. Beobachtung und Experiment in der Sprachpsychologie. *Die neueren Sprachen: Zeitschrift für den neusprachlichen Unterricht*. Ergänzungsband: Festschrift für Wilhelm Viëtor, 1910.

Thumb, A. Experimentelle Psychologie und Sprachwissenschaft. *Germanisch-Romanische Monatsschrift*, 1911, 3, 1–15, 65–74.

Thumb A., and Marbe, K. *Experimentelle Untersuchungen über die psychologischen Grundlagen der sprachlichen Analogiebildung*. Leipzig: Engelmann, 1901.

Trautscholdt, M. Experimentelle Untersuchungen über die Association der Vorstellungen. *Philosophische Studien*, 1882, 1, 213–250.

Uhlenbeck, E. M. An appraisal of transformational theory. *Lingua*, 1963, 12, 1–18.

Uhlenbeck, E. M. Some further remarks on transformational grammar. *Lingua*, 1967, 17, 263–316.

Veness, T. An experiment on slips of the tongue and word association faults. *Language and Speech*, 1962, 5, 128–137.

Verinis, J. S., and Cofer, C. N. Word recognition and set for association. *Psychonomic Science*, 1964, 1, 179–180.

Wallenhorst, R. Some relations between reaction time and choice of response in word association. *Psychological Reports*, 1965, 17, 619–626.

Warren, H. C. A *history of the association psychology*. New York: Scribner's, 1921.

Waterman, J. T. *Perspectives in linguistics*. Chicago: University of Chicago Press, 1963.

Watt, H. J. Ueber Assoziationsreaktionen, die auf optische Reizworte erfolgen. *Zeitschrift für Psychologie*, 1904, 36, 417–430.

Watt, H. J. Experimentelle Beiträge zu einer Theorie des Denkens. *Archiv für die gesamte Psychologie*, 1905, 4, 289–436.

Wechsler, D. *The range of human capacities*. Baltimore: Williams and Wilkins, 1935.

Wehrlin, K. The associations of imbeciles and idiots. In C. G. Jung, *Studies in word-association*. Trans. M. D. Eder. London: Heinemann, 1918. Pp. 173–205.

Wells, F. L. Linguistic lapses. *Archives of Philosophy, Psychology and Scientific Methods*, 1906, no. 6.

Wells, F. L. Some properties of the free association time. *Psychological Review*, 1911, 18, 1–23. (a)

Wells, F. L. A preliminary note on the categories of association reactions. *Psychological Review*, 1911, 18, 229–233. (b)

Wells, F. L. Practice effects in free association. *American Journal of Psychology*, 1911, 22, 1–13. (c)

Wells, R. S. De Saussure's system of linguistics. *Word*, 1947, 3, 1–31.

Wells, R. S. Predicting slips of the tongue. *Yale Scientific Magazine*, 1951, 26, 9ff.

Wheat, L. B. Free associations to common words. *Teachers College Contributions to Education*, 1931, no. 498.

Wheeler, B. I. *Analogy and the scope of its application in language*. Cornell University Studies in Classical Philology, no. 2. Ithaca, N.Y., 1887.

Whitney, W. D. *Language and the study of language*. New York, 1867. References are to the 5th ed., 1874.

Whitney, W. D. Steinthal and the psychological theory of language. *Oriental and Linguistic Studies*, series 1, pp. 332–375. New York, 1874. Also published as: Steinthal on the origin of language. *North American Review*, 1872, 114, 272–308.

Whitney, W. D. *The life and growth of language*. New York: 1875. References are to the reprinted ed., 1899.

Wickelgren, W. A. Context-sensitive coding, associative memory, and serial order in speech behavior. *Psychological Review*, 1969, 76, 1–15.

Wiggins, J. Two determinants of associative reaction time. *Journal of Experimental Psychology*, 1957, 54, 144–147.

Wilcocks, R. W. On substitution as a cause of errors in thinking. *American Journal of Psychology*, 1928, 40, 26–50.

Williams, H. M. Time characteristics in the word-association test. *University of Iowa Studies in Child Welfare*, 1937, 13, 51–60.

Wilson, D. P. An extension and evaluation of association word lists. Doctoral dissertation, University of Southern California, 1942.

Winter, W. Analogischer Sprachwandel und semantische Struktur. *Folia Linguistica*, 1970, 3, 29–45.

Wolfle, D. L. The relation of manual habits to the organization of a linguistic system. Master's thesis, University of Washington, 1928.

Wolfle, D. L. The relation between linguistic structure and associative interference in artificial linguistic material. *Language Monographs*, 1932, no. 11.

Wolfle, D. L. The relative stability of first and second syllables in an artificial language. *Language*, 1933, 9, 313–315.

Wolfle, D. L. The role of generalization in language. *British Journal of Psychology*, 1934, 24, 434–444.

Woodrow, H., and Lowell, F. Children's association frequency tables. *Psychological Monographs*, 1916, 22, no. 5.

Woodworth, R. S. *Experimental psychology*. New York: Holt, 1938.

Woodworth, R. S., and Schlosberg, H. *Experimental psychology*. (Rev. ed.) New York: Holt, Rinehart and Winston, 1954.

Woodworth, R. S., and Wells, F. L. Association tests. *Psychological Monographs*, 1911, no. 57.

Wreschner, A. Die Reproduktion und Assoziation von Vorstellungen. *Zeitschrift für Psychologie*, Ergänzungsband 3, 1907–1909.

Wundt, W. [Review of] Thumb and Marbe, *Experimentelle Untersuchungen* etc. *Anzeiger für indogermanische Sprach- und Altertumskunde (Beiblatt zu den Indogermanischen Forschungen)*, 1901, 12, 17–20.

Wundt, W. *Völkerpsychologie*, vols. 1, 2. *Die Sprache*. 3rd ed. Leipzig: Engelmann, 1911–1912.

Wynne, R. D., Gerjuoy, H., and Schifmann, H. Association test antonym-response set. *Journal of Verbal Learning and Verbal Behavior*, 1965, 4, 354–359.

Yum, K. S. An experimental test of the laws of assimilation. *Journal of Experimental Psychology*, 1931, 14, 68–82.

Ziehen, Th. Die Ideenassoziation des Kindes. *Sammlung von Abhandlungen aus dem Gebiete der pädagogischen Psychologie und Physiologie*, 1898, 1, no. 6; 1900, 3, no. 4.

Zipf, G. K. The meaning-frequency relationship of words. *Journal of General Psychology*, 1945, 33, 251–256.

INDEX

Aarsleff, H., 175n
Abercrombie, D., 59–60
Aborn, M., 114
Abstractions, control of, in linguistics and psychology, x
Ach, Narziss, 76–78, 111
Adelung, Johann Christoph, 14
Alexandrian school of grammarians, ln, 2, 3, 6, 7
Allport, Gordon W., 168
Allport-Vernon scale, 126
American Psychological Association, 156, 163
"Ambiguous sentences," Chomsky's notion of, 165
Analogía, 1, 5n
Analogical change. *See* Change, analogical
Analogical extensions, 159
Analogical formations: as blends, xii; and contamination, xii, 40n; causes of, xii, 152; and associations, xii, 65, 71, 202; examples of, 1; Merzdorf on, 28–30; inhibition of, 35; Paul on establishment of, 35–36; of children, 35, 47, 152, 194; Bloomfield on, 40n, 184–85; Misteli on, 47; Wheeler's classification of, into physiological and psychological processes, 50–51; Pipping's classification of, into conservative and creative, 62–63; experimental researches on, 64–84; Thumb on, 65, 68–69, 71, 72, 82; Marbe on, 68–69; grammatical, 68–69, 200; regularity of, 72; artificially produced, 80–81, 155; as solutions to pro-

portional equations, 151; Stern on, 152; Esper on, 202
Analogical process: and Saussure's doctrines, 177–78; origin of, in *parole*, 179
Analogical tendencies, distinguished from errors of discoordination, xii–xiii
Analogists, 2–3, 2n
Analogy: role of, in regularizing language, xii, 1, 16–18, 41, 150, 152, 176–77, 179, 188; Esper on, xii, xiii, 200–203; definitions of, xii, xiii, 6, 8, 76, 186–87, 200–203; treatment of, by psycholinguists, xii, 198–99; as a logical operation in form of equation, xii, 1–2, 8, 40, 153, 183–84, 185–86, 187, 193–94, 193n; role of, in language learning, xiii, 34–35, 157; normative use of, 1, 2, 5, 6n; the term, 2, 3; Alexandrians on, 3; Stoics on, 3; and usage, 5–6, 7, 12; and spontaneous speech, 6n; and meaning, 9–10; as creative force for new forms, 9n, 11, 15, 29–30, 179; and association, 12, 24, 30–31, 70–71, 140–42; as explanation of apparent exceptions or anomalies, 19, 22; Scherer on, 22, 23; and frequency, 23, 36; Curtius on, 29, 47; Merzdorf on, 29–30; Brugmann on, 30–33, 49–50; Paul on, 34–35, 36, 40, 41, 185–86; interaction of, with memory, 36; as supplementary to sound-laws, 47; Misteli on, 47, 76; Wheeler on, 51–55; Middleton on, 55–57; Thumb on, 70–71; Herzog on, 76; relevance of word-association experiments to problem of, 140–42; role

217

Association, outer and inner, 98
Association, paradigmatic, 57, 132, 133–34, 134–35, 137, 138, 139
Association, pure, 81
Association, reciprocal, 68, 68n, 96, 97
Association, rhyme and assonance, 100
Association, semantic, xiii
Association, sound, 83. *See also* Folk etymology
Association, spontaneous, 76–78
Association, syntagmatic, 132, 137, 139, 190
Association, verbal and habitual, 89–90
Association, word-completion, 99–100
Association experiments: on numerals, 72–73; history of, 85–144; first, 87–88; definitions, 93–94; use of artificial sound material in, 94, 142, 143; variables effecting results of, 96, 107, 120–21; group vs. individual tests in, 104–105; impossibility of free associations in, 107–108; controlled, 107–18; problem of set in, 112–13; methods of, 118–19, 136–37; reaction-time distributions in, 119–22, 125, 126–30; and behavior theory, 123–24; problem of individual differences in, 124–25; control of conditions in, 126; relevance of, to problem of linguistic analogy, 140–42. *See also* individual experimenters by name
Association of ideas: role of, in syntactical change, 55–56; and early work in psychology of learning, 93
Associationism, 12, 86, 88–89, 111, 112–13
Associative strength, 123, 124, 126
Associative theories of language, 162n
Autoclitics, 195–96

Back-formation, 188–89
Bailey, P., 189
Bain, Alexander, 86, 87
Baker, L. M., 116
Bawden, H. H., 58–59
Beauzée, Nicolas, 12
Behavior: neural basis of, xi; verbal, 161, 196n
Behavior theory, association experiments and, 123–24

Behaviorism: peripheralism of, xv; influence of, on associationism, 88–89
Behaviorists, controversy of, with mentalists, xv
Beneke, Friedrich Eduard, 87
Benfey, Theodor, 5n, 13, 14
Berko, association experiments of, 132–33
Bills, on controlled associations, 116
Blends and blending, xii, 140, 153; Hockett on, 189–90, 192, 194; Esper on, 201; Wells on, 202n
Bloch, Bernard, 194
Bloomfield, Leonard: on linguists' use of own data, xi; criticisms of Paul by, 37n; on linguistic change, 40n, 181–82; basic tenets of, 181; mentalism of, 181; on social reinforcement, 182–83; on analogies as proportional equations, 183–84, 193–94; on analogic change, 183–85; on contaminations, 185; objectivism of, 189; mentioned, ix, xiv–xv, 194
Bloomfieldians, quarrel of, with Chomskyans, 19n
Blumenthal, A. L.: conversion of, to Chomskyanism, ix; on Wundt, ix, xiv; on Chomsky, x
Boer, T. J. de, 68n
Boomer, D. S., on slips of the tongue, 59
Bopp, Franz: comparative grammar of Indo-European languages by, 14; Sanskrit grammar by, 18
Boring, E. G., xi, xv, 109
Borrowing: as source of linguistic disturbance, 15; neogrammarian view of, 25–26; Bloomfield's definition of, 182; mentioned, xiii, 200
Brain: mechanisms, x, xi; physiology, xv, 167; nature of storage in, 192–93. *See also* Mind; Thought and thinking
Braine, Martin, 170–71, 199
Bredsdorff, Jakob Hornemann, 16–17
Brentano, Franz, 86
Brown, Thomas: "secondary laws" of association of, 85; association experiments of, 87, 132–33; mentioned, 86, 164
Brugmann, Karl: on analogy, 30–33, 49–50, 186; on false analogy, 30–31, 33; on role of association in analogy, 30–

31, 46; on *Ursprache*, 31; on linguistic methodology, 32, 33, 50; on sound-laws, 32–33, 49; on linguistic change, 32–33, 61; on form associations, 32, 46; defense of neogrammarians by, 44–45, 49–50; on Leskien, 45; Misteli's reply to, 46–48; on relation of linguistics and philology, 48–49; on role of memory in speech, 49–50; mentioned, ix, 18, 24, 42, 45n, 64, 191

Bryant, S.: experiment on children's associations by, 79; investigation of free association by, 93; frequency table of, 93

Bücheler, Franz, 64

Burnett, James. *See* Monboddo, Lord

Carnegie Corporation, 131

Carroll, John B.: free-association experiments of, 117; report to Carnegie Corporation by, 131; mentioned, 154–55

Carton, A. S.: free-association experiments of, 117

Cason, E. B.: on controlled nature of associations in experiments, 108; on effect of experimenter's sex on results in association experiments, 120; association experiments of, 125

Cason, H.: on controlled nature of associations in experiments, 108; on effect of experimenter's sex on results in association experiments, 120; association experiments

Cattell, James McKeen: association experiments of, xiv, 79, 92–93, 116; use of chronoscope by, 93; frequency table of, 93; use of tachistoscope by, 119; handling of distribution of reaction-times by, 127–28; mentioned, 65, 94

Change, analogical: criteria for, xiii; neogrammarian view of, 25–26; as word-association process, 26; Leskien on, 27–28; relation of, to phonetic change, 27–28, 42–43, 182; Paul on, 35, 40; Osthoff on, 42–44; Wheeler's sixteen principles of, 55; Thumb on, 77, 78; prediction of, 77, 202, 202n; role of children in, 78; role of multiple responses in, 148; Esper on, 148, 154, 203; role of individual differences in,

149, 203; Wolfle on, 154; causes of, 154, 184; artificial production of, 172; Bloomfield on, 182–84; rejected by Chomskyan psycholinguists, 190–91, 190n; Winter on, 196; Thomason on, 196–97, 197n; Kurylowicz and Mańczak on, 202; morphological and functional, 203; mentioned, 140, 153, 158–59

Change, diachronic: distinguished from synchronic variation, 179

Change, linguistic: historical processes of, xii; Saussure's concept of, 180; Bloomfield's concept of, 181–83

Change, phonetic: neogrammarian's view of, 25–26; relation of, to analogic change, 27–28, 42–43

Change, semantic, 203

Chapanis, A., 92, 129

Charisius, definition of *analogía* by, 8n

Children: associations of, xiii, 78, 79, 83, 91, 104, 105–106, 132–35, 137; analogy-formations of, 35, 40, 47, 53, 71, 152, 162, 194; role of, in analogical change, 78; role of, in linguistic change, 79; syntactic sequences in speech of, 134; language learning by, 134–35, 158–59, 161–62, 169–70, 185; concept attainment of, 154n

Chomsky, Noam: rejection of Humboldt's theories by, ix; "Cartesian," abstract doctrines of, ix, x, 164; symbolic method of, x; speculations about hereditary mechanisms by, x; and Skinner, x–xi, 196n, 199; opposition to, 160, 161; opposition to "final-state" models of language by, 162; "ambiguous sentences" of, 165; theory of "creativity" or "productivity" of, 167; influence of, on Kirk Smith and Braine, 171; basic tenets of, 175n; on aim of grammar, 184n; Hockett's critique of, 190–92; mentioned, 6, 156, 168, 189n, 200. *See also* Chomskyan psycholinguists; Competence; Deep structures

Chomskyan psycholinguists: and dualism, ix; contempt of, for neogrammarians, ix, 19n; and spoken or "native" language, x, 200; contempt of, for empiricism, operationism, and positivism, x;

on brain mechanisms, x, 167, 193n; doctrines of, xiii, 159, 167; and Jenkins, 160, 161, 165–66; lack of interest of, in histories of languages, 166; and psychological science, 167–68; Hall and Hockett on, 168n; rejection of notion of analogical change by, 190–91, 190n; view of nature of language of, 202n. *See also* Chomsky, Noam; Competence; Deep structures

Chrysippus, doctrine of anomaly of, 4

Class formation, process of, 163

Classen, J., on analogist-anomalist controversy, 2

Cofer, C. N.: association experiments of, 106, 115, 117–18; methods of, 117n; on law of contiguity, 136; mentioned, 96n

Cognition, as distinguished from learning, 171

Collocations, as sources of linguistic change, 190

Competence: Chomskyan psycholinguists' preoccupation with rules of, x, 190n; and actual speech, 58n; Chomsky's notion of, 159, 166–67, 198, 199; "new" grammar model of, 164; as equivalent of Saussure's *langue*, 178; rigidity of, 179; Skinner on, 199

Concept attainment, 154n

Condillac, Etienne Bonnot de, 11–12

Constellation, role of, in word-association, 73

Contamination: Bloomfield on, 40n, 185; Herzog on, 41, 76; Marbe on, 41; Thumb on, 41, 65; Paul on operation of, 41–42; Middleton on, 56–57; Oertel on, 62; included in definition of analogy by Misteli, 76; Menzerath's experiments on, 83; Esper on, 148, 201; defined by Hockett, 188; mentioned, xii, 58, 70, 102n, 140, 142, 152, 153, 154, 155, 159

Contamination-associations, Saling on, 83–84

Contiguity, law of, 136, 137–38, 140

Contiguous usage, as cause of word-association, 114

Cornell University, seminar of, in psychology and linguistics, 131

Courtenay, Baudouin de, 175

Cramer, P., 104, 115

Crates of Mallos, 2, 3

Cratylus, Plato's, 3, 4

Creativity: Chomsky on, 167; Jenkins on, 193; Esper on, 201

Crossing, 153

Curtius, Georg: on analogy, 8n, 17–18, 29, 47, 50; on laws of sound change, 17–18; and neogrammarians, 18, 49–50; and Merzdorf, 29–30; mentioned, 24, 45n, 65

Darwin, Charles Robert, 39

Darwinism, as root of experimental psychology, 86

Dauber, J., 97–98

Davidson, E. H., 116–17

Deese, J.: rejection of law of contiguity by, 136, 137–38, 140; word-association experiments of, 136–37; on associative meaning, 137; on Ervin's findings, 137; use of statistics by, 137; on associations of nouns, 138–39; on associations of adjectives, 139; on cause of associations, 139–40; mentioned, xiv

Delacroix, H., 151–52

Descartes, René: innate ideas of, 11; influence of, on Chomsky, 175n; mentioned, 86

Deep structures, x, xiv, xv, 159–60, 165, 165n–66n, 182, 189, 195

Delbrück, B., 71, 181

Descriptive linguistics. *See* Linguistics, synchronic

Dialects: use of, to examine relation of analogy and association, 72; combining association and linguistic studies to examine, 74; association studies of, 76

Dialect-mixture: as cause of linguistic change, 32

Dissimilation, 58, 59, 188

Dixon, R. M. W.: on Chomsky, 159; on need to correlate verbal with other behavior, 196n; mentioned, 58n, 161, 195

Donatus, grammar of, 8n

Dualism, mind-body: and mentalistic psycholinguistics, ix–x, 178n; and psychology, 89; of Saussure, 175–76; mentioned, 67

Dunlap chronoscope, limitations of, for association experiments, 118

Durkheim, Emil: on group mind, 178n

Ebbinghaus, Hermann: "forgetting curve: of, 95; experiments on serial verbal learning and retention by, 93; constellation theory of, 111; linguistic training of, 131; mentioned, 64, 84, 94

Eberhart, V. L., miniature linguistic system experiments of, 169–70

Eberschweiler, A., 83, 84n

Eccles, J. C., 123

Editing: Hockett on, 192, 193, 194–96; Skinner on, 196n

Elliott, V. L., controlled-association experiments of, 116

Engram, the, xi

Entwisle, D. R.: experiments on children's associations by, 134–35; mentioned, 104

Errors, anticipatory, xii, xiii. See also Assimilations; Contamination; Dissimilation; Metatheses

Ervin, S. M.: on children's associations, 133–34; on syntagmatic association, 135; on prediction of associative responses, 135–36; Deese on findings of, 137; miniature linguistic systems experiments of, 169–70

Esper, Erwin A.: "mentalism" of, xi; polemical tone of writings by, xiv–xv; replication of Thumb's and Marbe's work by, 80, 131; on individual differences in analogical processes and linguistic systematization, 82, 148, 178–79, 203; miniature linguistic systems association experiments by, 107, 145–49, 151, 154, 155, 157, 158n, 171–72, 200, 201; on relevance of association experiments to problem of linguistic analogy, 140–42; on associations of the uneducated and children, 141; on role of multiple responses in analogic change and contamination, 148; Stern's use of experiments by, 150–51; experiments of, replicated by Wolfle, 153; on cause of analogic change, 154; overlearning in

experiments of, 155–56, 158n; results of, confirmed by Horowitz, 156; on individual learning methods, 158; Jenkins on, 162, 163; experiments of, corroborated by Foss, 169–70; definition and comparison of miniature linguistic systems and natural language by, 171–72; on significance of organization of miniature linguistic systems, 172; on status of language rules, 172–73; on linguists' misuse of Freud, 189; criticisms of Hockett by, 195–96; definition of analogy by, 200–203; on blends, 201; on contaminations, 201; on productivity or creativity, 201; on relation of word-associations to analogical formations, 202; mentioned, 154n, 155, 156, 199

Etymology, historical, 9n. See also Folk etymology

Experimental method, 81

Feeble-minded, associations of, 107

Fehling, Detlev, 2

Fichte, Johann Gottlieb, 13

Fodor, J., 167–68

Folk etymology, 54–55, 186, 188. See also Association, sound

Ford, T. J., association experiments of, 117–18

Forsyth, D. F., experiments on children's associations by, 134–35; mentioned, 104

Foss, D. J.: experimental corroboration of Esper by, 169–70; definition of miniature linguistic systems by, 171; mentioned, 105

Frequency: effect of, on operation of analogy, 36; and association, 70, 83, 85, 90–91, 96, 96n–97n, 97–98, 101–106. See also Marbe's Law

Frequency tables, 84n, 93, 101–106, 136

Freud, Sigmund: linguists' misuse of, 189; concept of "censor" of, 194; influence of, on Wells and Hockett, 202n

Friedrich, M., on method of least squares, 91

Functionalism, German, as root of experimental psychology, 86

Gagné, R. M., 154n
Galton, Francis: experimental investigation of association by, 87–88; on visual, histrionic, and verbal associations, 88, 89; on importance of associations established in childhood, 91; mentioned, 92, 94
Garrett, M., on relation of Chomskyan theory to psychological science, 167–68
Gaussian normal curve, 91
Gerjuoy, H., free-association experiments by, 117
German scholarship, influence on linguistics of, 13
German philology, 24
Gestalt psychology of language, 159
Gestaltists, 111, 112
Gibson, Eleanor, 154n
Godel, R., 178
Goldstein, M., on slips of the tongue, 59
Grammar: prescriptive, xiv, 1, 179; comparative, 9n, 34; transformational-generative, 131, 159–68; miniature, 163; generative, 190n
Grammarians, ancient, 8, 9, 9n, 12
Grimm, Jacob, 14, 22, 22n, 23, 24, 34
Group-mind fallacy, 178n

Hall, J. F., 129
Hall, R. A.: on Chomskyan linguistics, 160, 165n–66n, 166–67, 168, 168n; mentioned, 161
Haplology, xii, 58, 188, 190
Hartley, David, 86, 87, 88
Hawkins, A. S., 154n
Hegel, Georg Wilhelm Friedrich, 13, 178n
Heineman, C.: association experiment of, 120–24; theoretical account of association by, 122–23; statistical handling of reaction-times by, 128–29
Hellenism, 6
Helmholtz, Hermann von, 87
Herbart, Johann Friedrich, 38, 46, 174
Hermann, E., 196
Herodian, 5n
Herzog, E.: on contamination, 41, 76; criticisms of Thumb and Marbe studies by, 73–74, 75–76; definition of analogy

by, 76; on sources of associations, 78; on associations of children, 78; on role of children in linguistic change, 79; mentioned, 77
Hipp chronoscope, limitations of, for association experiments, 118
Hobbes, Thomas, 86, 87
Hockett, C. F.: on slips of the tongue, 60, 188, 189, 190; critique of Chomsky by, 168n, 190–92; on analogy, 187–90, 192, 193n, 194; on assimilation and dissimilation, 188; definition of contamination by, 188; on haplology, 188; on idiom formation, 188; definition of metanalysis by, 188; on metathesis, 188; on back-formation, 188–89; on Freud, 189; on recutting, 189; on blends, 189–90, 192, 194; on nature of brain storage, 192–93; on concept of "editing," 192–93, 194–96; Esper's criticisms of, 195–96; mentioned, 166, 202n
Homer, 1
Homonymy, 3
Horowitz, Arnold, 155, 156
Howes, D., 115, 137
Hull, C. L., x, 122, 154n
Humboldt, Wilhelm von: principles of analogy and association of, 14–15; conflict of a prioristic and objective tendencies in theory of, 15; contributions to linguistics by, 15–16; Whitney on, 19n; mentalism of, 174; influence on psycholinguists of, 175n; concept of "spirit of a nation" of, 178n; concept of "inner speech" of, 195; mentioned, ix, 19, 46
Hume, David, 86
Humphrey, G., 111

"Ideal speaker," 159
Idiom formation, 188
Imitation, in language learning, 43
Indiana University, psycholinguistic seminar at, 131–32
Individual differences: in associative responses, 82; in analogic change, 149, 203; in linguistic systematization, 178–79
Indo-European languages: relations

among, 14; Scherer on, 22–23; phonetic changes in, 35; analogic changes in, 67–68; Thumb and Marbe's use of parallels from, 71

Indogermanic languages, 28

Information theory, 115

"Innateness," doctrine of linguistic, 167

"Inner speech," Humboldt's concept of, 195

Irregular forms. *See* Anomaly

James, William, constellation theory of, 111

Jenkins, James J.: on association, 57, 142–43; association experiments of, 115; on mediation, 143–44, 157–58, 158n, 163; on experimental use of miniature linguistic systems, 157, 164–65; on Chomskyan doctrine, 160, 161, 165–66, 167–68; on psychology and psychological research, 161–62, 168; on Esper, 162, 163; on role of experimentation in psycholinguistics, 163–65; on competence, 164, 166; conception of language of, 168; survey of linguistics of Wundt, Paul, Watson, Allport, Skinner, Mowrer by, 168; on creativity and productivity, 193; mentioned, xiv, 104, 105, 106, 117n, 132, 133, 156, 168, 199

Jesperson, Otto, 16, 62, 194

Jones, Sir William, 11

Jung, Carl Gustav: classification of associations for diagnostic purposes by, 99–100; on delayed reaction-times, 128; mentioned, 81, 104, 107

Katz, J. J., ix–x

Kaeding, F. W., dictionary of frequencies by, 84n, 97, 98

Kant, Immanuel, 13

Kantor, J. R., xi

Kelley, T. L., on reaction-time distributions, 120

Kent, G. H. *See* Kent-Rosanoff list

Kent-Rosanoff list, 102–104, 120, 121, 124, 125

King, R. D., 190n

Kiparsky, P., 190n

Kjeldergaard, P. M., free-association experiments of, 117

Koff, R. H., association experiments with children by, 105–106

Koffka, K., attempts to secure free associations by, 107–108

Kraepelin, E., 66

Kroesch, Samuel, on semantic changes, 203

Kurylowicz, J.: on nature of analogy, 186–87; on cause of analogic changes, 202

Kulpe, Oswald, 64, 65, 108

Lafall, J., 59

Lang, J. B., 128

Langendoen, D. T., 7

Langue, 159, 175, 177, 178, 178n, 179, 200

Language: "native," Chomskyan technique applied to, x; natural, 11, 171, 172; role of analogy in, 11–12, well-constructed, 11–12; origin of, 11, 12–13; and nature of thought, 12; James Burnett on, 12–13; as constantly changing, 14; as object of study of scientific linguistics, 26–27; Paul on nature of, 34–35, 36–37; gestalt psychology of, 159; "finite-state" models of, 162; Lashley on, 162; physiological theory of, 162; sequential nature of, 162; histories of, 166; Esper's conception of, 171

Lapsus linguae. See Slips of the tongue

Lashley, K. S.: on problem of the engram, xi; on associationism, 113, 162n; on nature and theory of language, 162

Latencies. *See* Reaction-times

Laver, J. D., on slips of the tongue, 59

Lazarus-Steinthal school, answer to neogrammarians by, 37, 46–48

Learning: serial, xii, xiii, 93; general theory of, and research in verbal behavior, xiv, 161; Ebbinghaus on, 93; alleged neural correlates of, 113; concept of, 138; conditions of, 141; Horowitz' experiments concerning, 156; Esper on individual methods of, 158; experiments in maze-, 158n; traditional associative, 161, 171; as distinguished from cognition, 171

Learning, language: and association, xiii; and analogy, xiii, 40, 157; Paul on, 34–35, 40; role of imitation in, 43; Misteli on, 47–48; foreign vs. native, 48; by children, 134–35, 158–59, 169–70, 185; F. J. Smith on, 170; Kirk Smith on, 171; Rogge on, 185

Least squares, method of, 91

Lenneberg, E., 154n, 156, 164

Lepley, W. M., 96n

Leroy, M., definition of *langue* by, 179

Lersch, L., on analogy-anomaly controversy, 2, 7

Leskien, August: as co-founder of neo-grammarian school, 19; research methods of, 27; on relation of phonetic and analogic change, 27–28; on exceptionless sound-laws, 27–28; on *Ursprache*, 28; definition of language of, 45; mentioned, 23, 30, 45n, 47, 191

Linguistic change: role of unconscious in, 32; caused by dialect-mixture, 32; role of association in, 32–33; ascribed to speech activity, 38–39; originating in collocations, 190

Linguistic history, and psychology, 82

Linguistic morphology, rule-governed, 168–69

Linguistic Society of America, xv

Linguistic structure, children's acquisition of, 161–62

Linguistics: historical and comparative, ix, 11, 13–14, 17, 44–45; and psychology, ix, 21–22, 37, 48, 72, 82, 83, 131–32, 163–64, 168; synchronic, xi–xii, 158n, 179, 180, 181; and experimental psychology, xii, xiii, 72, 81, 196n, 200, 202n; polemics and controversy in, xiv–xv; and analogy-anomaly controversy, 7–8; inductive vs. deductive, 7–8, 19n; effect of natural sciences on, 13, 25–26, 44; scientific, 26–27, 38n, 181; methodology of, 32, 33, 34, 42, 44–45; and philology, 48–49; study of slips of the tongue in, 60; use of statistics by, 81; significance of word-association for, 131–32; and miniature linguistic systems, 156; mentalism of, 163, 174; in-

tuition in, 168n; rules in, 168n; structural, 174; diachronic, 179, 180, 181; misuse of Freud by, 189; treatment of analogy in, 198; role of semantics in, 202n

Lip-key, use of, in association experiments, 118–19

Locke, John, 11, 12, 86, 87

Loeb, Jacques, xv

Logic, formal: use of, in psychology, x; use of, in study of language, xiv

Loring, M. W.: controlled association experiments of, 109–10; on methods for measuring reaction-times, 118

Lotz, Rudolf Hermann, 87

Ludwig, C. F. W., 87

Lyons, J., 179

MLS. *See* Miniature linguistic systems

McGinnies, E., 126

Mańczak, W.: on analogical processes, 187; on analogical change, 202

Marbe, Karl: debt of, to Paul, 38n; on contamination, 41; linguistic experiments by, 64–84, 158n; on "imageless thought," 65; and Külpe, 65; and Wundt, 65, 74–75; on word-association, 65–66, 67, 73; on grammatical analogy-formations, 68–69; reply by, to Oertel's criticisms of Thumb and Marbe experiments, 73; criticisms of, by Schuchardt, Vossler, and Herzog, 73–74, 75–76; word-association experiment by, replicated by Esper, 80; association lexicon proposed by, 102n; on experimental methodology, 119; linguistic training of, 131; mentioned, xiv, 60, 73n, 78, 84, 94, 137, 143, 153, 154n, 199

Marbe's Law, 67, 70, 95, 121–22, 131. *See also* Reaction-times, associative

Marshall, J. C., xiv

Martius, Götz, 64

Marty, Anton, 174

May, M. A.: association experiments of, 110, 116; mentioned, 112

Mayer, A.: on mediated and spontaneous analogy, 76; Thumb and Ach confirm findings of, 77; association experiments of, 94

Mayer, Karl: on slips of the tongue, 57–58, 190

Maze-learning experiments, 158n

Mediation: place of, in stimulus-response theories, 89; role of, in word-association, 143; role of, in linguistic analogy, 143–44; Jenkins' and Palermo's concept of, 157–58, 158n

Mefferd, R. B., 80, 124

Memory: role of, in language learning, 35, 40; Paul on, 35, 36, 40, 41, 71; and analogy, 36, 71; operation of, in sound changes, 41; role of, with analogy in speech production, 49–50

Mentalism: of Esper, xi; of structural linguistics, 174–75; of Chomskyan linguistics, 175n; of Bloomfield, 181; of Rogge, 185; mentioned, ix, 201

Mentalists: controversy of, with behaviorists, xv; dualism of, 178n; mentioned, 88

Menzerath, P.: experiments on contaminations of, 83; mentioned, 120

Meringer, Rudolf: on slips of the tongue, 57–58, 58n, 82n; on speech mechanisms, 57n–58n; mentioned, 82, 190

Merzdorf, Reinhold: on analogical formations, 28–30; on sound-laws, 28–30; on false analogy, 29; and Curtius, 29–30

Messer, A.: association experiments of, 110

Metanalysis, 188

Metaphors, x

Metatheses, xii, 58, 59, 188, 190

Meumann, Ernst, 64

Middleton, G., 55–57

Mill, James, 86, 87

Mill, John Stuart, 86, 87

Miller, G. A., 113–14, 114n

Mind, free vs. mechanical activity of the, 48. See also Brain; Thought and thinking

Miniature linguistic systems: Esper's experiments using, 145–46, 147–49, 153, 171–72, 200, 201; Wolfle's experiments using, 149–50, 153–54; and analogy, 150, 155; Stern's discussion of, 150; Stevenson's experiments using, 150; psychologists' use of, 154–55n, 199; isolation of experiments using, 154n–55n; Horowitz's use of, 155, 156; Jenkins on use of, 156–57, 164–65; Lenneberg on use of, 164; "productiveness" of subjects in experiments using, 167; Eberhart's experiments using, 169–70; Palermo's experiments using, 169–70; Braine's experiments using, 170–71; F. J. Smith's experiments using, 170; Kirk Smith's experiments using, 170–71; definition of, 171; compared with natural languages, 172; significance of organization of, 172

Misteli, Franz: Osthoff and Brugmann answered by, 46–48; on sound-laws, 47; on language learning, 47–48; on analogy, 47, 48, 76; on free vs. mechanical activity of mind, 48; on role of psychology in linguistics, 48; on Paul's theories, 48; on contamination, 76; mentioned, 65, 69, 72

Monboddo, Lord (James Burnett), on origin of language, 12–13

Moran, L. J., association experiments of, 124

Morgan, Lloyd, 87

Müller, G. E., 84

Müller, Johannes, 87

Multiple responses, role of in analogic change and contamination, 148

Münsterberg, Hugo, 65, 66

Muuss, R., experiments on children's associations by, 134–35

Natural sciences, influence on linguistics of, 24, 25–26

Neogrammarians: basic tenets of, 19, 25–26; debt of, to von Raumer, 23; on exceptionless sound-laws, 23–24, 58n; on phonetic change, 24, 25–26; on analogic change, 25–26; on borrowing, 25–26; methods of, 44–45; answered by Misteli, 46–48; Brugmann answers Curtius' critique of, 49–50; on speech mechanisms, 57n–58n; criticized by Oertel, 60n; opponents of, 74; on role of analogy in linguistics, 131; Saussure on, 175; influence on Bloomfield of, 181; mentioned, ix, 18, 22, 182. See also Brugmann; Leskien; Merzdorf; Osthoff; Paul; Sievers

Pott, August Friedrich, 21, 47
Productivity: Jenkins on, 193; Esper on, 201
Proportion groups, formal and material, 40
Psycholinguists: mentalism of, ix; repudiate association, xii; treatment of analogy by, xii, 198–99; lack of interest of, in historical process of linguistic change, xii, Jenkins on experimentation by, 163–65; influences on, 175n
Psychologists, conversion to Chomskyan doctrines of, xiii–xiv
Psychology: mentalism of, ix; objectivism and behaviorism of, ix; and linguistics, ix, 21–22, 37, 48, 72, 82, 83, 131–32, 163–64, 168; and the nervous system, xi; and philology, 19, 24; use of, by neogrammarians, 24; Paul's theories of, 37–38; and problem of dualism, 89; of learning, 93; and miniature linguistic systems, 154–55, 156, 199; and transformational-generative grammar, 159–68; and Chomskyan theory, 161, 167–68; need for study of class-formation by, 163; treatment of analogy by, 198; interest in word-association of, 199. *See also* Psychology, associational; Psychology, experimental; Psychology, gestalt
Psychology, associational, 162, 168
Psychology, experimental: and word-association, xii, xiv, 69; on analogy-formation, xii, 64–84; and linguistics, xii, xiii, 72, 81, 196n, 200, 202n; Wundt as founder of, xiv; roots of, 86–87; remaining problems of, 161–62
Psychology, gestalt, 159

Quintilian, 6, 7, 8n

Rask, Rasmus Christian, 14
Raumer, Rudolf von, 23
Reaction-key, use of, in association experiments, 119
Reaction potential, 122, 123
Reaction-times, associative: studies of, 66; in mediated associations, 77, 99; distributions of, 91–92, 119–22, 125, 126–

30; in controlled vs. free associations, 116–17; variables effecting, 117–18, 120–21, 124, 126, 129; techniques for measuring, 118–19, 137; relation of, to response commonality, 121–22, 123, 124–25; delayed, 128. *See also* Marbe's Law
Recutting, 189
Reflexionspsychologie, 152, 175
Reinforcement theory, 123
Reinhold, F., 97, 102n
Riklin, Franz, 81, 99–100, 107
Rogge, C.: on language learning, 185; on analogy, 185–86
Romanticism, 24
Rosanoff, A. J., frequency tables of, 102–104
Roth, Rudolf von, 18
Rubenstein, H., 114
Russell, Bertrand, 12
Russell, W. A., 104, 105, 106, 117n

Saling, G.: on contamination-associations, 83–84; association lexicon of, 102n
Saussure, Ferdinand de: and separation of descriptive and historical linguistics, xi; as founder of structural linguistics, 174; main tenets of, 175; on neogrammarians, 175; dualism of, 175–76; on analogy, 176–77, 179, 180–81; concept of *langue* of, 177, 178, 178n; and psychology of language, 177–78; chess analogy of, 179; on opposition of synchronic and diachronic linguistics, 179–80; mentioned, 159, 166, 181, 200
Scheicher, August, 6
Schellenborg, P. E., 104, 106
Schelling, Friedrich Wilhelm Joseph von, 13
Scherer, Wilhelm: on analogy, 22–24; on false analogy, 23; positivism and determinism of, 23; nationalism of, 24; contributions of, 24; on nature of language, 25; on frequency as factor in analogy-formation, 61; mentioned, 17, 19, 44, 45n
Schifmann, H., 117
Schleicher, August: empiricism of, 13; on linguistic change, 22; on nature of language, 25; mentioned, 21, 27

Schlosberg, H.: association experiment of, 120–24; on word-association, 122–23; handling of reaction-times by, 128–29; mentioned, 104

Schmidt, Friedrich, association experiments of, 78, 79

Schuchardt, Hugo: criticisms of Thumb and Marbe experiments by, 73–74; on source of associations, 78; on role of children in linguistic change, 79; mentioned, 76

Scripture, E. W., 65, 72–73, 72n, 73n

Sechenov, I. M., 87

Selz, Otto: experiments on operation of set by, 110–13; on productive and reproductive thinking, 111–12

Sensationism, 12

Semantics, 19, 202n

Set: development of concept of, 108; experiments on operation of, 110–13

Sextus, on analogy and usage, 8

Shevitz, R., 96n, 106

Sievers, Eduard, 26–27

Skinner, B. F.: linguists' use of theories of, xi; Chomsky's views of, x–xi, 196n; on association, 106, 114; influence on Miller of, 114n; on social reinforcement, 182–83; definition of autoclitic by, 196; on self-editing, 196n; on verbal behavior, 196n; on competence, 199; mentioned, 113, 168

Slips of the tongue: distinguished from analogical tendencies, xii–xiii; Wheeler on, 51; and word-associations, 60; Thumb on, 82, 82n; Bloomfield on, 184, 185; Hockett on, 188, 189, 190; mentioned, 57–60, 67, 140–41, 201, 202n

Smith, F. J., miniature linguistic system experiments of, 170

Smith, Kirk: miniature linguistic system experiments of, 170–71; Chomsky's influence on, 171; on usefulness of artificial languages, 171; on language rules, 171, 172–73; on comparison of miniature linguistic systems with natural languages, 172; mentioned, 199

Sobel, R., association experiments of, 154n-55n

Social transmission, Esper's experiment on, 147

Social Science Research Council, Committee of, on Linguistics and Psychology, 131, 156

Sound change, laws of, 17–18

Sound-laws: regular, distinguished from phonetic assimilations, xii; neogrammarians on, 19, 23–24; exceptionless, 19, 23–24, 27–28, 28–29, 42–43, 44, 45n, 47, 58n; Leskien on, 27–28; Merzdorf on, 28–29, 29–30; Brugmann on, 32–33, 49; movement toward consistent application of, 34; Osthoff on, 42–43, 44; as supplementary to analogy, 47

Sound symbolism, 3

Speech mechanisms, 57n–58n

Statistics: Thumb on use of, by linguists, 81; use of, by Trautscholdt, 91; use of, in handling reaction-time distributions in association experiments, 91–92, 119–22, 126 30; use of, by Deese, 137

Steiner, T. E., association experiments of, 154n–55n

Steinthal, Heymann: on analogist-anomalist controversy, 2–3; on Quintilian's view of analogy, 7; quarrel of, with Whitney, 19n, 21–22; mentalism of, 174; distinction between *langue* and *parole* by, 174, 175; influence on psycholinguists, 175n; mentioned, 6n, 19, 21, 37, 46

Sterling, T. D., 114

Stern, Gustav: on analogy and multiple linguistic systems, 150; "combinative" analogy of, 150; on Delacroix's statements about analogy, 151–52; objection to Paul's "group theory" by, 151–52; on analogy-formations, 152; on "correlative" analogy, 152; three types of analogies of, 152–53; isolation and combination process of, 153, 167; on semantic analogy, 203; mentioned, 157

Stimulus-response theories: influence on associationism of, 88–89; and mediating processes, 89

Stimulus-response correlations, 201

Stevenson, H., miniature linguistic system experiment of, 150

Stoics of Pergamum, 2, 3, 4, 7

Stopwatch, limitations for use in association experiments of, 118
Stout, G. F., 79–80
Sturtevant, E. H., 194
Substitution, law of, 111n
Substitution class, 142
Syntactic novelty, doctrine of, 114
Syntagmatic relations, 177
Syntax, principle of analogy applied to, 55–57

Tachistoscope, use of, in association experiments, 119
Telescoping, 153
Thomason, Sarah, xiii, 196–97, 197n
Thorndike, E. L., 87, 96n, 100, 106
Thorndike-Lorge word-frequency count, 96n, 106
Thought and thinking: Würzburg school on processes of, 108–109; imageless, 111; reproductive and productive, 111; creative, 111–12; investigations of, by controlled-association experiments, 116. *See also* Brain; Mind
Thumb, Albert: debt of, to Paul, 38n; on contamination, 41, 65, 67; experimental studies of analogy by, 64–84; on analogy-formation, 65, 68–69, 71, 72, 80–81; on role of experimentation in word-association study, 69; on relation of association and analogy, 70–71, 72, 82; reply to critics by, 72, 73–74; on relation of psychology and linguistics, 72, 81, 83; and Schuchardt, 73–74; and Vossler, 73–74; and Herzog, 73–74, 75–76; and Wundt, 74–75; on study of dialects, 76; use of stopwatch by, 76; on mediated and spontaneous associations, 76–78; on analogical change, 77, 77n; on associations of children, 78; experiments by, corroborated by Schmidt, 79; on role of children in linguistic change, 79; Esper's replication of word-association experiment by, 80; proposes experiments using artificial sound formations, 80–81, 82–83, 145; on linguist's use of statistics, 81; proposes association lexicon, 82; on role of individual differences in

associative responses, 82; on slips of the tongue, 82n; on sound association, 83; on relation of frequency and reaction-times, 121–22; on conditions surrounding particular associations, 135; purpose of experiments of, 158n; mentioned, 73n, 84, 119, 131, 137, 141, 143, 153, 154n, 172, 199, 202
Transformation rules, 162
Transformational-generative grammar. *See* Grammar, transformational-generative
Transformational theory, 171
Transformationalism: and psychological research, 161–62
Trautscholdt, M.: methods of, 88, 90; on reaction-times, 90, 91; on frequency and latency of word-associations, 90–91; on children's associations, 91; on controlled association, 92; on "outer" and "inner" associations, 98; mentioned, 65, 66, 94

Ugelow, on relation of reaction-times to frequency of stimulus word, 129
Uhlenbeck, E. M., on transformational theory, 171
Unconscious, the: role of, in linguistic change, 25–26, 32; Paul on, 38, 69
Ursprache, 28, 31, 34, 44–45
Usage: and linguistic regularity, 5–6, 8; as cause of anomaly, 6; determines forms in natural language, 11; opposed to analogy, 12

Variability, as cause of word-associations, 142
Variation, synchronic: and diachronic change, 179
Varro, Marcus Terentius: on analogy, 1n, 4n, 6, 10, 12; inventor of analogist-anomalist controversy, 2; on anomaly, 4–5, 4n; distinguishes derivational from inflectional formations, 5; on regularity of language, 5; forerunner of Paul, Scheicher, rationalist grammarians, and Chomsky, 6–7; on principles governing all languages, 7; on linguistic change, 9n

Veness, T., on word-association, 59
Verbal organization, experiments on, using miniature linguistic-systems, 149–50
Verner, Karl Adolph, 45n
Voice-key, use of, in association experiments, 118
Vossler, Karl: "Tiefsinn" of, rejected by Thumb, xiv; Thumb and Marbe experiments attacked by, 73–74

Wallenhorst, R., 124
Watt, H. J.: on visual vs. auditory presentation of stimulus-words, 73; experiments on children's associations of, 79, 80; controlled-association experiments of, 108–109; mentioned, 110, 111, 112
Wechsler, D., 91–92
Wehrlin, K.. on associations of feeble-minded, 107
Wells, F. L.: on slips of the tongue, 58–59; diagnostic classification of associations by, 99–100; on freedom of associations in experiments, 108; controlled-association experiments of, 116; on associative reaction-times, 127; mentioned, 105, 120
Wells, Rulon: critique of Saussure by, 180; on prediction of analogical change, 202n; on blends, 202n
Wheat, L. B., word-association experiments with children of, 105
Wheeler, Benjamin Ide: on slips of the tongue, 51; classification of analogical phenomena by, 51–55; on children's analogies, 53; on folk-etymologies, 54–55; sixteen principles of analogical change of, 55; mentioned, 62
Whitney, William Dwight: as co-founder of neogrammarian school, 18–22; quarrel with Steinthal of, 19n, 21–22; on analogy, 20; Arens' assessment of, 20–21; on relation of linguistics and psychology, 21–22; as forerunner of behavioristic linguists, 22; on nature of language, 25; mentioned, 17
Wickelgren, W. A., 162n
Wieland, B. A., 80

Wiggins, J., association experiments of, 130
Wilcocks, R. W., 111n
Williams, H. M., 126
Winter, W., 196
Wolfle, D. L.: miniature linguistic system experiments of, 149–50, 153, 156; on stability of first and second syllables, 154; on association and analogic change, 154; mentioned, 155
Woodrow, H., 105
Woodworth, R. S.: on individual responses, 103; controlled-association experiments of, 116; on variables affecting experimental results, 120–21; on association, 199; mentioned, 100, 104, 107, 109, 111, 112, 116
Wreschner, Arthur: association experiments of, 94–97, 116; on mediating processes, 95; on reciprocal associations, 96; proposes association lexicon, 97; on memory-storage and association, 97; on "psychical meanings" of associations, 97; on stimulus-word familiarity, 98; mentioned, 107
Wundt, Wilhelm: mentalism of, ix; as founder of experimental psychology, xiv; Marbe's quarrel with, 65; classification of associations by, 66; on association of ideas, 69; criticisms of Thumb and Marbe studies by, 74–75; on *Totalkraft*, 75; on linguistics and psychology, 82; technique of "mental chronometry" of, 92; influence on psycholinguists of, 174–75, 175n; classification of analogical formations by, 185; mentioned, 37, 37n, 64, 72, 76, 79, 81, 88, 98, 168
Würzburg school, 65, 94, 108, 111
Wynne, R. D., free-association experiments of, 117

Yum, K. S., use of nonsense material by, 154n

Ziehen, Th., experiments on children's associations by, 79, 80
Zipf, G. K., 96n, 106
Zumpt, Karl Gottlob, grammar by, 8n